Student Workbook

Psychological Testing
Principles, Applications, & Issues

EIGHTH EDITION

Robert M. Kaplan
University of California, Los Angeles

Dennis P. Saccuzzo
San Diego State University

D0210015

Prepared by

Katherine Nicolai
Rockhurst University

WADSWORTH
CENGAGE Learning

Australia • Brazil • Japan • Korea • Mexico • Singapore • Spain • United Kingdom • United States

ISBN-13: 978-1-133-49207-8
ISBN-10: 1-133-49207-X

Wadsworth
20 Davis Drive
Belmont, CA 94002-3098
USA

Cengage Learning is a leading provider of customized learning solutions with office locations around the globe, including Singapore, the United Kingdom, Australia, Mexico, Brazil, and Japan. Locate your local office at: **www.cengage.com/global**

Cengage Learning products are represented in Canada by Nelson Education, Ltd.

To learn more about Wadsworth, visit **www.cengage.com/wadsworth**

Purchase any of our products at your local college store or at our preferred online store **www.cengagebrain.com**

Printed in the United States of America
1 2 3 4 5   17 16 15 14 13

Table of Contents

⊰ Note to Students ⊱

The Student Workbook to accompany Kaplan and Saccuzzo's *Psychology Testing: Principles, Applications and Issues 8th edition)* is designed to help you make the most out of your experiences in your psychological testing course. You can use the Workbook in several ways.

The Student Workbook can help you

structure your study time. Divide the time you spend on your psychological testing course each week into segments. Each segment will consist of reading a particular section of the text (denoted by a Roman numeral in your Workbook) and completing the corresponding section of the Workbook. In the first three weeks of class, keep track of how much time you devote to each segment. You might even want to note the time you spend next to each section in the Chapter Outline. Then, find the *average* amount of time you spend on a single segment. Use this average to plan your study schedule during the academic term.

prepare for class. If you complete the assigned reading and associated Workbook exercises before coming to class, you will be much better prepared to answer questions posed by your instructor during class. Additionally, if you find you have difficulty completing any of the Workbook exercises, you will be prepared to ask specific questions about material you did not understand.

prepare for exams. If you have kept up with your reading assignments and completed associated Workbook chapters, you will have a ready-made study guide. Furthermore, the practice quizzes at the end of every Workbook chapter will allow you to test what you know and identify areas that require further study.

practice skills you will need to complete assignments and projects. Numerous exercises and chapter assignments will help you develop the skills you will need to complete larger assignments, papers, and projects assigned by your instructor.

⊰ Acknowledgements ⊱

A number of people helped to bring the 8th edition of the Student Workbook to fruition. I want to express my gratitude to the Assistant Editor for Psychology at Cengage, Jessica Alderman, for her assistance with this edition of the Workbook. I am also grateful to Wilson Co, Ileana Shevlin, and Jennifer Keever, former Assistant Editors at Wadsworth, who edited previous editions of the Workbook, and especially to Marianne Taflinger, former Senior Editor at Wadsworth, who inspired me to pursue this project. I am very grateful to Bob Kauser and Roberta Broyer who obtained permission for me to use the measures presented in the Student Workbook.

I am also indebted to Rose Leising, a graduate of Rockhurst University and a former student in my Psychological Assessment course, for her insightful comments on the initial IRM prospectus, work on the data set, and compilation of the answer key for the Student Workbook. I have been fortunate to know many dedicated, creative and joyful instructors whose contributions to this project have been less tangible but no less valuable; in particular, I am grateful to my colleagues in the psychology department at Rockhurst University.

Finally, I would like to thank my Psychological Assessment students, both current and past, for their questions, insights and enthusiasm. The Student Workbook could not have been created without them.

Katherine M. Nicolai, Ph.D.
Rockhurst University
Kansas City, MO

~ *WORKBOOK CHAPTERS* ~

Each Workbook Chapter includes:

Chapter Exercises
Key Terms and Concepts
Practice Chapter Quiz
Chapter Assignment

⊸ CHAPTER 1: *Introduction* ⊶

Chapter One Outline

I.   Basic Concepts (text pp. 6-9)

      A. What a Test Is (text pp. 6-7)

      B. Types of Tests (text pp. 7-9)

II. Overview of the Book (text pp. 10-11)

      A. Principles of Psychological Testing (text p. 10)

      B. Applications of Psychological Testing (text pp. 10-11)

      C. Issues of Psychological Testing (text p. 11)

III. Historical Perspective (text pp. 11-22)

      A. Early Antecedents (text pp. 11-12)

      B. Charles Darwin and Individual Differences (text p. 12-13)

      C. Experimental Psychology and Psychophysical Measurement (text pp. 13-14)

      D. The Evolution of Intelligence and Standardized Achievement Tests (text pp. 14-17)

      E. Personality Tests: 1920-1940 (text pp. 17-19)

      F. The Emergence of New Approaches to Personality Testing (text pp. 19-20)

      G. The Period of Rapid Changes in the Status of Testing (text pp. 20-21)

      H. The Current Environment (text pp. 21-22)

CHAPTER 1 EXERCISES

I. BASIC CONCEPTS (text pp. 6-9)

A. What a Test Is (text pp. 6-7)
B. Types of Tests (text pp. 7-9)

1.   In the table on the next page, write in the term that matches each definition. The terms (and the page numbers on which they can be found) are listed below.

Test (p. 6)	*Ability Test* (p. 8)
Overt behavior (p. 6)	*Achievement Test* (p. 8)
Covert behavior (p. 6)	*Aptitude Test* (p. 8)
Scale (p. 7)	*Intelligence Test* (p. 8)
Trait (p. 7)	*Structured Personality Test* (p. 8)
State (p. 7)	*Projective Personality Test* (p. 8)
Individual Test (p. 7)	*Psychological Testing* (p. 9)
Group Test (p. 8)	

TERM	DEFINITION
	This broad category of tests measures human achievement, aptitude and/or intelligence.
	This is within an individual and cannot be directly observed (e.g., thoughts, feelings, etc.).
	This relates raw test scores to some theoretical or empirical distribution.
	A test that measures previous learning (e.g., a statistics exam).
	All the possible uses, applications and concepts of psychological and educational tests.
	This type of test measures an individual's potential for acquiring a certain skill.
	The specific condition or status (at a single point in time) of an individual.
	In this type of test, an ambiguous stimulus (e.g., an inkblot) is presented to an examinee who must provide a spontaneous response which is believed to reflect his or her unique characteristics.
	This type of test can be given to a large group of people by one examiner or test administrator (e.g., the SAT, an exam in class).
	This type of test measures a person's general potential to solve problems, adapt to changing circumstances, think abstractly, and acquire new knowledge.
	Enduring characteristics or tendencies to respond in a certain way across situations.
	A measurement tool or strategy used to quantify behavior or aid in the understanding and prediction of behavior.
	In this type of test, the examinee is given an objective statement about his or her thoughts, feelings or behaviors and is required to choose a response from a limited number of options (e.g., "Agree" or "Disagree", "True" or "False").
	This is an observable activity (e.g., crying, fighting, sleeping, eating, etc.).
	This type of test can be given to only one person at a time (e.g., a driver's test, some intelligence tests).

II. OVERVIEW OF THE BOOK (text pp. 10-11)

A. Principles of Psychological Testing (text p. 10)

The first section of the text covers basic principles and concepts that are central to all psychological and educational tests.

B. Applications of Psychological Testing (text pp. 10-11)

The second section of the text explores the characteristics and uses of many different kinds of tests, including achievement, intelligence, and personality tests.

C. Issues of Psychological Testing (text p. 11)

The third section of the text explores issues such as test bias, legal issues in testing, and the future of psychological testing.

III. HISTORICAL PERSPECTIVE (text pp. 11-22)

A. Early Antecedents

1.   The use of psychological tests and test batteries began in China more than 4000 years ago. How were test batteries used during the Ming Dynasty (1368-1644 C.E.)? _____

_____

_____

2.   During the 1800's, Great Britain, France, Germany and the United States all adopted China's testing model for what purposes? _____

_____

_____

B. Charles Darwin and Individual Differences (text pp. 12-13)

3.   Charles Darwin's *Origin of the Species*, published in 1859, exerted a tremendous influence on scientists' understanding of individual differences in ability and personality. According to Darwin, what is a necessary consequence of the fact that individual members of a species differ? _____

_____

_____

4.   Sir Francis Galton applied Darwin's theory to humans by studying individual differences in which aspects of functioning? _____

5.   James McKeen Cattell coined the term _____ _____ in his research based on Galton's work in individual differences.

C. Experimental Psychology and Psychophysical Measurement (text pp. 13-14)

6.   What important ideas about psychological testing emerged from the collective work of German psychophysicists Herbart, Weber, Fechner, and Wundt? _____

_____

_____

_____

D. The Evolution of Intelligence and Standardized Achievement Tests (text pp. 14-17)

7.   The figure below summarizes various aspects of the evolution of the Binet-Simon Scale in 1905 to the Stanford-Binet Scale in 1916. Complete the figure.

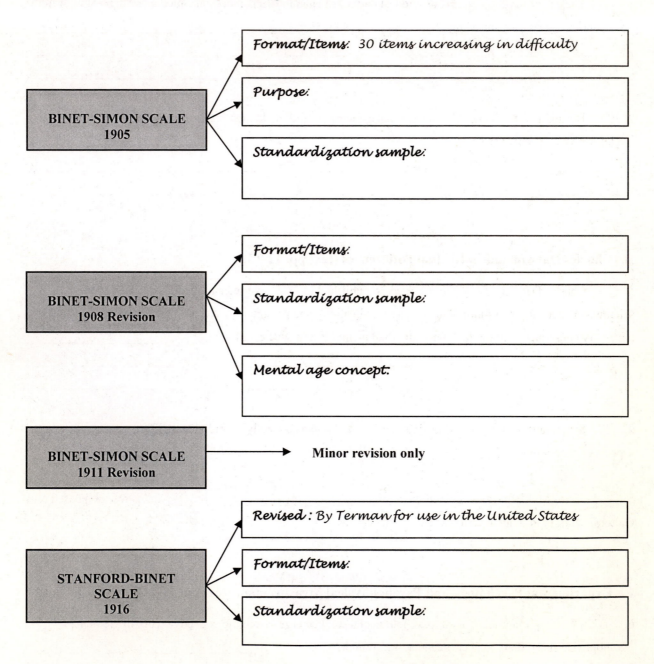

8.   What need spurred the demand for the development of large-scale group tests during World War I?

_____

_____

9.   Created by Robert Yerkes and others, Army Alpha and Army Beta were two group tests of ability. What distinguished these tests? _____

10.   Below, complete the list of benefits of standardized achievement tests, which were first developed in the early 1920's.

a. *They were easy to administer and to score* . _____ .

b. _____

c. _____

d. _____ .

E. Personality Tests: 1920-1940 (text pp. 17-19)

11.   Optimism is a *trait*, or a relatively enduring disposition that distinguishes one person from another. Give three more examples of traits. _____

12.   What is "structured" about a structured personality test? _____
_____

13.   Your text states that interpretation of the Woodworth Personal Data Sheet, the first structured personality test, was based on a now-discredited assumption. What is this assumption, and why has it been discredited? _____
_____
_____

14.   What are the primary differences between structured and projective tests of personality? _____
_____
_____

F. The Emergence of New Approaches to Personality Testing (text pp. 19- 20)

15.   In what important way was the Minnesota Multiphasic Personality Inventory (MMPI) an advance over early structured personality tests such as the Woodworth Personal Data Sheet? _____
_____

16. What is factor analysis? _____
_____
_____
_____

G The Period of Rapid Changes in the Status of Testing (text pp. 20-21)

17.   The "birth" of clinical psychology corresponds to a period of increased government funding providing for the training of psychologists who could develop and use applied psychological technology (e.g., psychological tests).   What date is given in your text for the "birth" of clinical psychology? _____

18.   A report by Shakow et al. (1947) was the foundation of the first formal training standards in clinical psychology. What were two important statements about psychological testing made in this report?

a. _____

b. _____

19.   Your text states that in the late 1940's and early1950's, testing was a major function of the clinical psychologist. However, psychologists often played a "complementary but secondary role vis-à-vis medical practitioners" (p. 21). In what way did psychologists play a "secondary role" to physicians? _____

_____

_____

_____.

20.   What prompted the "sharp decline" in the status of testing among psychologists and the public from the 1950's through the 1970's? _____

_____

_____

H. The Current Environment (text pp. 21-22)

21.   Your text identifies several branches or specialties of applied psychology that gained prominence in the last two decades of the 20th century. Summarize how these different specialties use psychological tests.

Specialty	*How psychological tests are used*
Neuropsychology	
Health psychology	
Forensic psychology	
Child psychology	

Key Terms, Concepts, and Names to Know from Chapter One

test	J. E. Herbart
psychological test	E. H. Weber
overt behavior	G. T. Fechner
covert behavior	Wilhelm Wundt
scale	G. Whipple
trait	Alfred Binet
state	Binet-Simon Scale(s)
individual test	standardization sample
group test	representative sample
ability test	mental age
achievement test	L. M. Terman
aptitude test	Stanford-Binet Intelligence Scale
intelligence test	Robert Yerkes
structured personality test	Army Alpha
projective personality test	Army Beta
psychological testing	standardized achievement tests
reliability	Stanford Achievement Test
validity	David Wechsler
test administration	Wechsler-Bellevue Intelligence Scale
interview	Woodworth Personal Data Sheet
test batteries	Rorschach inkblot test
Han Dynasty and Ming Dynasty	Sam Beck
American Civil Service Commission	Thematic Apperception Test
individual differences	Minnesota Multiphasic Personality Inventory
Charles Darwin	Factor analysis
Sir Francis Galton	Sixteen Personality Factor Questionnaire
James McKeen Cattell	

CHAPTER 1 QUIZ

1.   As part of her scholarship application for a summer dramatic arts program, twelve-year-old Sharon completed a test that assessed her potential for acquiring acting skills. Sharon has taken a(n) _____ test.

   a.   personality
   b.   intelligence
   c.   aptitude
   d.   achievement

2.   Evidence suggests that _____ developed the earliest systematic program of psychological testing.

   a.   China
   b.   Great Britain
   c.   Germany
   d.   the United States

3.   _____ applied the concept of "survival of the fittest" to the study of individual differences among human beings in his book, *Hereditary Genius*.

   a.   James McKeen Cattell
   b.   Charles Darwin
   c.   Wilhelm Wundt
   d.   Frances Galton

4.   In his research on individual differences in human functioning, Galton examined all of the following <u>except</u>

   a.   visual acuity.
   b.   reaction time.
   c.   verbal comprehension.
   d.   physical strength.

5.   Which of the following is <u>true</u> with regard to the work of German psychophysicists Herbart, Weber, Fechner and Wundt?

   a.   These researchers were primarily interested in the measurement of individual differences.
   b.   This body of work established the idea that psychological testing requires rigorous experimental control.
   c.   These researchers argued that human consciousness was too complex to be studied through the scientific method.
   d.   This body of work culminated in the development of the first intelligence test.

6. **The score of a child who took the 1908 revision of the Binet-Simon scale would probably be reported as a(n)**

   a. mental age.
   b. intelligence quotient.
   c. chronological age.
   d. performance IQ.

7. **A standardization sample is**

   a. typically not representative of the population.
   b. a set of deviant test scores.
   c. a comparison group.
   d. often unnecessary.

8. **For what primary reason were group tests of ability and personality developed?**

   a. to evaluate school children
   b. to identify career options for unemployed workers
   c. to assess mental patients
   d. to screen military recruits

9. **The _____ , a structured personality test, was developed through factor analysis.**

   a. 16PF
   b. MMPI
   c. TAT
   d. SAT

10. **Which of the following statements best captures the reason why the use of psychological testing declined among psychologists beginning in the 1950's through the 1970's?**

   a. The U.S. government failed to provide political or financial support for the development of psychological testing programs after World War II.
   b. Increasingly, the public criticized the potentially intrusive nature of psychological testing and feared the misuse of tests.
   c. Many psychologists rejected psychological testing because they associated the use of tests with a secondary role of technician in service of medical professionals.
   d. Both a. and b. are correct.
   e. Both b. and c. are correct.
   f. Both a. and c. are correct.

14

✍**Student Workbook Assignment 1.1**

⊸ **Constructing a Timeline of Major Events in the History of Testing** ⊷

♦ **DESCRIPTION OF THE ASSIGNMENT**

In this assignment you will create a timeline depicting significant events in the history of testing.

♦ **DIRECTIONS**

➔ **Before beginning this assignment, make sure you have read Chapter 1.**

(1) First, you will need to get a large sheet of blank legal-sized (8 ½" x 17") paper. Draw a line across the middle of the paper, length-wise. This will be the timeline you fill in with names, dates, and events.

(2) Begin by deciding on the units of time you will use. Centuries will probably work best, until you get to the 19th century. Then you should consider using decades as the time unit. If you change time units in the middle of your time line, simply draw a short double-slash through the time line at the point of change.

(3) Write the dates of historical events on your timeline first, to provide context for the testing-related dates and events.   Some examples of selected historical events between 1850 and 1950 are provided below.

(4) Then go to Chapter 1 and identify important testing-related dates and events (e.g., 1923: publication of the Stanford Achievement Test). Write these on the timeline.

Selected Historical Events Between 1850 and 1950.

1861 American Civil War begins
1865 American Civil War ends

1912 Titanic sinks

1914 World War I begins
1918 World War I ends

1927 Charles Lindbergh crosses the Atlantic

1929 Stock Market Crash/Great Depression begins

1939 World War II begins
1945 World War II ends

⊷ CHAPTER 2: *Norms and Basic Statistics for Testing* ⊶

Chapter 2 Outline

CHAPTER 2 EXERCISES

I. WHY WE NEED STATISTICS (text pp. 26-27)

⚑ Statistics are necessary to **describe** the meaning of test scores. Without statistics we cannot know whether a test score of 15, for example, is a good score or a poor score. Further, we can use statistics to make **inferences** about larger populations of individuals based on a representative sample of those individuals.   Chapter 2 reviews both **descriptive statistics** (such as the mean and standard deviation) and **inferential statistics** (such as correlation). Even if you have completed a statistics course, this chapter will serve as a good review. Moreover, you will discover many applications of familiar statistics that are unique to testing and measurement.

II. SCALES OF MEASUREMENT (text pp. 27-31)

1.   Measurement is defined as the application of _____ , or specific procedures, for assigning _____ to objects.

A. Properties of Scales (text pp. 27-29)

2.   Measurement scales differ from one another in terms of the properties of magnitude, equal intervals, and an absolute zero. Summarize the characteristics of each property below.

a. *magnitude*: _____

_____

b. *equal intervals*: _____

_____

c. *absolute zero*: _____

_____

B. Types of Scales (text pp. 29-30)

3.   In the table below, describe the type of scale listed, indicate (with a ✓) whether the scale possesses each of the three properties you summarized above, and give an example of the type of scale.

Type of Scale	Description	Magnitude	Equal Intervals	Absolute zero	Example
Nominal					
Ordinal					
Equal Intervals					
Ratio					

4.   Indicate whether each of the following scales is nominal, ordinal, equal intervals, or ratio.

• Time (e.g., hours, minutes, seconds): _____

• USDA stickers placed on cuts of meat (e.g., "prime," "lean"): _____

• Political party membership: _____

• Grade point average (be careful with this one!): _____

• Percentage scores on an exam: _____

18

C. Permissible Operations (text pp. 30-31)

5.　　　Mathematical manipulations cannot be applied to _____ data. Some mathematical operations can be applied to _____ data, but the results are sometimes difficult to interpret. On the other hand, most mathematical operations can be applied to _____ data, and all can be applied to _____ data.

III. FREQUENCY DISTRIBUTIONS (text pp. 31-34)

> ♩ **NOTE:** Several activities in Chapters 2-6 draw upon a fabricated data set of 15 scores on a hypothetical test called the University Aptitude Test (UAT). The UAT is a verbal analogies test consisting of 18 items.   Parts of the data set corresponding to specific activities are provided in each Workbook chapter.

UNIVERSITY APTITUDE TEST (UAT) SCORES	
Examinee	**UAT Raw Score**
Greg	16
Allison	7
Janine	10
Corey	17
Michelle	3
Thomas	11
Randall	14
Tina	10
LeeAnn	13
David	12
Marcia	4
Lance	9
Keisha	15
Blair	12
Joe	6

The table at left shows the raw scores of 15 examinees on the University Aptitude Test (UAT). The UAT consists of 18 verbal analogies items. In Chapter 2, exercises using the UAT data set emphasize descriptive statistics. You will use answers to Chapter 2 exercises in exercises utilizing the UAT data set in subsequent chapters. Therefore, be sure to compare your answers to the answer key to make sure you have done your calculations correctly.

1.　　　Using the template below, create a **histogram** depicting the distribution of UAT raw scores. The class interval is presented on the horizontal (x) axis and frequency of occurrence is presented in the vertical (y) axis.

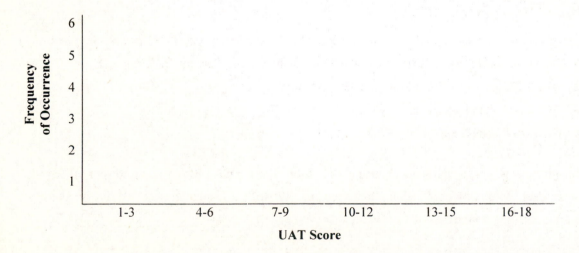

19

IV. PERCENTILE RANKS (text pp. 34-38)

1. **Percentile rank** answers the question: _____

_____?

After reading through text pp. 34-38 (and Box 2-1), you should be ready to calculate the percentile rank of selected UAT scores. Begin by arranging the scores in ascending order (the method suggested in Box-2-1) or in descending order (the method the Workbook author prefers!). Then use the formula for percentile rank shown below to find the percentile ranks corresponding to the UAT raw scores listed.

The formula for calculating percentile rank is:

$$P_r = \frac{B}{N} x100$$

where, P_r = percentile rank
X_i = the score of interest
B = the number of scores below X_i
N = the total number of scores

2. Calculate and record the percentile ranks corresponding to the following examinees' raw scores in the table below. The first is completed as an example.

Examinee Name	Raw Score (X_i)	B/N x 100	Percentile rank
Janine	10	5/15 x 100	33rd (or 33.33)
Keisha			
Thomas			
Joe			
Corey			
Marcia			

V. PERCENTILES (text pp. 38-39)

1. Percentiles are very closely related to percentile ranks. Percentiles are expressed as raw scores below which a certain percentage of scores fall. Identify the following percentiles from the UAT data set.

a. What UAT score is approximately the 33rd percentile? _____

b. What UAT score is approximately the 13th percentile? _____

c. What UAT score is approximately the 93rd percentile? _____

2. Imagine that you are a high school guidance counselor. One morning, Blair walks into your office and asks about her UAT score. Obviously, telling Blair "you got a 12" will mean nothing to her. Write a response to Blair's question using percentile rank and percentile. _____

_____

_____

VI. DESCRIBING DISTRIBUTIONS (text pp. 39-53)

A. Mean (text pp. 39-40)
B. Standard Deviation (text pp. 40-42)

1.   The **mean** is the average score in a distribution. What is the mean UAT score? _____

⤷ *The* ***standard deviation*** *is an approximation of the average deviation around the mean. Standard deviation is an extremely important statistic in psychological testing. Question 2. through 6. deal with standard deviation.*

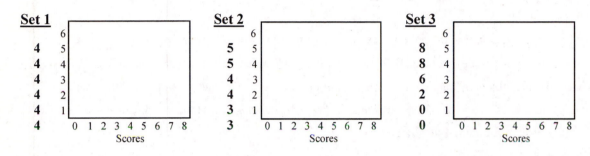

Data sets 1, 2, and 3 (the five numbers presented in columns under <u>Set 1</u>, <u>Set 2</u>, and <u>Set 3</u>) are scores on an 8-item math test administered to three different classes of second grade students who just completed a unit on arithmetic. The mean score of all three data sets (or all three arithmetic tests) is 4. If we used only the mean to assess how much arithmetic students in the three classes learned, we might be tempted to conclude that all 18 students learned about the same amount. However, simply looking at the three data sets is enough to tell us that the three classes of students are *not* the same in terms of their performance on the arithmetic test!

2.   On the templates shown above, draw the frequency distributions for each of the three data sets. These distributions graphically represent the fact that even though the data sets have the same mean score, 4, they are different in terms of _____ (or spread).

3.   At first, it seems as though measuring how much variation there is in a data set would be easy – all one would do is subtract each score in the data set from the mean score ($X - \overline{X}$). One could add up the "variations (more accurately, deviations) around the mean" and calculate the <u>average</u> deviation around the mean. Try this method of calculating variation or "spread" below.

Set 1	Set 2	Set 3
4 – 4 = ____	5 – 4 = ____	8 – 4 = ____
4 – 4 = ____	5 – 4 = ____	8 – 4 = ____
4 – 4 = ____	4 – 4 = ____	6 – 4 = ____
4 – 4 = ____	4 – 4 = ____	2 – 4 = ____
4 – 4 = ____	3 – 4 = ____	0 – 4 = ____
4 – 4 = ____	3 – 4 = ____	0 – 4 = ____

$\Sigma x_1 =$ ____, $\Sigma x_1/N =$ ____ $\Sigma x_2 =$ ____, $\Sigma x_2/N =$ ____ $\Sigma x_3 =$ ____, $\Sigma x_3/N =$ ____

4.   What you discovered is that the method used on the previous page to calculate variation or "spread" is not very useful! A better method might be to *square* the deviations around the mean – this will get rid of all the negative numbers. Go back to the previous page and square each of the values you found earlier (6 in each data set). Write these new values next to the old ones. Finally, add up the "squared deviations around the mean" and then calculate the <u>average</u> *squared deviation* around the mean: this is called the **variance**.

        a. variance of Set 1: _____

        b. variance of Set 2: _____

        c. variance of Set 3: _____

5.   The method you used in the previous exercise to estimate variation is better, but it still isn't as useful as it could be. After all, what does "squared deviation" really mean? What does a "squared deviation" look like? We can resolve this problem by taking the *square root* of the variance. This method will bring the resulting number back into the real world of raw score units, yielding an *approximation* of the average deviation around the mean, and this is the **standard deviation** (*voilà!*).

        a. standard deviation of Set 1: _____

        b. standard deviation of Set 2: _____

        c. standard deviation of Set 3: _____

Whether you realize it or not, you have just applied the formula $\sigma = \sqrt{\dfrac{\sum(X - \overline{X})^2}{N}}$ to calculate the standard deviations of the three data sets! But…there's just one problem. As you have read on text pp. 41-42, the formula shown above is used to calculate the standard deviation of a *population*, not a sample. In psychological testing, you will almost always use the formula that estimates the standard deviation of a sample, which looks like this:

$$S = \sqrt{\frac{\sum(X - \overline{X})^2}{N-1}}$$ or like this: $S = \sqrt{\dfrac{\sum X^2 - \dfrac{(\sum X)^2}{N}}{N-1}}$ (*note*: in most cases, this formula is much easier!)

6.   Go back and re-calculate the standard deviation for a *sample* this time. Use either formula shown above (although in this particular case, the one on the left may be easier).

        a. *S* of Set 1 = _____

        b. *S* of Set 2 = _____

        c. *S* of Set 3 = _____

   After completing the exercise above, go back and look at the frequency distributions of the three data sets you created earlier. Note that the set of data with the largest variance and standard deviation is *also* spread out a lot more than the other two. Whenever you encounter two or more data sets with approximately the same mean, but very different standard deviations, bring the image of these distributions into your mind's eye! For many students, *visualizing* statistics increases *understanding* of statistics.

Examinee	UAT Raw Score (X)	X²
Greg	16	
Allison	7	
Janine	10	
Corey	17	
Michelle	3	
Thomas	11	
Randall	14	
Tina	10	
LeeAnn	13	
David	12	
Marcia	4	
Lance	9	
Keisha	15	
Blair	12	
Joe	6	
N =	ΣX =	ΣX²=

7. Use the table at left to find the values you need to calculate the standard deviation of UAT scores.

Try using the raw score equivalent formula,

$$S = \sqrt{\frac{\sum X^2 - \frac{(\sum X)^2}{N}}{N-1}}$$

S = _____

✗ How are the mean and standard deviation used to interpret test scores? ✗

If you know the mean and standard deviation of scores on a test, you can interpret an examinee's test score in relation to the scores of others who have taken the test. The mean tells you what an "average" score is and the standard deviation can tell you if a score is more than just an average distance (or deviation) away from the mean.

For example, let's say several examinees were administered a measure of loneliness. On this measure, higher scores are associated with feeling more lonely. The mean score on the loneliness measure is 21 and the standard deviation is 3.5. If an examinee obtained a score of 21 on the loneliness measure, we would know that he or she probably feels an average level of loneliness. In fact, examinees who score within ± 1 standard deviation from the mean (i.e., who obtain any score between 17.5 and 24.5) would still be considered fairly average, since these examinees' scores fall within the "average deviation from the mean." On the other hand, if an examinee obtained a score of 29 on the loneliness measure, we might be very concerned about how lonely he or she was feeling. A score of 29 on this measure falls more than 2 standard deviations above the mean, suggesting that this examinee is significantly more lonely than others who took the test.

8. After reading the box above, identify the UAT scores that fall ± 1 standard deviation (SD) from the mean. Then identify scores that fall ± 2 SDs from the mean.

			14.82	
-2 SDs	-1 SD	Mean	+1 SD	+ 2 SDs

9.   Using your answers to 8. on the previous page, describe the following examinees' scores in *approximate* relation to the mean score (e.g., "Randall's UAT score of 14 is almost 1 standard deviation above the mean" or "Marcia's UAT score of 4 is about 1 ½ standard deviations below the mean.").

    a. Joe: _____

    b. Keisha: _____

    c. Thomas: _____

    d. Corey: _____

C. Z-Score (text pp. 42-43)

10.   Z scores transform raw test scores into _____ units that are easier to interpret.

✏ *Why* are Z scores easier to interpret? ✏

        As you will discover a bit later in this chapter, the mean of the Z score distribution is set at 0 and the standard deviation is set at 1. This means no matter what the raw score mean and standard deviation of a distribution happens to be, when those raw scores are converted to Z scores the distribution will have a mean of 0 and a standard deviation of 1. Always. So, if an examinee has a Z score of 0, we know that his or her raw score was right at the mean of the original (untransformed) score distribution.   If an examinee has a Z score of -1, it means that his or her raw score was exactly 1 standard deviation below the mean in the original score distribution.

        The bottom line is, the Z score is probably among the most efficient and useful scores you will ever encounter! The Z score is *efficient* because it combines information about the distribution's mean and the standard deviation into one score. The Z score is *useful* for many reasons, and here is just one of them: if two (or more) sets of raw test scores with different means and standard deviations are converted into Z scores, it is possible to compare relative performance across the two (or more) tests because both sets of scores are expressed in the same, or standardized, units. [Isn't that *brilliant*?]

---

11.   After reading through text pp. 42-43 (including the CES-D example), calculate and record the Z scores of the four examinees listed in the table below.

Examinee	UAT score (X)	$X - \overline{X}$	$Z = \dfrac{X - \overline{X}}{S}$
Joe			$Z =$ $= -1.09$
Keisha			
Thomas			
Corey			

↳ *Here's the fun part! Compare the Z scores you calculated above with your interpretations of the four examinees' raw scores in exercise 9., above. You should be able to see the resemblance!*

D. Standard Normal Distribution (text pp. 43-50)

↳ Examine the figure below, which is adapted from Figure 2-7 on text p. 46. This figure shows **the standard normal distribution** (also known as the "bell curve"). Theoretically, this bell-shaped curve describes the distribution in the population of scores on measures of most psychological constructs, including intelligence and personality traits. There are several things to note about this figure:

1. Units on the horizontal (x) axis are expressed as Z scores. As you know, Z scores have a mean of 0 and a standard deviation (SD) of 1.

2. The numbers inside the curve show the proportion of cases (or scores) that are expected to fall within ± 1 SD from the mean, ± 2 SDs from the mean, etc. These proportions can easily be turned into percentages – just multiply by 100. For example, the number of cases (or scores) we would expect to find between the mean score and the score that is one SD above the mean is 34.13% (because .3413 x 100 = 34.13).

3. The shaded area ± 1 SD from the mean contains about 68% of cases (or scores) in the normal distribution. Scores in this range are considered relatively average.

4. Scores that are more than ± 1 SD from the mean are, by definition, less frequently observed in the population. As the figure shows, less than 16% of scores in the distribution are in the area above +1 SD from the mean and below -1 SD from the mean (because .1359+.0214+.00135=.15865, or 15.87%). Therefore, a score that falls *outside* the shaded area in either direction might be considered significantly above average or significantly below average. Obviously, scores that are ± 2 SDs and ±3 SDs from the mean are considered even more unusual. Less than 3% of scores are above +2 SDs and below -2 SDs from the mean, and less than 1% of scores are above +3 SDs and below 3 SDs from the mean.

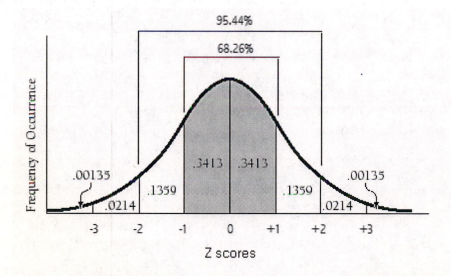

---

12.   When scores are normally or near-normally distributed, it is possible to convert Z scores into percentile ranks. For example, a Z score of 0 converts to the 50th percentile rank (since 50% of scores fall below a Z score of 0; see figure above). Identify the percentile ranks associated with the following Z scores below.

Z Score	Percentile Rank		Z Score	Percentile Rank
-3.00	_____		+1.00	_____
-2.00	_____		+2.00	_____
-1.00	_____		+3.00	_____

☙ *Because "real world" Z scores are rarely whole numbers like -3.00 or +1.00 (and are more often like -2.67 or +0.54) most Z score-to-percentile rank conversions require the use of special tables like those in* ***Appendix 1*** *in the back of your text. Exercises 13. through 15. will give you practice using these tables.*

Turn to Part I of Appendix 1 now. This table simply lists Z scores and corresponding percentile ranks.

13.   In a normal distribution, a Z score of .90 has a percentile rank of 81.59 (in other words, almost 82% of scores fall below a Z score of .90). Make sure you can find this value on Part I of Appendix 1. Then find the percentile ranks associated with the following Z scores:

Z Score	Percentile Rank		Z Score	Percentile Rank
-2.00	_____		+.50	_____
-1.30	_____		+1.80	_____
-0.50	_____		+2.00	_____

✎ *Using Part II of Appendix 1* ✎

         Turn to Part II of Appendix 1, in the back of your text, now. This table allows you to convert more specific Z scores (like +2.67 rather than +2.6) to percentile ranks. The four-digit numbers inside the table show the proportion of scores that are between a Z score of 0 (or the mean) and the *absolute value* of the Z score of interest. You can turn these proportions into percentages – just multiply by 100.

         For example, let's say you want to convert a Z score of +1.46 into a percentile rank. Find "1.4" in the far left column (and put your finger on it) and then find ".06" in the row at the top (and put your finger on it). Now, move one finger across the table and the other finger down the table – you should find a value of .4279. You can turn that proportion into a percentage: 42.79%. This is the percentage of scores between a Z score of 0 (or the mean) and a Z score of 1.46. But you are not finished yet! You are interested in converting a Z score of +1.46. into a percentile rank. Because 50% (or .5000) of scores fall below a Z score of 0, you must <u>add</u> .5000 and .4279. This sum equals .9279, so the percentile rank is 92.79. In other words, 92.79% of scores fall below a Z score of +1.46.

         Now let's say you want to convert a negative Z score, such as -1.46, into a percentile rank. Follow the same procedure as you did to find the Z score of +1.46—you will still find a value of .4279. Remember, this number tells you the proportion of scores between a Z score of 0 (or the mean) and a Z score of 1.46. Because you are interested in converting a Z score of -1.46 into a percentile rank, you must <u>subtract</u> .4279 from .5000 to find the proportion of scores that fall *below* a Z score of -1.46. Since .5000-.4279=.0721, the percentile rank corresponding to a Z score of -1.46 is 7.21. In other words, only 7.21% of scores are below a Z score of -1.46.

         <u>Important note!</u> Remember that you can convert Z scores into percentile ranks (and vice versa) using Part II of Appendix 1 *only* when scores are normally or near-normally distributed. Let's say you found the percentile rank of a raw score by using the formula $P_r = B/N \times 100$. Now let's say you found the Z score using the formula $Z = X - \overline{X} /S$. If the raw score distribution is normal or nearly normal, the percentile rank you find in Part II of Appendix 1 based on the Z score you calculated will be the same (or very close to) the percentile rank you found using the formula. On the other hand, if the raw score distribution is <u>not</u> normally distributed, the percentile rank you find in Part II of Appendix 1 based on the Z score you calculated will be different from the percentile rank you found using the formula. The degree to which the percentile ranks differ will depend on the extent to which the raw score distribution deviates from a normal distribution of scores.

14.   Using Part II of Appendix 1, find the percentile rank associated with the following Z scores.

Z Score	Percentile Rank	Z Score	Percentile Rank
-2.28		+.19	
-1.77		+1.55	
-0.63		+2.06	

15.   You can also use Part II of Appendix 1 to find Z scores associated with particular percentile ranks. For example, suppose you want to find the Z score that corresponds to the 82nd percentile rank. Because you know the Z score is going to be positive (since the percentile rank is over 50th), you need to find the value in the table closest to .8200-.5000, or .3200. The value in the table closest to .3200 is .3212. This value corresponds to a Z score of +.92. Make sure you can find this Z score.

Now let's say you want to find the Z score that corresponds to the 31st percentile rank. Because you know this Z score is going to be negative (since the percentile rank is less than 50th), you need to find the value closest to .5000-.3100, or .1900. The value closest to .1900 in the table is .1915. This value corresponds to a Z score of -.50. Make sure you can find this Z score.

Using Part II of Appendix 1, find the Z score associated with the following percentile ranks.

Percentile Rank	Z Score	Percentile Rank	Z Score
12th		95th	
62nd		29th	
44th		75th	

E. McCall's T (text pp. 50-51)

16.   Another type of standard score is **McCall's *T***. The *T* score distribution has a mean of 50 and a standard deviation of 10. *T* scores are employed by several prominent personality measures you will be reading about in Chapter 13, such as the Minnesota Multiphasic Personality Inventory (MMPI) and the California Psychological Inventory (CPI). Z scores can be transformed into *T* scores very easily, by using the formula: $T = 10Z + 50$. For example, if a Z score is +1.29, the corresponding *T* score would be 10(1.29)+50=62.9. If a Z score is -.17, the corresponding *T* score would be 10(-.17)+50=48.3.

First, go back to the figure on Workbook page 25 showing the standard normal distribution with Z scores indicated on the x axis. Underneath the label "Z scores" you will see a blank line. On that line, write "*T* scores." Then, under the specific Z scores indicated, write the corresponding *T* score. For example, under the Z score of 0, write "50." Under the Z score of -3, write "20," and so on.

Next, find the T scores associated with the following Z scores:

Z Score	*T* Score	Z Score	*T* Score
-2.28		+.19	
-1.77		+2.55	
-0.63		+3.06	

F. Quartiles and Deciles (text pp. 51-53)

17.   **Quartiles** divide the frequency distribution into equal _____, with Q1 at the 25th percentile, Q2 at the _____ percentile, Q3 at the _____ percentile, and Q4 at the _____ percentile.

18.   **Deciles** divide the frequency distribution into equal tenths, with D2 at the _____ percentile, D5 at the _____ percentile, D7 at the _____ percentile, etc.

19.   The **stanine system** converts scores to a scale ranging from ____ to ____; the term *stanine* comes from _____. Stanine distributions have a mean of _____ and a standard deviation of _____.

VII. NORMS (text pp. 53-62)

1.   **Norms** are used to interpret examinees' scores relative to the scores of individuals making up the standardization sample (also called the *norm group*). Both the mean and standard deviation are examples of norms. What are other examples? _____

2.   What assumptions are made about the relationship between characteristics of a test's standardization sample (or norm group) and characteristics of current test-takers? _____
_____
_____

⚲ **Psychological Testing in Everyday Life Box 2-4, *Within-Group Norming Controversy***
PTEL Box-2-4 discusses issues related to how tests are used by employers to evaluate job applicants of different racial and ethnic groups, given the fact that these groups do not have the same average level of performance on many tests. When tests are used to evaluate applicants, a higher percentage of white applicants are often selected than their representation in the general population would indicate. Essentially, the issue revolves around two goals of employers that sometimes are in conflict: (1) to enhance the racial and ethnic diversity of the workforce, and (2) to hire the applicants with the best individual qualifications. • What is *overselection*? • How did the U.S. Department of Labor remedy the problem of overselection based on GATB scores? • What are the opposing positions taken by the National Academy of Sciences and the Civil Rights Act of 1991 regarding within-group norming?

A. Age-Related Norms (text p. 54)

3.   Most intelligence tests, such as the Wechsler scales and the Stanford-Binet scales, have different normative groups for particular _____ groups.

B. Tracking (text pp. 55-59)

4.   Pediatricians often use age-related norms to assess whether children's growth (in height and weight) is occurring at expected rates. As they grow older, children tend to stay at about their same percentile level, relative to other children in their age group, in terms of their height and weight. This tendency is called

_____.

5.   Pediatricians use charts such Figure 2-9 on p. 57 and Figure 2-10 on p. 58 to assess whether children are growing at the expected rate. For example, Figure 2-9 (the tracking chart for boys) shows that a 9-month old baby boy at the 50th percentile for length is about 28.5 inches long. If the baby grows as expected (i.e., stays at the 50th percentile), at 27 months he should be about 35.5 inches long.   If a child does not stay on his "track" for growth, the pediatrician will take a closer look at potential causes and interventions, if necessary.

Look at Figure 2-10 (p. 58), the tracking chart for girls' growth. Complete the table below which summarizes length (height) information for four baby girls. Be sure to indicate whether the baby is growing at the expected rate (i.e., has roughly maintained her percentile rank).

Name of baby girl	Age (mos.)	%ile rank	Length (inches)	*Actual* length at 36 mos.	*Expected* length at 36 mos	Growing as expected? (Yes/No)
Cherie	6	75th	26.5	38	38.5	Yes
Madeline	18		31.0	36.5		
Fiona	24	95th		36.5		
Hannah		50th	34.0	37.5		

6.   If you were a pediatrician or a parent, which of the baby girls might you be concerned about? Why?

_____

_____

7.   Why is the application of tracking to education controversial? _____

_____

_____

_____

C. Criterion-Referenced Tests (text pp. 59-62)

8.   What are **criterion-referenced tests,** and how are the results of these tests used? _____

_____

_____

_____

Key Terms and Concepts to Know from Chapter Two

descriptive statistics

inferential statistics

properties of scales: magnitude

properties of scales: equal intervals

properties of scales: absolute zero

nominal scale

ordinal scale

interval scale

ratio scale

frequency distribution

percentile rank

percentile

variable

mean

standard deviation

variance

Z score

standard normal distribution

McCall's T score

quartiles

median

deciles

stanine system

norms

tracking

overselection

Section 106 of Civil Rights Act of 1991

norm-referenced test

criterion-referenced test

CHAPTER 2 PRACTICE QUIZ

1.   **If you lined children up according to their weight, from highest to lowest, you would be using a(n) _____ scale.**

      a. interval
      b. ordinal
      c. nominal
      d. ratio

2.   **The normative group, or standardization sample, is**

      a. the group to which current examinees can be compared.
      b. the population that scores in the extreme or "clinical" range on a test.
      c. the sample of people in a criterion validity study.
      d. typically not the target population for the test in question.

3.   **The score in the exact middle of the distribution of scores, such that equal numbers of scores fall above and below it, is the _____.**

      a. mean
      b. median
      c. standard score
      d. standard deviation unit

4.   **Suppose you are in the 87th percentile on a test. This means**

      a. you are in the group of 13 top-scoring people who took the test.
      b. 87% of the students got a score lower than your score.
      c. you got 87% of the items on the test correct.
      d. 87% of the students in the class scored higher than you did.

5.   **The Civil Rights Act of 1991**

      a. made it illegal for employers to use separate race-related norms for employment testing.
      b. made it legal for employers to use different cut-off scores on employment-related tests for the purposes of increasing racial diversity in the workplace.
      c. made overselection of particular racial groups illegal in employment settings.
      d. was deliberately vague regarding how employers could use tests to select employees.

Questions 6-9. relate to subjects' scores on the Green Test, described in the box below.

> Several subjects have just taken a test designed to measure the tendency to be envious of others, called the "Green Test." On the Green Test, higher scores indicate a greater tendency to experience envy. The test manual indicates that the original sample distribution (which conformed to the normal distribution) had a **raw score mean of 20** and a **standard deviation of 2.**

6.   **Pete received a raw score of 21 on the Green Test. His z-score would be _____ and his T-score would be _____.**

   a.   +1.50; 60
   b.   -1.50; 35
   c.   -.50; 40
   d.   +.50; 55

7.   **If Margie received a z-score of -1.00 on the Green Test, her percentile rank would be**

   a.   16.
   b.   50.
   c.   84.
   d.   97.

8.   **Daniel's percentile rank on the Green Test was 50. Therefore, his raw score was _____.**

   a.   18
   b.   20
   c.   22
   d.   24

9.   **Which is the correct order of subjects' tendency to be envious, as measured by the Green Test, from *least* envious to *most* envious?**

   a.   Pete, Margie, Daniel
   b.   Margie, Pete, Daniel
   c.   Daniel, Pete, Margie
   d.   Daniel, Margie, Pete
   e.   Margie, Daniel, Pete
   f.   Pete, Daniel, Margie

10.   **Although the use of_____ is accepted in medical settings, it is much more controversial in educational settings.**

   a.   Z score transformations
   b.   criterion-referenced tests
   c.   tracking
   d.   the stanine system

✍Student Workbook Assignment 2.1

⊸ Constructing a Grading System Using *Z* Scores and Percentiles ⊢

♦ DESCRIPTION OF THE ASSIGNMENT

This assignment provides a "real world" problem using Z scores and percentiles. It is modeled after *An example close to home* on pp. 49-50 of your text. It is very important that you go through this example carefully before you begin this assignment (including referring to Part II of Appendix 1 in the back of your text).

♦ DIRECTIONS

➔ **Before beginning this assignment, make sure you have read Chapter 2.**

Imagine that you are a teaching assistant for a professor who would like you to convert raw test scores into Z scores and then into letter grades. The professor gives you the following information about the test:

a. The test has 20 items.

b. There are 26 students in the class.

c. The professor grades on a curve that employs the following percentile cutoffs:

Grade	Percentiles
A	84-100
B	65-83
C	18-64
D	10-17
F	0 - 9

d. Scores on the test:

Student #	Score	Student #	Score
1	13	14	16
2	11	15	13
3	15	16	6
4	13	17	13
5	16	18	9
6	13	19	12
7	9	20	12
8	12	21	11
9	10	22	14
10	19	23	15
11	13	24	12
12	8	25	17
13	14	26	14

(1)   First, calculate the mean _____ and standard deviation _____.

(2)   In order to determine what grade each student should receive, you must first convert each of the professor's percentile cutoffs to z-score cutoffs.   First, find the value from Appendix 1, Part II, that corresponds to the lowest percentile rank for the particular grade.   Then write the Z score cutoff.   The first is done for you as an example.

Grade	Value from Appendix 1 Part II	Z-score cutoff
A	.3389	+.99
B	_____	_____
C	_____	_____
D	_____	_____
F	_____	_____

(3)   Now determine the z-scores and letter grades for each of the 8 students listed below.

Student #	Raw score	Z-score	Letter grade
2	_____	_____	_____
5	_____	_____	_____
7	_____	_____	_____
12	_____	_____	_____
16	_____	_____	_____
17	_____	_____	_____
21	_____	_____	_____
25	_____	_____	_____

⊶ CHAPTER 3: *Correlation and Regression* ⊷

Chapter 3 Outline

I. The Scatter Diagram (text pp. 66-68)

II. Correlation (text pp. 68-69)

III. Regression (text pp. 69-82)

    A. The Regression Line (text pp. 69-70)

    B. The Best-Fitting Line (text pp. 71-76)

    C. Testing the Statistical Significance of a Correlation Coefficient (text pp. 76-78)

    D. How to Interpret a Regression Plot (78-81)

IV. Other Correlation Coefficients (text pp. 81-83)

V. Terms and Issues in the Use of Correlation (text pp. 84-88)

    A. Residual (text p. 84)

    B. Standard Error of Estimate (text p. 84)

    C. Coefficient of Determination (text p. 85)

    D. Coefficient of Alienation (text p. 85)

    E. Shrinkage (text pp. 85-86)

    F. Cross Validation (text p. 86)

    G. The Correlation-Causation Problem (text p. 86)

    H. Third Variable Explanation (text p. 86)

    I. Restricted Range (text pp. 86-88)

VI. Multivariate Analysis (Optional) (text pp. 88-93)

    A. General Approach (text pp. 88-89)

    B. An Example Using Multiple Regression (text pp. 89-90)

    C. Discriminant Analysis (text pp. 90-91)

    D. Factor Analysis (text pp. 91-93)

CHAPTER 3 EXERCISES

I. THE SCATTER DIAGRAM (text pp. 66-68)

1. When researchers examine whether two variables are related to each other, they often begin by plotting the data on a scatter diagram. Imagine you are a researcher interested in the question of whether examinees' scores on the University Aptitude Test (UAT) are related to their grade point averages at the end of their first year at Ivy League University. Create a scatter diagram of the *bivariate distribution* of UAT scores and first-year GPA for the 15 examinees. Both the data table and the scatter diagram template are on the next page.

Examinee	UAT Score	1st year GPA
Greg	16	3.65
Allison	7	2.65
Janine	10	2.50
Corey	17	3.40
Michelle	3	2.75
Thomas	11	3.80
Randall	14	3.20
Tina	10	3.60

Examinee	UAT Score	1st year GPA
LeeAnn	13	3.35
David	12	3.55
Marcia	4	2.95
Lance	9	3.00
Keisha	15	3.90
Blair	12	3.10
Joe	6	2.30

SCATTER DIAGRAM: UAT Scores and GPA

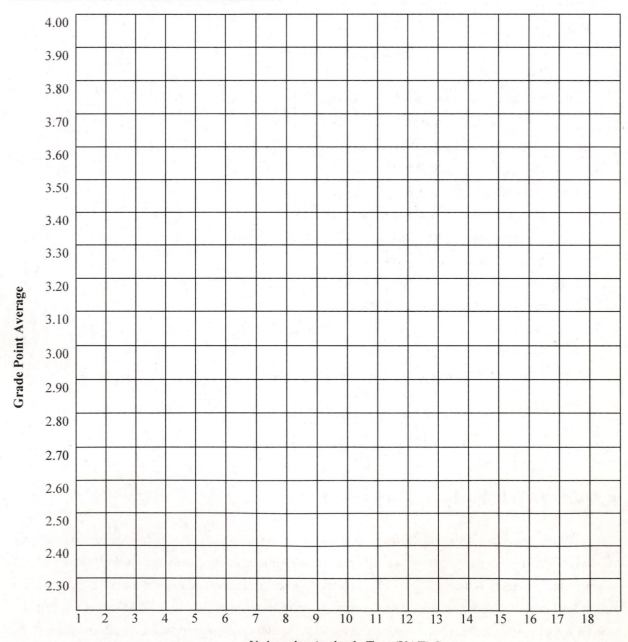

Grade Point Average

University Aptitude Test (UAT) Score

36

II. CORRELATION (text pp. 68-69)

1.   Look at the scatter diagrams shown below. Identify the type of relationship (positive correlation, negative correlation, no correlation) illustrated in each diagram.

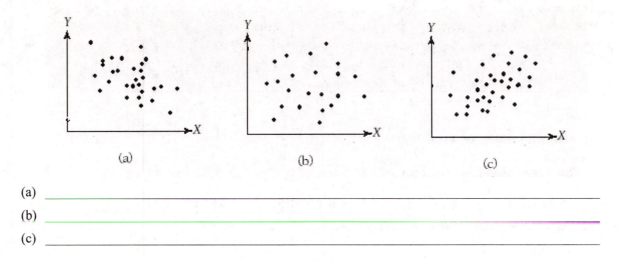

(a)

(b)

(c)

(a) _____

(b) _____

(c) _____

2.   Compare the scatter diagram you created on the previous page to the scatter diagrams shown above. Which of these three relationships (a, b, or c) appears to best characterize the bivariate distribution of UAT scores and first-year GPA at Ivy League University? _____.

3.   How would you describe the relationship between UAT scores and GPA? _____

_____

_____

✎ How are correlation coefficients interpreted? ✎

A correlation coefficient is simply the number that describes the relationship between two variables. The correlation coefficient tells you two things about the relationship between variables: its *magnitude* (strong or weak) and its *direction* (positive or negative).

First, the absolute value of the correlation coefficient will always be between 0.00 and 1.00 (in other words, it can range from -1.00 to +1.00). The strength, or magnitude, of the relationship between two variables is determined by looking at the absolute value of the correlation coefficient. A coefficient that is closer to 0.00 indicates a weaker, or possibly no, relationship between the variables. Let's say a correlation coefficient for two variables is 0.02 (or -0.02, because we only care about the absolute value of the coefficient when we examine its magnitude). In this case, the two variables are essentially unrelated. What this means is that *knowing the value of one variable tells you nothing about the value of the other variable.* For example, IQ and favorite ice cream flavor are unrelated variables. If you knew a person's IQ score, would it help you predict his or her favorite ice cream flavor? Of course not! But perhaps knowing the person's IQ score would help you predict some other variable, such as high school grade point average. This is because the magnitude of the correlation between IQ scores and high school GPA is substantially greater than 0.02 (although it still does not come close to 1.00).

(Continued on the next page)

A positive correlation between two variables simply means that as the value of one variable increases, the value of the other variable increases. A positive correlation *also* means that as the value of one variable decreases, the value of the other variables decreases. In other words, a positive correlation means that the values of the two variables are "traveling" in the same direction. Examples of positively correlated variables include: height and weight, clumsiness and accidents, and IQ score and grade point average. A negative correlation between two variables means that as the value of one variable increases, the value of the other variable decreases. In other words, a negative correlation means that the value of the two variables are "traveling" in opposite directions. Examples of negatively correlated variables include: happiness and depression, cautiousness and accidents, and exercise and amount of body fat.

III. REGRESSION (text pp. 69-82)

A. The Regression Line (text pp. 69-70)

1.   Regression is a technique closely related to correlation that is used to make _____ about scores on one variable from knowledge of scores on another variable.

2.   The regression line is the _____ straight line through a set of points in the scatter diagram.

3.   Go back to the scatter diagram of examinees' UAT scores and GPAs you created on page 36. Use the "eyeball method" and draw a **regression line**, or the best-fitting line, through the data points. (This will be only your best guess at the best-fitting line, of course!)

4.   Based on the regression line you drew, what *approximate* GPA would you predict for an individual who obtained a score of 14 on the University Aptitude Test? _____

5.   How does your prediction compare to the GPA obtained by Randall, the examinee who *actually* scored a14 on the UAT? _____

_____

🏃 *Very soon you will calculate the **regression equation**, the statistical (vs. the "eyeball") method that will enable you to draw a more exact best fitting line through the data points and make predictions about GPA based on University Aptitude Test scores. First, however, it is important for you to take a few minutes and think about the components of the regression equation. Read through text pages 69-70. This is challenging material, so take your time! If you still have questions about the components of a regression equation, read "What does a regression equation mean?" on the next page, which summarizes information presented on text pp. 69-70 in a slightly different way.*

What does the regression equation mean?

First of all, the regression equation looks like this: $\mathbf{Y' = a + bX}$. You might recognize it from your mathematics courses, because the regression equation is really just the equation for a straight line.

In this equation, **Y'** ("Y prime") is the score on variable Y, such as GPA, that you want to predict. On the previous page, question 4., you used the "eyeball" method to find Y'. Note that Y' and Y (the *actual* score on variable Y) are hardly ever the same. This is because there will always be error in predicting variable Y from knowledge of variable X. You discovered this on the previous page, in question 5, when you found that Randall's actual GPA was different from the GPA you would have predicted based on the "eyeballed" regression line. (We'll discuss this point a bit more later, but for the moment, keep in mind that the difference between Y and Y' is called the ***residual***.)

The most important component of the regression equation is ***b*****,** or the regression coefficient, which tells you the slope of the line. The absolute value of standardized coefficient *b* can range from 0.00 (which would be a horizontal line) to 1.00 (which would be a perfect diagonal line). Look at the diagram shown below (and on text p. 78), which illustrates the slopes of regression lines with different values of standardized *b*. If *b* = 0.0, it means that there is no relationship between X and Y. In other words, knowing the value of X (such as an examinee's UAT score) tells you absolutely nothing about the value of Y (the criterion score, such as GPA). The closer the value of standardized *b* is to 1.0, the better the regression equation is at predicting the value of Y from knowledge of X. (Of course, just as one rarely sees a "perfect" correlation coefficient of 1.00, one hardly ever comes across a "perfect" standardized *b* of 1.00!)

Something that is not illustrated on the diagram is the fact that, just like a correlation coefficient, *b* can be positive <u>or</u> negative. Look back to the three scatter diagrams labeled (a), (b) and (c) on Workbook page 33. Whereas a regression line with a positive *b* (for example, *b*=.50) might fit scatter diagram (c), a regression line with a negative *b* (for example, *b*=-.80) might fit scatter diagram (a).

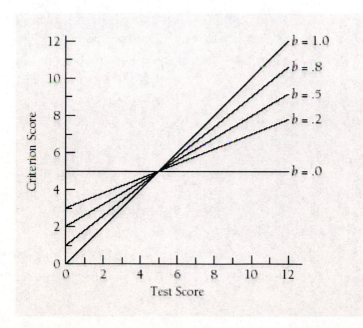

The next component of the equation is ***a***, the intercept, which is where the regression line crosses the y axis. It is the value of Y when X is 0. In the diagram above, you can see that in the regression line whose *b* is 0.0, *a*=5. In the regression line whose *b* is .8, *a*=1.

Finally, ***X*** is simply the observed or known value of X (such as UAT score) on the basis of which you will predict GPA (or Y').

B. The Best-Fitting Line (text pp. 71-76)

The moment you have been waiting for has arrived (☺)! You will calculate the **regression equation**, the statistical (vs. the "eyeball") method that will enable you to draw a more exact best fitting line through the data points and make predictions about GPA based on University Aptitude Test scores. On the next page, you will see Worksheet 1: *Values Needed for Calculating the Correlation Coefficient and Regression Line.* Use this worksheet to help you find all the values you need to plug into the regression equation.

The equation for the regression line is **Y'=a + bX**   where,   Y'=the predicted value of Y (GPA)
                                                                                                                                             a = the y-intercept
                                                                                                                                             b = the slope of the regression line
                                                                                                                                             X = the observed score (UAT score)

The formulas for calculating *b* (the slope of the regression line) and *a* (the y-intercept) are:

$$b = \frac{N(\sum XY) - (\sum X)(\sum Y)}{N\sum X^2 - (\sum X)^2}$$

$$a = \overline{Y} - b\overline{X}$$

(See Appendix 3-1 in the text for step-by-step directions on how to calculate the regression equation.)

6.   The equation for the regression line is **Y'** = _____ + _____**X**

7.   Using the regression equation, what first-year GPA at Ivy League University would you predict for examinees who obtained the following scores on the University Aptitude Test?

		Y (actual GPA)
a. UAT = 4	**Y'**= _____	_____
a. UAT = 10	**Y'**= _____	_____
b. UAT = 17	**Y'**= _____	_____

8.   Now, compare each Y' with its respective Y. In the space next to each Y' above, write the actual GPAs of examinees who obtained UAT scores of 4 (Marcia), 10 (Janine and Tina), and 17 (Corey). Notice there are differences between the predicted GPAs (Y') and the actual GPAs (Y) held by examinees with particular UAT scores. The difference between the actual and the predicted GPA (Y-Y') is called the **residual** (see text pp. 84-85).

9.   Correlation is a special case of regression in which scores on both variables are in

_____ or _____ units. This is useful because it means that in correlation, the intercept is always 0.

WORKSHEET 1

<u>Values Needed for Calculating the Correlation Coefficient and Regression Line</u>

Examinee	X UAT Score	Y GPA	X^2	Y^2	XY
Greg	16	3.65			
Allison	7	2.65			
Janine	10	2.50			
Corey	17	3.40			
Michelle	3	2.75			
Thomas	11	3.80			
Randall	14	3.20			
Tina	10	3.60			
LeeAnn	13	3.35			
David	12	3.55			
Marcia	4	2.95			
Lance	9	3.00			
Keisha	15	3.90			
Blair	12	3.10			
Joe	6	2.30			
	$\Sigma X=$	$\Sigma Y=$	$\Sigma X^2=$	$\Sigma Y^2=$	$\Sigma XY=$

N = _____ $(\Sigma X)^2 =$ _____

$\overline{X}$ = _____ $(\Sigma Y)^2 =$ _____

$\overline{Y}$ = _____ $(\Sigma X)(\Sigma Y) =$ _____

C. Testing the Statistical Significance of a Correlation Coefficient (text pp. 76-78)

10.   Use Appendix 4 in the back of your text to determine whether the correlation coefficients in the table below are statistically significant (i.e., that the associations found between sets of variables was not the result of chance). If the correlation is statistically significant, use the Table to determine whether it is significant at the .05 or the .01 level for a two-tailed test. Both N (number of pairs of observations) and *r* (the correlation coefficient) are given. You will use this formula to calculate the t value: $t = r\sqrt{\dfrac{N-2}{1-r^2}}$

N	*r*	*T*	Statistically significant? (Yes/No)	If yes, at what level for a two-tailed test? (.05 or .01)
10	.23			
40	.23			
80	.23			
200	.23			

D. How to Interpret a Regression Plot (78-81)

11.   When the slope of the regression line is 0, variable X (the predictor) and variable Y (the criterion) are essentially _____.

12. In the case described above, your best guess at the criterion score is going to be what? _____
_____.

IV. OTHER CORRELATION COEFFICIENTS (text pp. 81-83)

1.   For each type of variable, give two examples not listed in the text.

   a. continuous: _____

   b. true dichotomous: _____

   c. artificial dichotomous: _____

2.   In the table below, indicate with a "✓" the correlation coefficient(s) that would be appropriate to assess the relationships between the following pairs of variable types.

Pairs of Variable Types	Pearson's *r*	Biserial *r*	Point biserial *r*	Tetrachoric *r*	Phi
Continuous & artificial dichotomous					
True dichotomous and true dichotomous					
Both artificial dichotomous					
True dichotomous and continuous					
Both continuous					

V. TERMS AND ISSUES IN THE USE OF CORRELATIONS (text pp. 84-88)

1.　　Define (or describe) and give an example and/or formula that illustrates each term in the table below.

TERM	DEFINITION OR DESCRIPTION	EXAMPLE
Residual (p. 84)		
Standard Error of Estimate (pp. 84-85)		
Coefficient of Determination (p. 85)		
Coefficient of Alienation (p. 85)		
Shrinkage (pp. 85-86)		
Cross-Validation (p. 86)		
Correlation-Causation Problem (p. 86)		
Third Variable Explanation (p. 86)		
Restricted Range (pp. 86-88)		

VI. Multivariate Analysis (Optional) (text pp. 89-94)

🔖 *Note: Be sure to ask your instructor if he/she would like you to complete this section of the Workbook.*

A. General Approach (text p. 89)

1.   Multivariate analyses allow researchers to examine the relationship between several _____ and one _____, or criterion.

2.   Multivariate analyses use _____ combinations of variables, which are weighted composites of the original variables.

B. An Example Using Multiple Regression (text p. 90)

3.   If you were going to conduct a multiple regression analysis to examine variables that might predict the extent to which you felt a first date was successful (on a scale of 1 to 10), which three predictor variables would you choose? How would you weight each of these variables (e.g., x1, x2, x3, x4, etc.)

Variable	Weight
a. _____	_____
b. _____	_____
c. _____	_____

4.   For what reason(s) would you likely transform raw scores on the predictor variables into Z scores?
_____
_____

5.   Under what circumstances would you be cautious about interpreting regression coefficients (or *b*'s)?
_____
_____
_____

6.   Do the circumstances you described above apply to the three variables identified in question 3?
Explain. _____
_____
_____

C. Discriminant Analysis (text p. 91)

7.   Under what circumstances would you use discriminant analysis, rather than multiple regression, to predict a criterion or outcome variable? _____
_____

D. Factor Analysis (text pp. 91-93)

✶ *The best way for you to study factor analysis is to read through **Focused Example 3-2, The Factors of Trust**, on pp. 92-93. Then complete the exercise below.*

Factor analysis is a technique frequently used by test developers. Essentially, factor analysis allows test developers to identify whether the items they created "act" as intended. For example, if a test developer believes she has created a test that measures three dimensions of a construct, and she writes items designed to measure each of these three dimensions, she hopes the items will "act" as intended. Specifically, she hopes items she wrote for dimension A will correlate most highly with other items written for dimension A, rather than with items written for dimensions B or C. In the language of factor analysis, this test developer hopes items will **load** most highly onto Factor A (versus Factor B or Factor C). In this way, factor analysis can offer construct-related evidence of the validity of a test, since this technique *confirms* whether the structure of the test matches the test developer's beliefs about the construct on which the test is based. Sometimes test developers are not sure how many dimensions make up the construct, so they subject their test data to a factor analysis as a way to *explore* the number of dimensions (or factors) that emerge.

For example, let's say a researcher constructs a test of food preferences. He writes 40 items related to what people like about the food they eat. Then he gives his test to a large sample of people and subjects his data to a factor analysis. Answer the following questions based on the factor analysis table shown (note: only the first 9 items are shown).

8. Which items loaded most highly on Factor I? _____

Factor II? _____ Factor III? _____

9. When you examine the content of the items, what would you name each of the factors?

Factor I: _____

Factor II: _____

Factor III: _____

	Factors		
	I	**II**	**III**
1. Food tastes better when it looks appealing on the plate.	.15	.28	.47
2. I would much rather eat an overly-spiced meal than a bland one.	.49	.21	.09
3. The way food is served to me does not influence whether I will like it.	-.22	.04	-.41
4. I enjoy the scent of a freshly cooked meal almost as much as I enjoy eating it.	.25	.37	.20
5. Even if I was very hungry, I would rather eat a small but attractively prepared meal than a less attractive, large meal.	.08	.-11	.43
6. As far as I'm concerned, the more my eyes water when I eat spicy-hot food, the better I like it.	.42	.27	.12
7. I do not care how food smells, as long as it tastes good.	-.29	.-53	.08
8. I prefer mild-tasting cheeses and meats to strong-tasting ones.	-.41	-.18	.05
9. How food smells really influences how it will taste to me.	.33	.44	.15

Key Terms and Concepts to Know from Chapter Three

scatter diagram

correlation

correlation coefficient

positive correlation

negative correlation

regression

regression line

regression coefficient

sum of squares

covariance

slope

intercept

best-fitting line

residual

principle of least squares

Pearson product moment correlation coefficient

statistical significance of a correlation coefficient

criterion validity

Spearman's rho

true dichotomous variables

artificially dichotomous variables

biserial correlation

point biserial correlation

phi coefficient

tetrachoric correlation

residual

standard error of estimate

coefficient of determination

coefficient of alienation

shrinkage

cross validation

correlation-causation problem

third variable explanation

restricted range problem

multivariate analysis

multiple regression

standardized regression coefficients

raw regression coefficients

discriminant analysis

factor analysis

principal components

factors

item loading

factor loading

method of rotation

CHAPTER 3 PRACTICE QUIZ

1. Correlation is a special case of regression in which scores on both variables are

    a. standardized.
    b. squared.
    c. estimated.
    d. ordinal.

2. If people who are taller also tend to be heavier, then the <u>most</u> <u>likely</u> value of the Pearson product moment correlation coefficient between height and weight is

    a. +1.50.
    b. -0.50.
    c. +0.50.
    d -1.50.

3. In the regression equation, *a* is the _____ and *b* is the _____ .

    a. slope; variance
    b. intercept; slope
    c. intercept; variance
    d. variance; slope

4. If the correlation between scores on an intelligence test and annual income is .30, the coefficient of determination is

    a. .06.
    b. .09.
    c. .15.
    d. .60.

5. A psychologist examined the correlation between scores on a test of verbal reasoning (variable X) and years in school (variable Y). The psychologist administered the verbal reasoning test to a group of 11th grade students. The psychologist will find

    a. a correlation close to 1.00, due to restriction of range on variable X.
    b. a correlation close to 0.00, due to restriction of range on variable Y.
    c. a correlation close to 1.00, due to restriction of range on variable Y.
    d. a correlation close to 0.00, due to restriction of range on variable X.

6.   In regression, the difference between the predicted Y (Y') and the observed or actual Y is the

   a. residual.
   b. standard error of estimate.
   c. coefficient of alienation.
   d. critical value.

7.   Which of the following is a true dichotomous variable?

   a. passing or failing a statistics exam
   b. eye color
   c. right or left handedness
   d. weight

8.   The correlation between two continuous variables is found using

   a. Spearman's rho.
   b. point biserial r.
   c. tetrachoric r.
   d. Pearson's r.

9.   Suppose you wanted to predict success in graduate school using a combination of three variables: undergraduate GPA, intelligence test scores, and professor ratings. The statistical method that you would most likely use is

   a. multiple regression.
   b. factor analysis.
   c. bivariate correlational analysis.
   d. item-total analysis.

10.   A researcher who wants to find out how many underlying dimensions are represented in his 100-item personality test would probably use

   a. discriminant analysis.
   b. factor analysis.
   c. multiple regression.
   d. cross validation.

✍Student Workbook Assignment 3.1

⊷ Scatter Diagrams & the Eyeball Method of Estimating Correlation Coefficients ⊶

♦ DESCRIPTION OF THE ASSIGNMENT

Visual inspection of data is a very important step in data analysis. Researchers use scatter diagrams to show the relationship between two variables. In this assignment, you will use the "eyeball method" to estimate the direction and magnitude of relationships between two variables.

♦ DIRECTIONS

➔ **Before beginning this assignment, make sure you have read Chapter 3.**

(1)   Examine scatter diagrams A-E, then answer the following questions.

    a.   Which of the scatter diagrams depicts a *positive relationship* between variable X and variable Y? Briefly explain your answer.

    b.   Which of the scatter diagrams depicts a *negative relationship* between variable X and variable Y? Briefly explain your answer.

    c.   Which of the scatter diagrams depicts *no relationship* between variable X and variable Y? Briefly explain your answer.

    d.   Which of the scatter diagrams depicts the *strongest relationships* between variable X and variable Y? Briefly explain your answer.

    e.   Take a guess at what the correlation coefficient might be for each of the relationships shown. (This is just a broad estimate of course; focus on what the coefficients might be relative to each other). Briefly explain your answers.

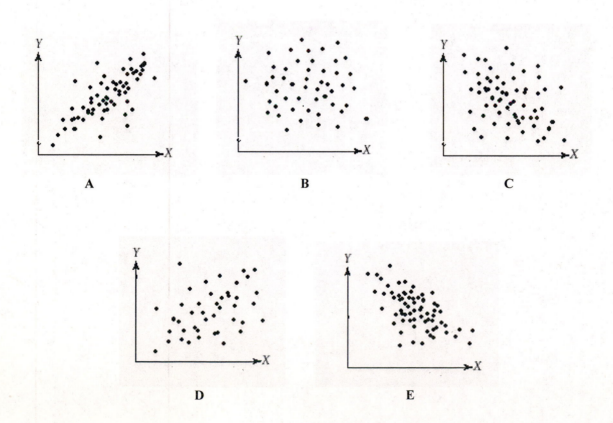

A   B   C

D   E

⊣ CHAPTER 4: *Reliability* ⊢

Chapter 4 Outline

CHAPTER 4 EXERCISES

I. HISTORY AND THEORY OF RELIABILITY (text pp. 102-105)

1. In the language of psychological testing, the term *error* refers to discrepancies that will <u>always</u> exist between _____ ability and the _____ of ability.

2. Tests that are relatively free of measurement error are said to be _____, whereas tests that have "too much" error are deemed _____.

A. Conceptualization of Error (text pp. 102-103)

3. Throughout Chapter 4, the text authors use the analogy of the "rubber yardstick" in reference to psychological tests and measures. Explain why this is a fitting analogy. _____

_____

_____

B. Spearman's Early Studies (text p. 103)

4.   Many advances in the field of psychological measurement were made in the late 19th and early 20th centuries. Combining Pearson's research on the _____ with De Moivre's notions on sampling error, _____ published the earliest work on reliability theory in his 1904 article, "The Proof and Measurement of Association Between Two Things."

C. Basics of Test Score Theory (text pp. 103-105)

5.   The most basic assumption of classical test score theory is reflected in the symbolic equation below: Fill in the terms beneath each component of this equation.

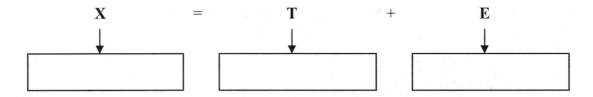

6.   Another major assumption of classical test theory is that errors of measurement are _____, rather than systematic.

⚡ *Read through the shaded box below, which introduces and explains the symbolic equation, X=T+E, in simple terms. Then carefully read the text section entitled "Basics of Test Score Theory" on pp. 103-105 before moving to the Workbook questions on the following page.*

$$\text{⚡ } X = T + E \text{ ⚡}$$

Imagine the most perfect, accurate psychological measurement device in the universe. This device could peer into your mind and identify your *true* level of intelligence, your *true* degree of extraversion or introversion, your *true* knowledge of Chapters 1-4 of this textbook, and other characteristics. Perhaps this device could be passed over your head, then on a small screen a score would appear—your *true score (T)* on the characteristic in question.

Of course, no such perfect psychological measurement device exists. And although, in theory, each one of us has thousands or more true scores on an abundance of psychological characteristics, all these true scores are unknowable. The best we can do is use our imperfect measuring devices—psychological tests—to estimate people's true scores. The score yielded by any psychological test, whether it is an intelligence test, a personality test, or a test you take in this course, is called the *observed score (X)*. The degree to which observed scores are close to true scores varies from test to test. Some tests yield observed scores that are very close to true scores, whereas some yield scores that are not at all close to true scores. In other words, some tests yield scores that reflect, or contain, less *error (E)* than others. Another way of saying this is that some tests are more reliable than others.

At this point you are probably wondering how we could possibly figure out the extent to which a test measures true scores rather than error, since true scores are unknowable. Furthermore, if true scores are unknowable, then isn't the amount of error reflected in observed test scores unknowable as well? Great questions! The following exercises over text pp. 103-105 will help you find the answers!

Read through the futuristic study presented in the box below and then answer the questions related to classical test theory that follow it.

> A subject with a strange-looking helmet on his head sits at a desk in a laboratory. The helmet is able to completely erase the subject's memory[1] of the previous 30 minutes. An experimenter hands the subject a test labeled "Test A" and directs the subject to complete it. After 25 minutes, the subject finishes Test A. The experimenter presses a button on the helmet and the subject immediately loses all memory of taking Test A. Then the experimenter once again places Test A in front of the subject and directs him to complete it. The subject completes the test, the experimenter presses the button on the helmet, and the subject forgets he ever saw Test A. The experimenter *again* places Test A in front of the subject, directs him to complete it....and so on. Imagine the subject takes Test A over 100 times.

7.   Will the subject's *observed score* on repeated administrations of Test A be the same every time? Explain your answer: _____

_____

_____

8.   In the space below, draw the distribution curve of the subject's observed scores on Test A.

9.   Explain why the mean of this hypothetical distribution is the best estimate of the subject's *true score* on Test A. _____

_____

_____

_____

↳ *If the mean observed score in a distribution of repeated tests is the best estimate of the true score, it should make sense that all the other scores in the distribution reflect, or contain, some amount of error. So, observed scores that are ± 1 SD from the mean of this distribution are better reflections of true scores than are scores ± 2 SDs from the mean. Scores that are ± 3 SDs from the mean reflect even more error.*

10.   Classical test theory uses the standard deviation of this distribution as a basic measure of error called the _____ _____ of _____,

which tells us, on average, how much an observed score deviates from the true score.

---

[1] For the purposes of this example, assume the helmet wipes out the subject's explicit *and* implicit memories of the previous 30 minutes!

11.   The figure below (and on text p. 105) shows three different distributions of observed scores, each with a unique standard deviation.

a. Which distribution (a, b, or c) depicts scores that reflect the *least* amount of error? _____

b. Which distribution (a, b, or c) depicts scores that reflect the *most* amount of error? _____

c. Most important, explain in your own words <u>why</u> you gave the answers above. _____

_____

_____

_____

_____

_____

(a)   (b)   (c)

12.   Because we cannot know actual true scores or actual error in measurement, we must estimate them. In practice, the _____ of the <u>observed</u> scores and the reliability of the test are used to estimate the standard error of measurement.

II. THE DOMAIN SAMPLING MODEL (text pp. 105-106)

1.   Because it is not feasible to create and administer tests containing every possible item related to a domain, trait, or skill (it would take a lifetime to create this test, let alone take it!) we must create tests consisting of a representative _____ of items from the domain.

2.   Reliability analyses estimate how much _____ there is in a score from a shorter test that is meant to mirror the longer (impossible-to-create) test containing all possible items.

3.   If three random samples of items are selected from the entire domain of all possible items, each of the three samples <u>should</u> yield an unbiased estimate of the _____ related to the domain.

4.   We know, however, that the three samples will <u>not</u> give the same estimate. Therefore, to estimate reliability, we can do what? _____

_____

_____

III. ITEM RESPONSE THEORY (text pp. 106-108)

1.   One reason classical test theory may be less than satisfactory as a basis for assessing reliability is that it requires that exactly the same test items be administered to each person. This means that for any particular examinee, only a handful of the test items will actually tap into his or her exact (unique) ability level. Yet the reliability estimate is for the entire test, including all the items that were too easy or too difficult for that particular examinee.

a.   Explain how tests are developed on the basis of item response theory (IRT). _____

_____

_____

_____

_____

b.   Describe the "overall result" of IRT-based procedures regarding test reliability. _____

_____

IV. MODELS OF RELIABILITY (text pp. 108-117)

1.   Reliability coefficients are _____ coefficients that can also be expressed as the ratio of the _____ on a test to the _____ on a test.

2.   Reliability coefficients can be interpreted as the proportion of variation in observed scores that can be attributed to *actual differences* among people on a characteristic/trait versus *random factors* that have nothing to do with the measured characteristic/trait. Interpret the hypothetical reliability coefficients in the table below.

RELIABILITY COEFFICIENT	INTERPRETATION
The reliability coefficient of an intelligence test is .82.	*This means that 82% of the variation in IQ test scores can be attributed to actual differences in IQ among people, and 18% of the variation can be attributed to random or chance factors that don't have much to do with IQ.*
The reliability of women's ratings of men's physical attractiveness is .70.	
The reliability coefficient of the weight scale in the university fitness center is .97.	
The reliability of a self-esteem measure is .90.	

A. Sources of Error (text pp. 108-109)

3.   Have you ever taken a test (e.g., an exam in one of your classes, a standardized test such as the SAT or GRE, etc.) and felt that the observed score you obtained did not really reflect your true score (i.e., your true knowledge of the subject being tested)? In your opinion, what were *sources of error* in your observed test score?

_____

_____

_____

4.   Reliability coefficients estimate the proportion of observed score variance that can be attributed to true score variance versus error variance. There are several ways of estimating test reliability because there are several different sources of variation in test scores. Briefly describe three methods of estimating test reliability:

a. *test-retest method*: _____

_____

b. *parallel forms method*: _____

_____

c. *internal consistency method*: _____

_____

B. Time-Sampling: The Test-Retest Method (text pp. 109-110)

5.   Test-retest methods of estimating reliability evaluate measurement error associated with administering the same test at two different times; this method is appropriate *only* when it is assumed the trait being measured does not _____.

6.   If you were to use the test-retest method to estimate the reliability of a test, what specific <u>actions</u> would you take? _____

_____

_____

7.   _____ effects occur when something about taking the test the first time influences scores the second time the test is taken; these effects can lead to _____ of the true reliability of a test.

8.   Give an example of a circumstance under which the effects described in 7 above would <u>not</u> compromise the reliability coefficient. _____

_____

9.   It is very important to consider the time interval between two administrations of the test in the interpretation of the test-retest reliability coefficient. What are three possible interpretations of a low test-retest coefficient (e.g., $r=.60$) of an anxiety measure that was administered to college students in March and then again in July (4 months later)?

a. _____

b. _____

c. _____

C. Item Sampling: Parallel Forms Method (text pp. 110-111)

⤷ Look at the figure below. Imagine that the large oval represents the boundary of a hypothetical content domain, such as information from Chapters 1-3 of this text. Each of the dots inside the large oval represents one item in the content domain. (In reality, the content domain of Chapters 1-3 probably contains thousands of dots, or possible items.) Now imagine that the circle bounded by the dashed line represents the sample of items that appear on a test over Chapters 1-3.

Content domain: All possible items from text Chapters 1-3

Items sampled for test over Chapters 1-3

10.   For what reason would the test over Chapters 1-3 probably be deemed unreliable with regard to item sampling? _____

_____

11.   Imagine another sample of items was drawn from the content domain depicted above. This set of items could comprise a *parallel form* of the test over Chapter 1-3. So now we have Test Form A (the original test) and Test Form B. Describe what <u>actions</u> you would take to estimate the reliability of Form A of the test using the parallel forms method. _____

_____

_____

_____

⤷ *In practice, most test developers do not estimate reliability using the parallel forms method. More often, they estimate reliability by examining the internal consistency of items on a single test. Text pages 111-116 describe three primary ways internal consistency reliability is evaluated: (1) split half, (2) KR_{20}, and (3) coefficient alpha.*

D. Split-Half Method (text pp. 111-113)

12.   Describe what <u>actions</u> you would take to estimate the reliability of a 20-item test using the split-half method. _____

_____

13.   For what reason does the basic split-half method underestimate the reliability of a test? _____

_____

14.   Apply the *Spearman Brown formula* (presented below and on text p. 112) to estimate what the correlation between the two halves of a 20-item test with a split-half correlation coefficient of .69 would have been if each half had been the length of the whole test.

$$r = \frac{2r}{1+r}$$

The Spearman Brown formula is: Corrected split-half reliability = _____

E. KR$_{20}$ Formula (text pp. 113-115)

15.   The Kuder-Richardson formula 20 (or KR$_{20}$) splits items all possible ways, so this method of estimating internal consistency reliability avoids the problem of _____ variances between arbitrary splits of a test into two halves (a problem sometimes presented with use of the split-half method).

> **↳ NOTE:** Several activities in Chapters 2-6 draw upon a fabricated data set of 15 scores on a hypothetical test called the University Aptitude Test (UAT). The UAT is a verbal analogies test consisting of 18 items. The UAT is designed to predict college-level academic performance.

On the next page you will see a worksheet that will help you find the values you need to calculate the internal consistency reliability of the University Aptitude Test (UAT) using the KR$_{20}$ formula.   For each item, "1" means the answer given by the student is correct and "0" means the answer given by the student is incorrect. For the purposes of this exercise, imagine that the UAT is only 10 items instead of 18 items. This means that you will need to calculate S^2, or the variance of UAT scores, even if you already calculated the UAT's standard deviation in Chapter 2 (because in Chapter 2 you calculated the SD based on the 18-item UAT).

The formula to find KR$_{20}$ requires calculation of the variance, or S^2.

$$S^2 = \frac{\sum X^2 - \frac{(\sum X)^2}{N}}{N-1} \qquad\qquad S^2 = \underline{\hspace{2cm}}$$

The KR$_{20}$ formula is shown below.

$$KR_{20} = \frac{N}{N-1}\left(\frac{S^2 - \sum pq}{S^2}\right)$$

where   KR$_{20}$ = the reliability estimate (r)
         N = the number of items on the test
         S^2 = the variance of the total test score
         p = the proportion of people getting each item correct
         q = the proportion of people getting each item incorrect

16.   **The KR$_{20}$ coefficient for the 10-item UAT =** _____

Worksheet to find KR₂₀ for the 10-item University Aptitude Test

	University Aptitude Test (UAT): Item numbers										X	X²
Examinee	**#1**	**#2**	**#3**	**#4**	**#5**	**#6**	**#7**	**#8**	**#9**	**#10**		
Greg	1	1	1	1	1	1	0	1	1	1		
Allison	1	1	1	1	0	1	0	0	0	0		
Janine	1	1	1	1	0	1	0	0	1	0		
Corey	1	1	0	1	1	1	1	1	1	1		
Michelle	0	0	1	1	0	0	0	0	0	0		
Thomas	0	1	1	1	0	1	1	0	1	0		
Randall	1	1	1	1	0	1	1	1	1	1		
Tina	0	0	1	1	0	0	1	0	0	0		
LeeAnn	1	1	1	1	0	1	1	0	1	1		
David	0	1	1	1	0	1	1	0	1	0		
Marcia	0	0	0	1	0	0	0	0	1	0		
Lance	1	1	1	1	0	1	1	0	1	0		
Keisha	1	1	1	1	0	1	0	1	1	1		
Blair	0	1	1	1	0	1	0	0	0	1		
Joe	0	0	1	1	0	0	0	0	0	0		
# correct												
P												
Q												
pq												
Σpq =											$\sum X =$	$\sum X^2 =$

F. Coefficient Alpha (text pp. 115-116)

17.   Under what circumstances is *coefficient alpha*, rather than KR_{20}, the appropriate measure of the internal consistency reliability of a test? _____

_____

18.   All measures of internal consistency – split-half, KR_{20}, and coefficient alpha – evaluate the extent to which the different items on a test _____.

19.   If a test is designed to measure several different traits or characteristics, _____ is a good way to examine whether items within subgroups or components are internally consistent.

G. Reliability of a Difference Score (text pp. 116-117)

20.   Under what circumstance might a researcher be interested in finding the *reliability of a difference score*?_____

_____

21.   When a reliability of the difference score is computed, the scores of both tests must be transformed into _____ units.

22.   For what reasons is the reliability of a difference score expected to be lower than the reliability of either score on which it is based? _____

_____

_____

_____

23. Using the formula presented below (and on text p. 116), find the reliability of a difference score between two measures with reliabilities of .87 and .92, respectively. The correlation between the two measures is .80.

The formula for the reliability of a difference score is: $r = \dfrac{\frac{1}{2}(r_{11} + r_{22}) - r_{12}}{1 - r_{12}}$

where, r_{11} = the reliability of the first measure
r_{22} = the reliability of the second measure
r_{12} = the correlation between the first and the second measures

The reliability of the difference score = _____

V. RELIABILITY IN BEHAVIORAL OBSERVATION STUDIES (text pp. 118-119)

1.   Why are behavioral observations frequently unreliable? _____

_____

_____

2.   *Interrater* or *interjudge reliability* estimates consider the consistency among different _____

who are rating the _____ behavior.

3.   Two reasons are given for why recording the percentage of times that two or more observers agree is
not a good method of estimating interrater reliability. What are they?

a. _____

b. _____

4.   The best method for estimating interrater agreement among several observers is the _____

statistic, which requires the use of nominal scales and corrects for _____ agreement.

VI. CONNECTING SOURCES OF ERROR WITH RELIABILITY ASSESSMENT METHODS (text pp. 119-120)

1.   Complete the diagram below, which re-organizes information presented in Table 4-2, *Sources of Error and Methods of Reliability Assessment*, presented on text p. 120.

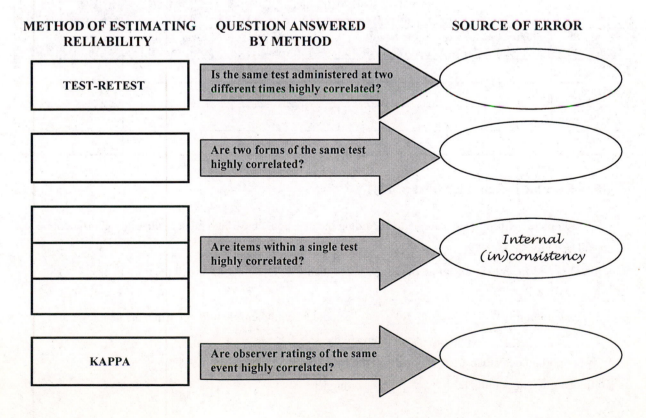

METHOD OF ESTIMATING RELIABILITY	QUESTION ANSWERED BY METHOD	SOURCE OF ERROR
TEST-RETEST	Is the same test administered at two different times highly correlated?	
	Are two forms of the same test highly correlated?	
	Are items within a single test highly correlated?	*Internal (in)consistency*
KAPPA	Are observer ratings of the same event highly correlated?	

VII. USING RELIABILITY INFORMATION (text pp. 120-129)

A. Standard Errors of Measurement and the Rubber Yardstick (text pp. 120-124)

1.   A larger standard error of measurement corresponds to a lower certainty that _____

_____, whereas a smaller standard error of measurement

corresponds to a higher certainty that _____.

2.   If the standard deviation of scores on a self-esteem test is 1.90, and the reliability coefficient of the test

is .85, what is the standard error of measurement?

The formula for calculating the standard error of measurement is: $S_m = S\sqrt{1-r}$

where S_m = the standard error for the measurement
        S = the standard deviation of scores
        r = the reliability coefficient

The S_m for the self esteem test = _____.

3.   The standard error of measurement is used to form confidence intervals around observed scores. These

confidence intervals allow us to estimate the probability that the _____ falls within a

certain interval.

4.   Find the 68% and 95% confidence intervals around the following scores on the self-esteem test:

Name of Examinee	Score on Self Esteem Test	Self Esteem Test 68% Confidence Interval		Self Esteem Test 95% Confidence Interval	
		Lower bound of interval	Upper bound of interval	Lower bound of interval	Upper bound of interval
Clint	15				
Marianne	11				
Jennifer	19				
Anthony	8				

B. How Reliable is Reliable? (text p. 124)

5.   Complete the following statements regarding the question, "how high must a reliability coefficient be to

be considered high enough?"

a. Reliability coefficients in the range of .70-.80 are probably high enough for measures used in basic

_____.

b. Tests that are highly _____ should have higher reliability coefficients than tests of

_____ constructs such as creativity.

c. When important decisions are to be made on the basis of test scores (in clinical settings, for example),

reliability coefficients should be _____ or higher.

C. What To Do About Low Reliability (text pp. 126-129)

6.   Explain why adding more items to a test can increase its reliability.

_____

_____

_____

_____ .

7.   Use the *Spearman-Brown prophecy formula* shown below (and on text p.126) to estimate how many items would have to be added to the 10-item University Aptitude Test to raise its reliability to .90. Use the KR_{20} coefficient you calculated for the UAT (question E.16, on p. 58) as r_o, the observed level of test reliability. (**Important note**: Remember that the Spearman-Brown prophecy formula does <u>not</u> give you the number of items that need to be added to the test. It gives you *the number of tests the same length of the current test* to bring the reliability up to the desired level. This means you must multiply the answer you get using the formula by the number of items on the current test, which in this case is 10. Then you must subtract 10 from this to yield the total number of *new* items that must be added to the UAT to bring its reliability up to .90).

The Spearman-Brown prophecy formula is: $N = \dfrac{r_d(1-r_o)}{r_o(1-r_d)}$

where,

$N =$	the number of tests of the current version's length that would be needed to have a test of the desired reliability
$r_d =$	the desired level of reliability
$r_o =$	the observed level of reliability (of the current version of the test)

Number of items that must be added to the UAT to raise its reliability to .90 = _____

8.   What assumptions are made about the new items being added to the test in order to raise its reliability?

_____

_____

9.   Another way to increase the reliability of a test is to remove items that decrease its reliability. Briefly describe two ways this can be accomplished.

a. _____

b. _____

10.   What is the purpose of using the *correction for attenuation*? _____

_____

_____

_____

Key Terms and Concepts to Know from Chapter Three

Reliable/reliability

Error

Classical test score theory

$X = T + E$

Standard error of measurement

Domain sampling model

Reliability coefficient (general)

Test-retest method/reliability coefficient

Carryover effect

Practice effects

Parallel forms method/reliability coefficient

Spit-half method/reliability coefficient

Spearman-Brown formula

KR_{20} formula

Coefficient alpha

Difference score

Reliability of a difference score

Interrater/interscorer/ interjudge reliability

Kappa statistic

Sources of error (associated with different methods of estimating reliability)

Standard error of measurement

Two approaches to deal with low reliability

Factor and item analysis

Correction for attenuation

➤ CHAPTER 4 PRACTICE QUIZ ➤

1.   **KR$_{20}$ and coefficient alpha are both measures of**

    a. the extent to which items on a test are clearly related to the construct being measured.
    b. the extent to which items on a test are intercorrelated.
    c. the extent to which items on a test are of an appropriate level of difficulty.
    d. the extent to which items on a test are truly measuring what they purport to measure.

2.   **Administering a test to a group of individuals, re-administering the same test to the same group at a later time, and correlating test scores at times 1 and 2 demonstrates which method of estimating reliability?**

    a. test-retest method
    b. alternative forms method
    c. split-half method
    d. internal consistency method

3.   **A test has a reliability coefficient of .77. This coefficient means that**

    a. 77% of the variance in test scores is true score variance, and 23% is error variance.
    b. 77% of items on this test are reliable and 23% of the items are unreliable.
    c. 23% of the variance in test scores is true score variance, and 77% is error variance.
    d. 77% of the variance in scores is unexplained variance, and 23% is error variance.

4.   **Test constructors can improve reliability by**

    a. increasing the number of items on a test.
    b. decreasing the number of items on the test.
    c. retaining items that measure sources of error variation.
    d. increasing the number of possible responses to each item.

5.   **Administering two supposedly equivalent forms of test (e.g., Form A and Form B) to the same group of individuals yields a correlation coefficient indicating**

    a. test-retest reliability.
    b. split-half reliability.
    c. alternative forms reliability.
    d. internal consistency reliability.

6.   **A reliability of a difference score is expected to be**

a. lower than the reliability of either test on which it is based.
b. higher than the reliability of one test and lower than the reliability of the other test on which it is based.
c. higher than the reliability of both tests on which it is based.
d. unrelated to the reliability of either test on which it is based.

7.   **Strong interrater (or interjudge) reliability is probably MOST important to which type of test?**

a. Behavior rating scales
b. Structured (objective) personality tests
c. Achievement tests
d. Aptitude tests

8.   **The relative closeness of a person's observed score to his/her true score is estimated by the**

a. test-retest reliability coefficient.
b. internal consistency reliability coefficient.
c. standard deviation.
d. standard error of measurement.

9.   **Sources of error associated with time-sampling (e.g., practice effects, carry-over effects) are best expressed in _____ coefficients, whereas error associated with the use of particular items is best expressed in _____ coefficients.**

a. test-retest reliability; internal consistency reliability
b. alternate forms reliability; interrater reliability
c. internal consistency reliability; test-retest reliability
d. split-half reliability; alternate forms reliability

10.   **Which of the following allows test developers to estimate what the correlation between two measures would have been if they had not been measured with error?**

a. standard error of measurement
b. reliability of a difference score
c. correction for attenuation
d. Spearman-Brown prophecy formula

✍Student Workbook Assignment 4.1

⊣ Explaining Reliability Coefficients ⊢

♦ DESCRIPTION OF THE ASSIGNMENT

In this assignment, you will identify and describe reliability studies that must be conducted by the researchers in each of the mini-cases shown below. This is a good way to learn about information each reliability method provides, as well as sources of error examined by each method.

♦ DIRECTIONS

➔ **Before beginning this assignment, make sure you have read Chapter 4.**

For each mini-case described below,

(1) identify the <u>method</u> of estimating reliability the researcher should use.
(2) describe the <u>actions</u> that must be taken to find the reliability coefficient.
(3) describe the <u>information</u> that is provided by the reliability coefficient, including sources of error.

CASE A   A research group was asked to provide a test publisher with the internal consistency reliability coefficient for a 100-item, dichotomously-scored (correct/incorrect) measure of intelligence they created.

CASE B   Dr. Bates is using a published behavioral rating scale in her research on children's social aggression on the playground. She has four research assistants who will spend approximately 50 hours each observing and recording the children's behavior, using the rating scale. Dr. Bates wants to make sure the research assistants are recording and scoring the children's behavior in the same ways.

CASE C   Researchers who developed a measure of optimism want to show that their test measures a stable personality characteristic that changes very little over time.

CASE D   Dr. Ludlow is interested in gathering reliability data for a creativity test he recently developed. Items on the test were scored from 1 to 5, with 5 indicating a very creative response and 1 indicating a non-creative response. Dr. Ludlow's primary interest is whether all the items on the test measure the same thing.

CASE E   Dr. Gladeau is approached by a teacher in the local public school system who asks him to help her with a problem. Specifically, the teacher states that she teaches two different third-grade math classes and uses different unit tests in each. "I need to provide evidence that my two math tests are measuring the same thing—that even though the items themselves are different, the tests are functionally the same."

CASE F   Dr. Veverka is interested in whether the items on her 50-item multiple-choice exam are of similar difficulty, or whether they increase in difficulty.

⊷ CHAPTER 5: *Validity* ⊷

CHAPTER 5 EXERCISES

I. DEFINING VALIDITY (text pp. 134-135)

1.   What did the Supreme Court rule in the case of *Griggs v. Duke Power* (on p. 134)? _____

_____

_____

2.   In the first brief section of Chapter 5 (p. 134) the authors present several ways to define *validity*. Which definition makes the most sense to you? _____

_____

_____

3.   What are the three primary types of evidence that can support a test's validity?

_____

_____

II. ASPECTS OF VALIDITY (text pp. 135-154)

A. Face Validity (text p. 136)

1.   In the table on the next page, write a face valid item that might be included on each measure listed. An example is provided for you.

Characteristic the test measures	Response or scoring options	Example of a "face valid" item
Eating disorders	True/False	*Sometimes after eating a large meal, I make myself vomit or take laxatives to "get rid" of the food.*
Skill at changing a flat tire	Excellent/ Good/ Poor	
Knowledge of basic statistics	Correct/ Incorrect	
Depression	Always/ Sometimes/ Never	
Procrastination	Agree/ Disagree	

2.   What is a potential *benefit* of using a highly face valid test? _____

_____

_____

3.   Can you think of a potential *limitation* of using a highly face valid test? _____

_____

_____

4.   Why is face validity not considered a "true" form of validity? _____

_____

_____

B. Content-Related Evidence for Validity (text pp. 136-137)

5.   In order to provide *content-related* evidence for the validity of a test, one must show that items on the

test: _____

_____

6.   On page 137, your text states that like evidence for face validity, evidence for content-related validity is *logical* rather than statistical. List two ways that such evidence might be gathered.

a. _____

b. _____

7.   Define *construct under-representation*: _____

_____

8.   Describe construct under-representation on a hypothetical test covering material from text Chapter 4.

_____

_____

_____

9.   Define *construct-irrelevant variance*: _____

_____

10.   Give an example of construct-irrelevant variance that might have influenced *your* score on an exam taken in the last year: _____

_____

C.   Criterion-Related Evidence for Validity (text pp. 138-148)

> ✎ **What is the "criterion" in criterion-related evidence for validity?** ✎
>
> A criterion is typically a "real-world" indicator of the thing the test is attempting to measure. Your text states that "the reason for gathering criterion evidence is that the test or measure is to serve as a 'stand-in' for the measure we are really interested in" (p. 138). In other words, a test score does not have much meaning in and of itself; it is simply a number. What *does* have meaning is how well a test score corresponds to something of interest (e.g., a behavior, a performance level, a diagnosis, an outcome, etc.) out there in the real-world. And this something of interest is the "criterion" in criterion-related validity.
>
> For any one test, there may be several potential criteria. An important key to gathering evidence of criterion-related validity is to identify a criterion that is both *meaningfully related to the purpose of the test* and *measurable*. Let's say we want to find criterion-related evidence for the validity of a Leadership Skills Inventory, which will be used by Company X to identify workers best suited for the role of project team leader. In this example, the obvious criterion is "success in team leadership position." How will this criterion be measured? Perhaps evaluations of team leaders by team members, or team productivity. If the Leadership Skills Inventory works well as a "stand-in" for an estimate of team leader success—in other words, if scores on the Leadership Skills Inventory are highly correlated with evaluations of team leaders—then there is criterion-related evidence for the validity of the test.

Predictive and concurrent evidence

11.   Read the hypothetical studies below and indicate whether they reflect attempts to establish *predictive* or *concurrent* types of criterion-related validity evidence by placing a check mark (✓) in the appropriate column.

STUDY	Predictive Evidence	Concurrent Evidence
a. Day-care workers completed behavior rating scales on children enrolled in a pre-school program. Correlation coefficients were calculated between scores on the rating scale and teacher evaluations of the children's behavior in first grade.		
b. Researchers administered a Science Aptitude Measure (SAM) to 1200 college students. The researchers compared SAM scores to grades received by the same group of students in a required science course they completed the previous year.		
c. Employees at a large greeting card manufacturing company completed a test of artistic potential. Researchers found that compared to employees who scored low on the test, employees with high scores were significantly more likely to work in the design department (vs. packaging, marketing, sales, etc.).		
d. Researchers administered the Relationship Commitment Inventory (RCI) to 100 newly-married couples. Three years later, the researchers collected information from the couples with regard to whether they were still married, separated, or divorced.		

♀ Focused Example 5-2, *Validation of a Self-Report Measure of Depression*
This Focused Example explores the criterion-related validity evidence for two measures of depression: the CES-D and the IDD. • Compare the evidence for validity of the CES-D with the evidence of validity of the IDD. Which is stronger, in your opinion? • In what situations or contexts might the CES-D be a more useful measure? The IDD?

Validity coefficients

12.   What is a validity coefficient, and what information does it provide? _____

_____

_____

_____

13.   Validity coefficients in the range of _____ to _____ are considered high, although coefficients much lower than this can still be statistically significant, which means that: _____

_____

_____

14. Answer the following questions about the meaning of a validity coefficient reported in the manual of a hypothetical test called STASS.

> **The manual for the Stanton Test of Attitudes Toward Social Service (STASS) reports a validity coefficient of .36 (or *r* = .36) for predicting the number of service hours students voluntarily complete during four years of college. Universities whose mission is to "teach the leaders of tomorrow" use the STASS to identify students who will be invited to join an honors leadership program.**

In this example, the predictor is _____ and the criterion is

_____. The validity coefficient is _____, so the coefficient of determination is

_____. The coefficient of determination means that _____ of the variation in

_____ can be explained (or predicted) by _____.

Other explanations (or predictors) of variation in the criterion might include _____

_____.

> ♀ **Focused Example 5-3, *The Testing Industry and the Public***
> This Focused Example presents a controversy that has great relevance to most students who hope to attend college, graduate or professional school. Do tests such as the SAT, GRE, LSAT and MCAT actually predict success in college and graduate school? After examining the results of research on this question, the Educational Testing Service (the test publisher) and Ralph Nader (consumer advocate) came to markedly different conclusions. ● What are the strengths and weaknesses of Nader's challenges to ETS? What about ETS's response to Nader's charges? ● What do you think? Do universities place too much emphasis on test scores in making selection decisions?

> ♀ **Focused Example 5-4: *Why the University of California rejected the SAT-I***
> Based on the results of a major study, the University of California system announced in 2001 that it would no longer require the Scholastic Reasoning Test-I for freshman admission. ●What does the SAT-I and SAT-II measure, respectively? ●What were the results of the study on which the UC system's decision was based?

Evaluating validity coefficients

15. In the exercise on the next two Workbook pages, you will apply the recommendations made in *Standards for Educational and Psychological Testing* for interpreting validity coefficients (see text pp. 143-148) to a hypothetical measure called the **Collegiate Athletic Promise Scale**, or the CAPS. In the CAPS manual, several studies are reported indicating the measure's predictive validity for identifying high school students who go on to play collegiate-level sports. For each recommendation, (a) briefly describe what information or data you would need to evaluate hypothetical validity coefficients in the context of the particular recommendation, and (b) give an example of information or data that would lead you to question the meaning or usefulness of the validity coefficient. An example is provided.

RECOMMENDATION #1: *Look for changes in the cause of relationships* (pp. 143-144)
Information needed to evaluate the CAPS validity coefficient: *Need to know the extent to which conditions of the original validity studies on the CAPS are similar to or different than current test conditions.*
Example of information leading to questions about the meaning and usefulness of the CAPS validity coefficient: *If the validity studies on the CAPS were conducted several decades ago, the usefulness of the reported validity coefficients would be questionable. Practices for recruiting college athletes are different today than they were several decades ago (e.g., today's recruiters cast a wider net, have more money to spend on athletes, and may place less emphasis on academic criteria). The CAPS may or may not be valid for predicting involvement in contemporary collegiate athletics.*

RECOMMENDATION #2: *(Ask) What does the criterion mean?* (p. 144)
Information needed to evaluate the CAPS validity coefficient
Example of information leading to questions about the meaning and usefulness of the CAPS validity coefficient

RECOMMENDATION #3: *Review the subject population in the validity study* (p. 144)
Information needed to evaluate the CAPS validity coefficient
Example of information leading to questions about the meaning and usefulness of the CAPS validity coefficient

RECOMMENDATION #4: *Be sure the sample size was adequate* (p. 145)
Information needed to evaluate the CAPS validity coefficient
Example of information leading to questions about the meaning and usefulness of the CAPS validity coefficient

RECOMMENDATION #5: *Never confuse the criterion with the predictor* (pp. 145-146)
Information needed to evaluate the CAPS validity coefficient
Example of information leading to questions about the meaning and usefulness of the CAPS validity coefficient

RECOMMENDATION #6: *Check for restricted range on both predictor and criterion* (pp. 146-147)
Information needed to evaluate the CAPS validity coefficient
Example of information leading to questions about the meaning and usefulness of the CAPS validity coefficient

RECOMMENDATION #7: *Review evidence for validity generalization* (p. 147)
Information needed to evaluate the CAPS validity coefficient
Example of information leading to questions about the meaning and usefulness of the CAPS validity coefficient

RECOMMENDATION #8: *Consider differential prediction* (pp. 147-148)
Information needed to evaluate the CAPS validity coefficient
Example of information leading to questions about the meaning and usefulness of the CAPS validity coefficient

16.   .Summarize the results of studies examining the question, *How well does the Graduate Record Exam (GRE) predict success in graduate school?* _____

_____

_____

_____

_____

_____

♀ Focused Example 5-5, *The Cholesterol Test: Predictive Validity Evidence*
This is an excellent example of validity as applied to medical tests. ● In the studies described in this Focused Example, what is the predictor? The criterion? ●Can you explain why cholesterol tests are considered valuable predictive tools, even though they account for only 1% of the variance in mortality in some studies?

D. Construct-Related Evidence for Validity (text pp. 148-154)

17.   Identify three *constructs* other than those mentioned in the text for which there are no established criteria (or "gold standards") _____

_____

18.   Describe the two primary ways that convergent evidence for construct validity is obtained.

a. _____

_____

b. _____

_____

♀ Focused Example 5-6, *The Meaning of Love*
Read this Focused Example carefully, because it is an extremely helpful illustration of the process of construct validation. ● What steps did Zick Rubin take as he prepared to write items for his love scale? ● What three factors emerged when all the items on the love scale were submitted to a factor analysis? ● What did the factor analysis reveal about items on the liking scale? ● What hypotheses about the love scale did Rubin test? What were the results of these studies? ● In what ways did Rubin's research provide construct-related evidence for the validity of his love scale?

---

19.   Your text presents many examples of how researchers provided convergent construct-related evidence for a health index by testing hypotheses about how the health index should "act" in relation to other measures and variables associated with health status. Complete the table on the next page by filling in the results of studies examining several hypotheses about the relationships between health index scores and other measures.

HYPOTHESIS RELATED TO	RESULTS
a. Individuals' ratings of their own health status	*The correlation between health index scores and self-ratings of health were strong.*
b. Symptoms and chronic medical conditions	
c. Age	
d. Visits to doctors	
e. Disabled vs. non-disabled people	
f. Physiological measures of disease	
g. Effects of treatment	

♀ Focused Example 5-7, *Construct Validity of the Women's Health Initiative Insomnia Rating Scale*
Results of validity studies on the WHIIRS are described in this Focused Example. ●How did the results of these studies provide construct-related validity evidence for the WHIIRS?

Discriminant evidence

20. What is one very practical reason why test developers are interested in providing *discriminant* evidence of construct validity (also called divergent validation)? _____

_____

_____

21. To demonstrate discriminant evidence for validity, a test should have _____ correlations with measures of _____ constructs; this shows that the test does not measure something *other* than what it was designed to measure.

Read the information presented below about a hypothetical measure of optimism/pessimism, and then answer the questions that follow.

The Pollyanna Optimism Test (POT) is a 25-item measure of optimism/pessimism. The test developers have provided a table, or matrix, in the POT manual showing correlation coefficients which they believe provide evidence of both convergent and discriminant construct validity. Information provided in the POT manual includes the following:

    ☐ The *Optimism-Pessimism Scale (OPS)* is a reliable, well-validated measure of optimism/ pessimism. This test has 150 items, so some test users feel it is too long and unwieldy for their purposes.

    ☐ The *Banner Self-Esteem Inventory (BSEI)* measures global self-esteem. The POT manual points out that self-esteem and optimism/pessimism are certainly related, but represent very different constructs.

The correlation matrix presented in the POT manual is shown below.

	POT	BSEI	OPS
POT	1.00		
BSEI	.21	1.00	
OPS	.78	.30	1.00

22.   Which correlation coefficient(s) relate to the POT's convergent validity? _____

23.   Do you believe evidence for convergent construct-related validity of the POT had been provided in the matrix? Explain your answer. _____

_____

_____

_____

_____

_____

24.   Which correlation coefficient(s) relate to the POT's discriminant validity? _____

25.   Do you believe evidence for discriminant construct-related validity of the POT had been provided in the matrix? Explain your answer. _____

_____

_____

_____

_____

_____

Criterion-referenced tests

26.   Briefly compare procedures for establishing the validity of norm-referenced tests with those of criterion-referenced tests. _____

_____

_____

_____

_____

E. Relationship between Reliability and Validity (text pp. 154-155)

27.   Calculate the maximum validity coefficient that could be obtained for a test with a reliability coefficient of .85 and a second test (or criterion measure) with a reliability coefficient of:

    .90_____

    .80_____

    .70_____

    .60_____

    .50_____

28.   Describe a pattern of evidence indicating that a measure (of intelligence, for example) is highly reliable, but not valid: _____

_____

_____

_____

_____

Key Terms and Concepts to Know from Chapter Five

Griggs v. Duke Power (1971)

Validity

Face validity

Content validity evidence

Construct underrepresentation

Construct-irrelevant variance

Criterion validity evidence

Predictive validity evidence

Concurrent validity evidence

Validity coefficient

Issues of concern when evaluating validity coefficients (8 of them)

Construct validity evidence

Convergent evidence (for construct validity)

Discriminant evidence (for construct validity)

Criterion-referenced tests

CHAPTER 5 PRACTICE QUIZ

1.   **As a result of the Supreme Court's ruling in *Griggs v. Duke Power*, employers must be able to provide evidence that tests used to make selection and promotion decisions**

   a.   measure capabilities specific to particular jobs or situations.
   b.   improve the overall quality of the workforce.
   c.   can be easily administered and scored by company managers or supervisors.
   d.   are well-established general measures of intelligence.

2.   **Validity is best understood as**

   a.   the ability of the test to measure consistently across time and cultures.
   b.   the extent to which the test measures what it claims to measure.
   c.   the collection of information and evidence available about a test.
   d.   the degree to which a test's measurements are free of errors.

3.   **The most we could say about a self-esteem test consisting of the items "I feel I deserve to be treated with respect" and "I think I am worthless" is**

   a.   it shows content-related evidence of validity.
   b.   it shows criterion-related evidence of validity.
   c.   it shows face validity.
   d.   it shows construct-related evidence of validity.

4.   **If researchers found a criterion validity coefficient of .40 for an achievement test, it would mean**

   a.   40% of the variation in achievement test scores can be explained by variation in the criterion.
   b.   16% of the variation in the criterion can be explained by variation in achievement test scores.
   c.   16% of the variation in achievement test scores can be explained by variation in the criterion.
   d.   40% of the variation in the criterion can be explained by variation in achievement test scores.

5.   **After taking an exam in a psychology course, a student makes this comment: "All the questions on the test came from Chapter Three, but the professor said the exam was over material in Chapters One through Six! What a waste of study time!" The student's criticism of the professor's exam is most obviously related to _____ evidence of validity.**

   a.   construct-related
   b.   concurrent criterion-related
   c.   content-related
   d.   predictive criterion-related

6.   Which of the following is <u>not</u> a recommendation regarding the evaluation of validity coefficients found in the *Standards for Psychological and Educations Testing?*

    a. Check that both predictor and the criterion scores have adequate variability.
    b. Review evidence that findings of the validity study do not apply only to that particular study situation.
    c. Be sure the validity coefficient is sufficiently strong, at least .40 or better.
    d. Be sure the validity study was conducted on a population representing the group to which inferences will be made.

7.   Developers of a sensation-seeking scale found that scores on the scale were highly correlated with self-reported frequency of alcohol and drug use. This finding most clearly provides _____ evidence for the validity of the sensation-seeking scale.

    a. concurrent criterion-related
    b. convergent construct-related
    c. discriminant construct-related
    d. content-related

8.   *Construct-irrelevant variance* is closest to which of the following concepts?

    a. measurement error
    b. standard deviation
    c. coefficient of determination
    d. cross-validation

9.   Dr. Lansing found that the correlation between scores on a measure of anxiety she developed and scores on an existing measure of depression was .82. It is likely that reviewers of Dr. Lansing's anxiety measure will view this correlation as evidence *against* _____ validity.

    a. predictive criterion-related
    b. discriminant construct-related
    c. convergent construct-related
    d. content-related

10.   A measure can be _____ yet not _____.

    a. valid; reliable
    b. useful; valid
    c. reliable; valid
    d. trustworthy; useful

Student Workbook Assignment 5.1

⊸ Evaluating Validity Coefficients ⊢

♦ DESCRIPTION OF THE ASSIGNMENT

You learned in Chapter 5 that an informed test consumer knows the right questions to ask about the meaning of validity coefficients to enable him/her to correctly interpret them. These questions, adapted from recommendations provided in *Standards for Educational and Psychological Testing*, and presented on text pp. 143-147, include the following:

(1)	Are there changes in the cause of relationships?
(2)	What does the criterion mean?
(3)	Does the subject population represent the group to which inferences will be made?
(4)	Was the sample size adequate?
(5)	Is the criterion confused with the predictor?
(6)	Does either the predictor or the criterion have restricted range?
(7)	Is there evidence for validity generalization?
(8)	Is differential prediction an issue?

In Assignment 5.1, you will apply these questions to a hypothetical test-related situation. Specifically, you will take the role of an administrative board member who must help the other members understand information about the validity of a particular hypothetical test.

♦ DIRECTIONS

→ **Before you do this assignment, make sure you have read Chapter 5.**

(1) Read through the case on the next page.

(2) Identify *four* of the eight questions from the list above (and on pp. 143-147) that you think are most important to the evaluation of the validity coefficients presented in the case.

(3) For each of the four questions you selected, discuss *in language the other board members will understand*:

    (a) why the question is particularly relevant, citing specific examples from the case, and
    (b) how the validity coefficient(s) might be interpreted or evaluated in the context of the particular
        question.

(4) Finally, describe two examples of criterion-related evidence for the test's validity that might lead you to feel more confident in the board's adoption of it.

⊣ Evaluation of Validity Coefficients Reported in the *Poe Potential for Violence Scale* Manual ⊢

Imagine that you are on the administrative board of Lage Correctional Facility, a medium security prison housing 400 female inmates. The board is trying to decide whether it should approve the use of a measure of violence potential to help identify which inmates are at highest risk for harming other inmates or prison staff. If the measure is adopted it will be used by Lage Correctional Facility officials to make decisions about restrictions placed on particular high-risk inmates. As it happens, you are the only board member with any knowledge of psychological testing, so you have been asked to evaluate the validity evidence for a particular test under consideration.

The test being considered by the administrative board is the Poe Potential for Violence Scale (PPVS), which measures a person's risk for engaging in violence against other individuals. The PPVS is a self-report measure consisting of 100 true/false items such as, "When I'm upset other people had better stay out of my way if they know what's good for them," "Sometimes when I lose my temper I break things," and "I truly believe there are some laws that are meant to be broken." The PPVS manual reports a test-retest (one week interval) reliability coefficient of .90 and a Cronbach's alpha coefficient of .86.

Three criterion-related validity studies are reported in the PPVS manual. The first validity study was conducted in 1960, very soon after the first edition of the PPVS was published. PPVS scores were collected from 173 male inmates at a maximum security prison. The researchers also examined each inmate's records and counted the number of physical incidents (e.g., assaults) involving the inmate in the previous year. PPVS scores were significantly correlated with number of physical incidents (r=.30).

In another study, 400 male inmates housed in three correctional facilities were administered both the PPVS and the Destructive Potential Interview Schedule (DPIS), a structured interview that yields categorical ratings of the potential to destroy property (Low potential, Moderate potential, and High potential.) Reliability and validity data regarding the DPIS were not provided in the description of this study. The correlation coefficient found for the relationship between PPVS scores and DPIS ratings was .38, which was statistically significant.

The final study reported in the PPVS manual examined the ability of the PPVS to predict the proportions of sentences served by female inmates in a minimum security prison. The researchers hypothesized that since parole boards base their recommendations for parole or continued confinement in part on the inmate's risk of committing violent crimes in the community, amount of time served by inmates would be a good criterion against which PPVS scores could be compared. The PPVS was administered to 26 female inmates immediately after they began serving two-to five-year sentences. At the end of the five-year period, the researchers examined the records of the inmates to determine the amount of time each inmate had served. Records for only 20 inmates were complete. Five of the inmates from the initial sample had been transferred to medium-security facilities and their status was unknown, and one inmate had died as a result of injuries inflicted during an altercation with another inmate while in prison. Therefore, in their analyses the researchers used only the data from the 20 inmates whose records were complete. Contrary to expectations, PPVS scores were not related to amount of time served. Inmates who scored lower on the PPVS were released on parole no earlier and served no less of their sentences than inmates who scored higher on the PPVS.

The Lage Correctional Facility board members have asked you to translate "into English" both the information presented in the PPVS manual and your own expert evaluation of that information in the context of the board's potential adoption of the scale.

<u>Note</u>: Both the Poe Potential for Violence Scale (PVS) and the Destructive Potential Interview Schedule (DPIS) are fabricated tests whose descriptions were created by the author for the purposes of this assignment.

✍ **Student Workbook Assignment 5.2**

↤ **Designing a Construct-Related Validity Study** ↦

♦ **DESCRIPTION OF THE ASSIGNMENT**

As you have read in Chapter 5 on pp. 149-151, convergent evidence for the construct-related validity of a measure can be demonstrated in two ways: (1) by showing that the test is correlated with other established and validated tests of the same construct, and (2) by showing that the test really measures what it purports to measure because test scores are associated in specific ways to relevant non-test variables. Focused Example 5-6 (on text pp. 148-149) describes Zick Rubin's efforts to obtain this second type of convergent evidence to support the construct-related validity of his love scale. Rubin hypothesized that if his scale really was measuring love, then high-scoring relationship partners should spend more time gazing into each other's eyes than should low-scoring relationship partners. And this is exactly what Rubin found, lending support to his contention that the love scale really did measure love. Assignment 5.2 asks you to design a study that gathers convergent evidence for the construct-related validity of one of three measures. The directions for the assignment are provided below.

♦ **DIRECTIONS**

→ **Before beginning this assignment, make sure you have read Chapter 5.**

(1) Read through the descriptions of the three measures on the next page. The three measures are: Desire for Control on Examinations (Measure A), Tendency to Gossip Questionnaire (Measure B), and The Objectivism Scale (Measure C). You will design a study that reflects the second method of obtaining convergent evidence of construct-related validity (described in Introduction to the Assignment, above) for <u>one</u> of the three measures. The choice of Measure A, B, or C is completely up to you. [Note: Your instructor may adapt this assignment to fit his or her specific objectives, so be sure to identify any alterations to these directions before you complete the assignment.]

Be sure to address the following seven items in your write-up of Assignment 5.2:

(1)   Identify the measure on which you are basing your study.

(2)   Identify one hypothesis about the relationship between scores on the measure and some other non-test variable(s).

(3)   Briefly describe the sample for your study.

(4)   Briefly describe how you would measure the variables in your study.

(5)   Briefly describe the procedure you would use to collect data for your study.

(6)   Identify the outcome (or pattern of results) you would expect if your hypothesis was supported.

(7)   Briefly discuss what conclusions you might reach about the measure if your hypothesis was supported.

Description of Measures for Assignment 5.2

⊣ MEASURE A ⊢

Name of measure: Desire for Control on Examinations

Construct measured: Individuals' desire to exert control in academic testing situations.

Description of measure: The Desire for Control on Examinations (DCE) scale consists of 13 statements such as "I would like to have a say in whether a class exam is take-home or administered in class" and "It is important for me to know beforehand what types of items will be on an exam (e.g., multiple choice, essay)". Respondents indicate on a 5-point scale the frequency with which the statements apply to them (ranging from 1= *Never applies to me* to 5= *Always applies to me*.) Higher scores indicate greater motivation to be in control in an examination context. The authors of the DCE suggest the scale might be useful in the identification of variables that influence performance on academic tests.

Wise, S., Roos, L., Leland, V., Oats, R. & McCrann, T. (1996). The development and validation of a scale measuring desire for control on examinations. *Educational and Psychological Measurement, 56*, 710-718.

⊣ MEASURE B ⊢

Name of measure: Tendency to Gossip Questionnaire

Construct measured: Individuals' disposition to gossip.

Description of measure: The Tendency to Gossip Questionnaire (TGQ) asks respondents to indicate on a 7-point scale (ranging from *Never* to *Always*) the extent to which each of 20 statements characterize their behavior. These statements include the following: "Talk with friends about other people's personal appearance," "Analyze with friends the compatibility of couples," and "Tell friends about interesting details of others." Higher scores on the TGQ indicate a stronger tendency to gossip.

Nevo, O., Nevo, B., & Derech-Zehavi, A. (1993). The development of the Tendency to Gossip Questionnaire: Construct and concurrent validation for a sample of Israeli college students. *Educational and Psychological Measurement, 53*, 973-981.

⊣ MEASURE C ⊢

Name of measure: The Objectivism Scale

Construct measured: A cognitive style characterized by a tendency to make decisions on the basis of empirical (observable) facts and logical considerations rather than nonobjective information.

Description of measure: The Objectivism Scale consists of 11 items including "I think the answers to most questions in life can be found through careful, objective analysis of the situation" and "I gather as much information as possible before making decisions." Responses to items are on a 5-point scale ranging from *Not at all characteristic of me* to *Extremely characteristic of me*. Higher scores indicate a more objective style.

Leary, M., Sheppard, J., McNeil, M., Jenkins, B., & Barnes, B. (1986). Objectivism in information utilization: Theory and measurement. *Journal of Personality Assessment, 50*, 32-43.

⇥ CHAPTER 6: *Writing and Evaluating Test Items* ⇤

CHAPTER 6 EXERCISES

I. ITEM WRITING (text pp. 158-170)

1.   After reading through the guidelines for writing test items on text p. 158, examine the following portion of a hypothetical "School Anxiety Scale" designed for children between the ages of 8 and 14. Under each item, indicate whether it is <u>acceptable</u> as written or <u>unacceptable</u> because it violates one or more of the item-writing guidelines presented. If the item is unacceptable, explain why and then re-write it to be more effective.

(a) In the morning before school, I feel nauseated or like I might throw up.

☐ Always of almost always   ☐ Sometimes   ☐ Rarely/Once in a while   ☐ Never

---

(b) When I think about going to school I hyperventilate.

☐ Always or almost always   ☐ Sometimes   ☐ Rarely/Once in a while   ☐ Never

---

(c) Thinking about school makes me feel dizzy and my head hurt.

☐ Always or almost always   ☐ Sometimes   ☐ Rarely/Once in a while   ☐ Never

---

(d) In the morning before school, I pretend to be sick because I can't stop thinking about all the bad things that might happen to me or to my parents while I am at school and away from home.

☐ Always or almost always   ☐ Sometimes   ☐ Rarely/Once in a while   ☐ Never

---

A. Item Formats (text pp. 159-167)

2.　　Choose an item from the "School Anxiety Scale" on the previous page and write it in a **dichotomous** format. _____

3.　　What are the:

a. *advantages* of the dichotomous item format? _____

_____

b. *disadvantages* of the dichotomous item format? _____

_____

4.　　How is the **polytomous** item format different from the dichotomous item format? _____

_____

5.　　What are the advantages of the polytomous item format? _____

_____

_____

6.　　Test developers must choose *distractors*, or incorrect response options, for their polytomous format items very carefully. How might one determine that a distractor is ineffective? _____

_____

7.　　What are the risks of using ineffective distractors on a test? _____

_____

_____

_____

8.　　Complete the following statements related to *guessing* on a polytomous format test.

a. On a standard multiple-choice test with four choices per item, examinees would be expected to answer

　　　_____% of them correctly just by chance.

b. Students should probably guess on multiple-choice items when they do not know the answer <u>if</u> a

_____ for _____ is not applied (if it is applied, then random

guessing has the same effect as not answering the item at all).

c. The _____ _____ is a term that describes the chances that a

low-ability test taker will obtain each score, and is determined through technical mathematical methods.

9.   This exercise will make the importance of selecting good distractors on a test very clear to you! Four items from the Testwiseness Scale (Weiten, 2000) are presented below. The distractors for each item are so poorly written that you should be able to guess the correct answers without knowing anything at all about history, the subject of the test. In other words, if you are "test wise" you should get a score of 100% on this test! Answer the four items, then identify specific reasons why the distractors for each item are ineffective.

TESTWISENESS SCALE (ABRIDGED)

1.   The Osten Manifesto aimed to

   a. discourage Southern expansionism.
   b. prevent expansion in the South.
   c. aid in Southern expansionism.
   d. all of the above

Item 1. distractors are ineffective because: _____

_____

2.   The dispute between Great Britain and the United States over the boundary of Maine was settled by

   a. the treaty of Quebec.
   b. the treaty of Niagra.
   c. the Webster-Ashburton Treaty.
   d. the Pendleton-Scott Treaty.

Item 2. distractors are ineffective because: _____

_____

3.   The Webster-Ashburton Treaty settled a long-standing dispute between Great Britain and the United States over

   a. the Maine boundary.
   b. numerous contested claims to property.
   c. damages growing out of the War of 1812 and subsequent conflicts.
   d. fishing rights on the Great Lakes and in international waters.

Item 3. distractors are ineffective because: _____

_____

4.   Men who opposed the "Ten Hour Movement" in British factory history

   a. was a leader in the dominant political party.
   b. is convinced that shorter hours of work are bad for the morals of the laboring class.
   c. is primarily motivated by concern for his own profits.
   d. were convinced that intervention would endanger the economic welfare of Britain.

Item 4. distractors are ineffective because: _____

_____

From Weiten, W. (2000). Testwiseness scale. *Personal Explorations Workbook.* (p. 3-5) .Pacific Grove, CA:Wadsworth: Used with permission.

10.   **Likert format** scales are frequently employed in the measurement of attitudes and personality. Your text presents examples of Likert scales using responses that vary along the dimension of *agreement* (Strongly disagree to strongly agree.). Likert scales might consist of responses that vary along other dimensions as well. For example, responses to the Likert-type items on the "School Anxiety Scale" vary along the dimension of *frequency* (Always to Never). For each of the three Likert-scale items that might be seen on a "Smoking Cessation Inventory," come up with the remaining response choices (also called "anchors").

How <u>confident</u> are you about being able to quit smoking?

4	3	2	1
Completely confident			

How <u>strong</u> is your urge to smoke after you wake up in the morning?

5	4	3	2	1
			Weak, but still noticeable	

How <u>supportive</u> are significant people in your life (e.g., family, close friends) of your goal to quit smoking?

6	5	4	3	2	1
		Slightly supportive			

11.   The **category format** is similar to the Likert format except that the category format typically (a) employs a wider range of choice points, and (b) specifies or describes only the end points on the scale. Complete the following statements related to the category format.

a. Researchers have found that both the _____ of people and the things being _____ influence responses to items on a 10-point category scale.

b. Category scales are most effective when the _____ of the scale are clearly defined and raters are frequently _____ of these ratings.

c. A rating scale with _____ points or categories usually provides enough discrimination.

d. As shown in Figure 6-1 on text p. 166, a _____ _____ scale presents raters with a 100-centimeter line; raters then place a mark between two well-defined endpoints.

12.   Both **checklists** and **Q-sorts** ask examinees to look at a set of adjectives (or descriptors) and identify whether or to what extent each describes himself/herself, some other person, or something else entirely. On the next page, identify 8 adjectives that might be seen on a checklist or Q-sort used to assess examinees' perceptions of their parents' style of raising children. (Two adjectives are provided to get you started).

Adjectives on a "Perceptions of Parenting Style" Checklist or Q-Sort

Over-protective _____   _____

Affectionate _____   _____

_____   _____

_____   _____

II. ITEM ANALYSIS (text pp. 170-183)

A. Item Difficulty (text pp. 170-172)

1. Item difficulty is: _____.

2. Calculate the **item difficulty** levels for the first five items on the University Aptitude Test. For each item, "1" means the item was answered correctly and "0" means the item was answered incorrectly. Write your answers in the spaces provided at the bottom of the table.

Examinee	Item 1	Item 2	Item 3	Item 4	Item 5	Total Score
Greg	1	1	1	1	1	16
Allison	1	1	1	1	0	7
Janine	1	1	1	1	0	10
Corey	1	1	0	1	1	17
Michelle	0	0	1	1	0	3
Thomas	0	1	1	1	0	11
Randall	1	1	1	1	0	14
Tina	0	0	1	1	0	10
LeeAnn	1	1	1	1	0	13
David	0	1	1	1	0	12
Marcia	0	0	0	1	0	4
Lance	1	1	1	1	0	9
Keisha	1	1	1	1	0	15
Blair	0	1	1	1	0	12
Joe	0	0	1	1	0	6
Item Difficulty						

3. How is "optimum difficulty level" of items defined? _____

_____

4. All the items on the UAT have five response choices. Using the formula presented on text p. 171, calculate the optimum item difficulty level for UAT items. Write your answer here: _____

5. For most tests, items in the difficulty range of _____ to _____ maximize information about differences among examinees.

B. Discriminability (text pp. 172-174)

6.   Assessment of **item discriminability** determines what? _____

_____

_____

✦ Two ways of evaluating item discriminability are presented in the text: (1) the *extreme groups method*, and (2) the *point biserial method.* The exercises in this section ask you to calculate the item discriminability level, or **discrimination index**, for the first five items on the University Aptitude Test (UAT).

7.   The *extreme group method* identifies the discrimination index for each item by comparing examinees who performed well on the test (e.g., the top third) to those who did poorly on the test (e.g., the bottom third). The difference between the proportion of "top" examinees and the proportion of "bottom" examinees who answered the item correctly is the discrimination index for that particular item.

Directions:

→ Find the discrimination indexes for the first five items of the UAT by using the extreme group method. In this exercise, you will identify the top-scoring third of examinees (or the top 5, since there are 15 examinees) and the lowest-scoring third of examinees (i.e., the bottom 5).

→ Use the data table provided on the previous page to find the top- and bottom-scoring groups. Total scores for each examinee are listed in the far right column of the table.

→ Record the names of the five top-scoring and the five bottom-scoring examinees below. (The first in each group is provided for you).

Examinees in the top third of the group	Score		Examinees in the bottom third of the group	Score
Corey	17		Michelle	3
_____	___		_____	___
_____	___		_____	___
_____	___		_____	___
_____	___		_____	___

→ Now find and record the discrimination index for each item in the table on the next page. Be sure to refer to Box 6-1 on text p. 173 for step-by-step directions on how to calculate discrimination indexes.

Item number	Proportion Correct for Examinees in the Top-Third of the Group (P_t)	Proportion Correct for Examinees in the Bottom Third of the Group (P_b)	Discrimination Index $(d_i = P_t - P_b)$
1			
2			
3			
4			
5			

8.   Based on the findings of the extreme group method, evaluate the extent to which UAT items 1-5 discriminate well (again, be sure to read through all of Box 6-1 on text p. 173).

Item 1: _____

Item 2: _____

Item 3: _____

Item 4: _____

Item 5: _____

9.   The *point-biserial method* identifies item discriminability by examining the correlation between performance on an item and performance on the test as a whole. (Make sure you have read through text pp. 172-174.) The formula for the point-biserial correlation is shown below. You will again use UAT data provided on p. 79 of the Workbook.

Point-biserial correlation formula:

$$r_{pbis} = \left[\frac{\overline{Y_1} - \overline{Y}}{S_y}\right]\sqrt{\frac{P_x}{1 - P_x}}$$

where r_{pbis} = point biserial correlation (or discrimination index)
$\overline{Y_1}$ = the mean score on the test for those who got item 1 correct
$\overline{Y}$ = the mean score on the test for all persons
S_y = the standard deviation of exam scores for all persons
P_x = the proportion of persons getting the item correct

Directions:

→ Go back to Workbook Chapter 2 and find the mean UAT score you calculated and recorded on p. 21.

→ Then find the standard deviation you calculated on Workbook p. 23.

→ You have already calculated P_x (the difficulty index) for each item in Exercise A.2, on p. 91.

→ Find $\overline{Y_1}$ by calculating the mean (total) UAT score only for examinees who got Item 1 correct. Then do the same for Items 2-5. Write these mean scores in the spaces on the next page.

Item number	Number of examinees who answered the item correctly	Mean UAT score of examinees who answered the item correctly
1	_____	_____
2	_____	_____
3	_____	_____
4	_____	_____
5	_____	_____

→ Now plug the values you found for each item into the point-biserial correlation formula.

→ Record the point-biserial correlations you found for each item in the spaces provided. Then identify which items are good or effective and which should be eliminated, based on guidelines presented on text p. 174.

Item number	Point-biserial correlation	Evaluation of item discriminability
1	_____	_____
2	_____	_____
3	_____	_____
4	_____	_____
5	_____	_____

C. Pictures of Item Characteristics (text pp. 174-180)

10. Figure 6-5 from text p. 176 is shown below. This figure depicts five different **item characteristic curves** (Items A through E). Certain items are more sensitive in particular ranges than others. Also, certain items are better than others (and certain items might be downright bad). On the next page, describe the characteristics of each item, including ranges at which it is more and less sensitive, and whether it would be considered a "good" or a "bad" item. The characteristics of Item C are described, as an example.

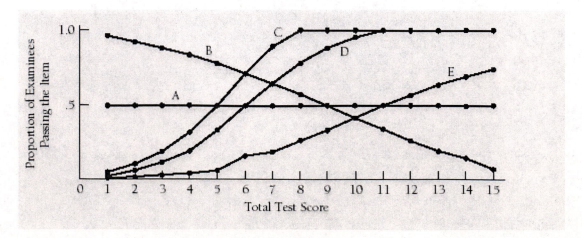

Item	Description of Item Characteristics
A	
B	
C	*The Item C curve rises steadily until it reaches a total score of 8, so it seems to be sensitive up to the mid-range of performance. Then it flattens out completely, suggesting that all test takers performing at the mid-range or better got the item correct. So, Item C discriminates at lower but not at higher levels of performance.*
D	
E	

11.   In the table below, you will see that total UAT scores have been divided into four classes, or score intervals. First, determine what proportion of the people in each score category got each item correct. Then plot the item characteristic curves on the graph provided one the next page. Be sure to label each item.

	Proportion of Examinees Passing Item, by Total UAT Score				
Total Score	Item 1	Item 2	Item 3	Item 4	Item 5
1-6					
7-10					
11-14					
15-18					

Item Characteristic Curves for Items 1-5

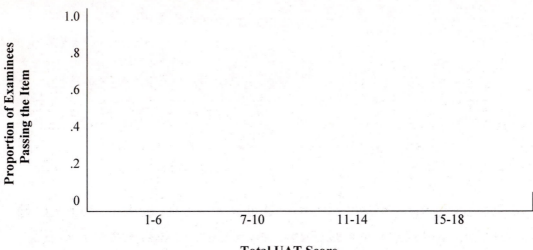

12.   Describe the characteristics of each UAT item, including ranges at which it is more and less sensitive, and whether it would be considered a "good" or a "bad" item.

Item   **Description of Item Characteristics**

1   _____

      _____

2   _____

      _____

3   _____

      _____

4   _____

      _____

5   _____

      _____

✦ Another way of depicting item characteristics is shown in the figure on the next page (also on text p. 177). *Item Difficulty* (or percent passing) is on the Y axis and *Item Discriminability* is on the X axis. Item 12 had a Difficulty level of about 46 (i.e., 46% of examinees got the item correct) and a Discriminabity level of about .60

(i.e., the correlation between item passage and total test score was .60). Your text notes on p. 177 that "good" items usually fall within a difficulty range of 30% to 70% and have a discriminability index above .30.

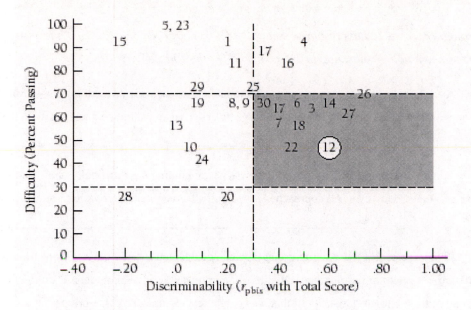

13.　　Complete the graph below which depicts both Item Difficulty and Item Discriminabilty (using the point-biserial correlations you found on p. 94) of UAT items 1 through 5. Use the figure above as a guide.

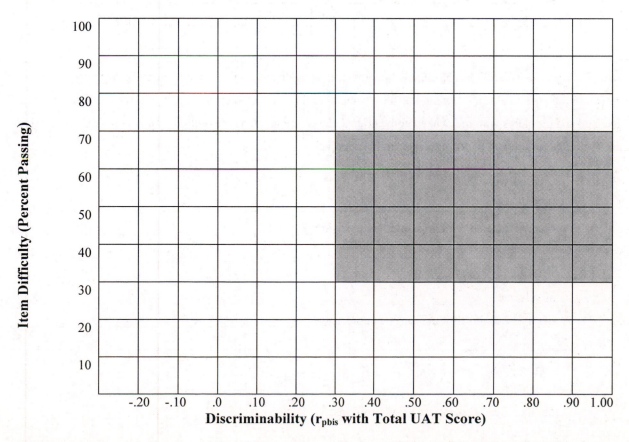

14.   Which UAT items:

should be retained? _____

should be eliminated? _____

❧ *Questions 15. through 18. relate to **item response theory (IRT)**, that has been described as "the most important development in psychological testing in the second half of the 20th century" (p. 178).*

15.   As compared to classical test theory in which an examinee's test score equals the total number of items answered correctly, approaches based on item response theory (IRT) derive an examinee's test score on the basis of what? _____

16.   Tests that are constructed using IRT use several approaches, including item difficulty and discriminability, to select items. However, all approaches based on IRT grade items in relation to the probability that: _____

17.   One primary advantage of IRT-based tests is that they can be adapted for computer administration. Imagine that you took a traditional multiple-choice statistics test administered on a computer. Then imagine that you took an IRT-based multiple-choice statistics test that was computer-administered. Describe how your experience taking the latter test would probably be different from your experience taking the former test.

_____

_____

_____

18.   Figure 6-9 on text p. 178 depicts how precisely examinees' abilities can be measured using conventional ("peaked" and "rectangular") vs. computer-adaptive approaches to testing. Describe types of items selected and problems with the peaked conventional and the rectangular conventional approaches. Then describe the "solution" offered by the computer-adaptive approach.

Peaked conventional approach

Items selected: _____

Problem associated with measurement precision:_____

_____

Rectangular conventional approach

Items selected: _____

Problem associated with measurement precision:_____

_____

Computer adaptive approach

Items selected: _____

Solution to measurement precision problems: _____

_____

D. Linking Uncommon Measures (text pp. 179-181)

19.   For what reason are "linkages" needed between different versions of the same test (e.g., different versions of the SAT, the GRE, the LSAT, etc.)? _____

_____

_____

20.   For what reason might "linkages" be needed between two completely different tests (e.g, between the ACT and the SAT; between a mathematics achievement test and a writing competency test)?_____

_____

_____

E. Items for Criterion-Referenced Tests (text pp. 181-182)

21.   What is the first step in creating items for a criterion-referenced test? _____

_____

_____

22.   How should one evaluate items on a criterion-referenced test? _____

_____

_____

23.   Figure 6-10 on text p. 182 shows a hypothetical distribution of scores on a criterion-referenced test. What does the bottom of the "V" represent and how is it used? _____

_____

_____

24.   How would you feel if your university started using criterion-referenced tests instead of traditional (norm-referenced) tests? In your opinion, what would be the benefits and limitations? _____

_____

_____

_____

F. Limitations of Item Analysis (text pp. 182-183)

25.   Summarize the main problem regarding the adequacy of tests based on item analysis procedures.

_____

_____

_____

Key Terms and Concepts to Know from Chapter Six

Dichotomous format

Polytomous format

Distractors

Guessing threshold

Likert format

Category format

Visual analogue scale

Checklist format

Q-Sort format

Item analysis

Item difficulty

Item discriminability

Extreme group method

Point biserial method

Item characteristic curve

Item response theory

Criterion referenced test

Antimode

Cutting score

CHAPTER 6 PRACTICE QUIZ

1.   **A test comprised of items such as "I usually feel rested when I wake up in the morning" to which examinees must respond "True" or "False" is an example of**

       a. a polytomous format.
       b. a Likert-scale format.
       c. a category format.
       d. a dichotomous format.

2.   **Which of the following is <u>not</u> a potential problem created by the inclusion of ineffective distractors on a test?**

       a. They can decrease the reliability of a test.
       b. They can give clues to examinees about the correct response.
       c. They can decrease the time examinees spend on items.
       d. They can decrease the validity of a test.

3.   **If a correction for guessing is used on a test, it means that**

       a. test scores will be adjusted to take into account the percentage of items examinees are expected to answer correctly by chance alone.
       b. examinees who guess on items they do not know the answer to will receive lower test scores than if they had simply left the unknown items blank.
       c. test scores are curved to reflect the percentage of examinees who are expected to guess on 50% or more of test items.
       d. test scores of examinees who make random guesses will be artificially inflated compared to the scores of those who do not make random guesses.

4.   **A test comprised of items to which responses can vary on a 6-point scale ranging from "Strongly agree" to "Strongly disagree" is an example of**

       a. a polytomous format.
       b. a Likert-scale format.
       c. a category format.
       d. a dichotomous format.

5.   **Researchers have found that a _____ scale on a test employing a category format is sufficient for discriminating among individuals.**

       a. 5-point
       b. 10-point
       c. 20-point
       d. 100-point

6.   Dr. Marcus analyzed items on his physics test by calculating the proportion of students who got each item correct. Dr. Marcus was examining

   a. item difficulty.
   b. the guessing threshold.
   c. item discriminability.
   d. the antimode.

7.   Which of the following item characteristic curves represents the best item?

   a. A curve that rises steadily to the midpoint of test performance and then falls steadily to the highest performance levels (i.e., an inverted U-shaped curve).
   b. A curve that is flat to the midpoint of test performance, rises sharply after the midpoint, and then flattens out at the highest performance levels.
   c. A curve that drops steadily to the midpoint of test performance and then rises steadily to the highest performance levels (i.e., a U-shaped curve).
   d. A curve that rises steadily and smoothly to the highest performance levels.

8.   On a multiple choice test with four response options, the optimum item difficulty level is about

   a. .250.
   b. .500.
   c. .625.
   d. .875.

9.   If Dr. Hamline wants to know whether the most difficult items on the statistics test she created were answered correctly only by the top-performing students in her class, she would need to assess

   a. item difficulty.
   b. the guessing threshold.
   c. item discriminability.
   d. the antimode.

10.   Tests based on Item Response Theory (IRT)

   a. yield scores reflecting the level of difficulty of items examinees were able to answer correctly.
   b. are less adaptable to computer administration than are traditional tests.
   c. may be more biased toward examinees who are slow in completing tests.
   d. define total test scores in term of the number of items examinees answered correctly.

✍Student Workbook Assignment 6.1

⊶ Writing Multiple Choice Items for Your Next Exam ⊶

♦ DESCRIPTION OF THE ASSIGNMENT

This assignment will encourage you to think about the differences between good and poor multiple-choice (polytomous format) test items. You will construct 10 multiple-choice items based on material from one or more text chapters. Be sure to pay attention to the guidelines for writing test items presented on text p. 158 and Table 6-2 on text pp. 168-169.

♦ DIRECTIONS

➔ Before beginning this assignment, make sure you have read Chapter 6.

(1) If your instructor asks you to complete this assignment, he or she will tell you which chapter(s) will serve as the content domain for the items you create.

(2) Write 10 multiple-choice (polytomous format) items for your next exam. Remember that poor distractors decrease the reliability of test, so pay attention to the quality of the distractors you choose!

(3) Make use of Table 6-1 (pp. 168-169), which provides advice on item writing, as you construct your items.

⊷ CHAPTER 7: *Test Administration* ⊷

Chapter 7 Outline

CHAPTER 7 EXERCISES

I. THE EXAMINER AND THE SUBJECT (text pp. 186-198)

A. The Relationship Between Examiner and Test Taker (text pp. 186-187)

1. Your text reports the findings of several studies examining whether the behavior of the examiner can affect children's ability test scores. In the table below, summarize the methods and results of these studies.

Study	Method	Results
Feldman & Sullivan (1960)		
Witmer, Bernstein, & Dunham (1971)		
DeRosa & Patalano (1991)		
Fuchs & Fuchs (1986)		

2. What does research suggest about live interview versus self-report questionnaire methods of gathering information from examinees? _____

_____

_____

B. The Race of the Tester (text pp. 187-189)

3. What reason is given for the lack of evidence that the examiner's race affects intelligence test scores?

_____

_____

4. Under what circumstances is it more likely that the race of the examiner might influence test scores?

_____

_____

5. What variations in the administration of ability tests have been shown to increase the performance of disadvantaged test takers? _____

_____

C. Language of Test Taker (text p. 189)

6. Identify two challenges with regard to testing non-English speakers. _____

_____

_____

D. Training of Test Administrators (text pp. 189-190)

7. Typically, assessment instruments such as Structured Clinical Interview for DSM-IV (SCID) or complicated tests such as the Wechsler Adult Intelligence Scale-Revised (WAIS-R) are administered by licensed _____ or _____ .

8. What did Patterson et al. (1995) discover about the training and proficiency level of graduate students with regard to administering the WAIS-R? _____

_____

_____

E. Expectancy Effects (text pp. 191-192)

9.   What is the Rosenthal (expectancy) effect? _____

_____

10.   Overall, what have researchers found about the consistency and magnitude of expectancy effects in experimental studies? _____

11.   Describe ways in which expectancy effects could influence students' test scores. _____

_____

_____

_____

F. Effects of Reinforcing Responses (text pp. 192-195)

12.   Your text reports the findings of several studies examining the effects of reinforcing responses on test scores. In the table below, summarize these findings.

Study	Findings
Sweet (1970)	
Bergan, McManis & Melchert (1971)	
Schultz & Sherman (1976); Terrell, Taylor, & Terrell (1978)	
Cannell & Henson (1974)	

13.   What specific information should test manuals provide about test administration? _____

_____

_____

_____

 Psychological Testing in Everyday Life Box 7-2, *The Incentive Scoreboard*
Box 7-2 (text p. 194) summarizes Sattler's (1988) review of research on the effects of reinforcements or incentives on test performance. • What did Sattler find?

G. Computer-Assisted Test Administration (text pp. 195-196)

14. What are the advantages of computerized test administration? _____

_____

_____

_____

15. What were the results of a study comparing levels of disclosures of personal information among individuals tested with one of three methods (computer, questionnaire, and personal interview)?

_____

_____

_____

16. What are the disadvantages or potential problems associated with computerized test administration?

_____

_____

_____

_____

H. Mode of Administration (text pp. 196-197)

17. Your text reports research findings indicating that when health-related measures are administered to people by an interviewer or over the telephone, their health scores are higher than when they complete health-related measures on their own. In a few sentences, explain why these differences in health scores might exist.

_____

_____

_____

18. On the other hand, researchers have not found clear evidence that the mode of administration of _____ tests has an impact on scores.

I. Subject Variables (text pp. 197-198)

19. List subject variables considered to be sources of error affecting test scores: _____

_____

_____

_____

II. BEHAVIORAL ASSESSMENT METHODOLOGY (text pp. 198-201)

1.   Under what circumstances might behavioral assessment methodologies be more useful than psychological testing procedures? _____

_____

_____

_____

_____

_____

A. Reactivity (text p. 199)
B. Drift (text p. 199)
C. Expectancies (text pp. 199-200)

2.   Imagine that you accepted a part-time job conducting behavioral assessments at a local elementary school. In the table below, define each term and then describe examples of how you might experience (a) reactivity, (b) drift, and (c) expectancies, as you complete your assessments of the children.

Reactivity	Definition:
	Example:
Drift	Definition:
	Example:
Expectancies	Definition:
	Example:

D. Deception (text pp. 200-201)

3.   So-called "integrity tests" are designed to evaluate the honesty and integrity of employees. The use of these tests in employment decision-making continues to be very controversial. Why? _____

_____

_____

_____

_____

_____

_____

4.   Your text describes the views of Ones, Chockalingam, and Schmidt (1995) with respect to the use of integrity tests in the workplace. Describe the views of these researchers (including evidence they drawn upon to support their argument).

_____

_____

_____

_____

_____

E. Statistical Control of Rating Errors (text p. 201)

5.   What is the *halo effect* and why might it be important to control statistically in studies of behavioral rating accuracy? _____

_____

_____

_____

_____

_____

_____

Key Terms and Concepts to Know from Chapter Seven

Examiner/interviewer effects

Race of examiner/tester effects

Effects of language of test taker

Test administrator training effects

Expectancy effects/ Rosenthal effects

Effects of reinforcing responses

Computer-assisted test administration

Subject variables (such as test anxiety)

Functional behavioral assessment (FBA)

Reactivity

Observer drift

Contrast effect

Expectancies (in behavioral observation)

Detection of deception/honesty

Employee Polygraph Protection Act

Halo effect

CHAPTER 7 PRACTICE QUIZ

1. **The ability test score of ten-year-old Stacy is most likely to be highest if her examiner**

    a. is familiar to her, does not initiate conversation, and does not comment on her performance.
    b. is unfamiliar to her, does not initiate conversation, and does not comment on her performance.
    c. is familiar to her, initiates conversation, and praises her performance.
    d. is unfamiliar to her, initiates conversation, and praises her performance.

2. **Research on the effects of the examiner's race on children's IQ test performance indicates**

    a. substantial negative effects when the examiner is African-American and the child is white.
    b. substantial negative effects when the examiner is white and the child is African American.
    c. substantial positive effects when the examiner and the child are the same race.
    d. minimal, if any, effects.

3. **A study of 22 graduate students found that scoring errors on the WAIS-R diminished only after the students had completed _____ or more practice sessions.**

    a. 3
    b. 5
    c. 8
    d. 10

4. **In one study, graduate students were told that ambiguous responses to intelligence test items were given by either "bright" or "dull" people. In fact, the responses were exactly the same. When they scored the tests, the graduate students gave more credit to responses they believed were from bright examinees. The findings of this study illustrate**

    a. expectancy effects.
    b. reactivity.
    c. incentive effects.
    d. drift.

5. **Which of the following has NOT been found with regard to the effects of reinforcement on test performance?**

    a. Culturally-relevant verbal reinforcement has a significant effect on IQ test scores of African-American children.
    b. Children's socioeconomic class and gender are related to effects of reinforcement on test performance.
    c. Effects of tangible reinforcements such as money and candy are significantly greater than effects of verbal praise on test performance.
    d. None of the above reflects the research findings on the effects of reinforcement on test performance.

113

6.   **Computer-assisted test administration**

   a. is generally less reliable than traditional assessment.
   b. requires that the same items be presented in the same order to test takers.
   c. typically yields test scores somewhat lower than those of paper-and-pencil tests.
   d. yields lower rates of scoring errors than traditional assessment procedures.

7.   **Reactivity results in**

   a. more accurate observer ratings.
   b. less accurate observer ratings.
   c. more test-taker deception.
   d. less test-taker deception.

8.   **Although Hal was trained in a standardized method of behavioral observation six months ago, his ratings of the same behavior have changed over time. This illustrates the problem of observer _____.**

   a. expectancies
   b. drift
   c. reactivity
   d. bias

9.   **One of the primary concerns about the use of integrity tests is**

   a. their remarkable ability to predict future criminal behavior.
   b they all require very expensive equipment and extensive training.
   c. that scores on these tests are highly correlated with IQ.
   d. the number of false positives identified by the tests.

10.   **In the context of psychological assessment, the halo effect is an example of a**

   a. subject variable.
   b. scoring or rating error.
   c. standardized procedure.
   d. self-serving bias.

✍Student Workbook Assignment 7.1

⊸ Identifying Issues in Test Administration ⊶

◆ DESCRIPTION OF THE ASSIGNMENT

As you know, many factors influence test scores. In this assignment, you will identify errors introduced by characteristics of the testing situation, the tester, and/or the test-taker.

◆ DIRECTIONS

➔ **Before beginning this assignment, make sure you have read Chapter 7.**

(1) Read the case presented below and continued on the next page.

(2) Identify three aspects of the testing situation, including characteristics and behaviors of both tester and test-taker, that might have introduced error into the test score.

(3) Briefly comment on how you think these sources of error might influence the test-taker's score.

Dr. Frakes, a clinical psychologist, was asked to administer intelligence tests to children in a local public school district. The purpose of the testing was to identify children in grades 1-5 whose intelligence test scores qualified them for the district's talented and gifted (TAG) program.

The school district directed Dr. Frakes to administer a newly-developed individual test of children's intelligence, called the Children's Experimental Aptitude Test (CEAT). Because the test was so new, Dr. Frakes had never actually seen it. The school district paid for Dr. Frakes to attend a 6-hour training workshop on the CEAT the weekend before the testing was to take place. Dr. Frakes attended the training workshop and was relieved to discover that the CEAT was very similar to a children's intelligence test with which he was familiar. As part of the training, Dr. Frakes gave one practice administration of the CEAT to another workshop participant.

Dr Frakes went to the testing center, which was located in an elementary school classroom. As Dr. Frakes was entering the school, he saw the Dean of the college where he taught part-time (and hoped to teach full-time in the future) walking into the school holding a young boy's hand. The Dean approached Dr. Frakes and introduced him to nine-year-old Howie, the Dean's son. "Howie is the brightest student in his class," said the Dean, "and I know he's going to ace this IQ test of yours!"

Howie was the third student Dr. Frakes tested that morning. When Howie entered the classroom, Dr. Frakes made a special attempt to chat with him and make him feel comfortable. However, Howie seemed very uninterested in being tested. He yawned and looked away several times when Dr. Frakes was explaining what would happen during the testing session. Then the session began.

Several of the CEAT subtests were timed; the test manual specified exactly how much time should be given to items on these subtests. However, because Dr. Frakes was still unfamiliar with the test, he had to consult the manual several times to remind himself of the amount of time Howie should receive to answer the items. Therefore, Howie completed a few of tests in the allotted amount of time, but had considerably more than the allotted time on several other tests.

continued on next page

Because Dr. Frakes knew that Howie was considered one of the brightest children in his second-grade class, he was surprised when the boy answered relatively easy items incorrectly or when he said he did not know the answer to an easy item. For example, one CEAT subtest required the examinee to identify the most important part missing from a picture of a common object. One picture showed a bicycle with several spokes missing from the rear wheel. Howie stared at the picture for about 20 seconds and then said he could not see anything missing from it. Dr. Frakes commented, "This one is a little tough…look *really* closely at the wheels on the bicycle. What is missing?" Howie was then able to give the correct answer.

As he was testing Howie, Dr. Frakes became increasingly certain the boy would qualify for the TAG program. Furthermore, he thought the program would be good for Howie's motivation level. Dr. Frakes had these thoughts in mind when he scored the test and wrote up the results in the summary report.

◄ CHAPTER 8: *Interviewing Techniques* ►

Chapter 8 Outline

I. The Interview as a Test (text pp. 206-207)

II. Reciprocal Nature of Interviewing (text p. 208)

III. Principles of Effective Interviewing (text pp. 208-217)

        A. The Proper Attitudes (text pp. 208-209)

        B. Responses to Avoid (text pp. 209-210)

        C. Effective Responses (text pp. 211-212)

        D. Responses to Keep the Interaction Flowing (text pp. 212-215)

        E. Measuring Understanding (text pp. 215-217)

IV. Types of Interviews (text pp. 217-225)

        A. Evaluation Interview (text pp. 217-218)

        B. Structured Clinical Interviews (text pp. 218-223)

        C. Case History Interview (text pp. 223-224)

        D. Mental Status Examination (text pp. 224-225)

        E. Developing Interviewing Skills (text p. 225)

V. Sources of Error in the Interview (text pp. 225-230)

        A. Interview Validity (text pp. 226-229)

        B. Interview Reliability (text pp. 229-230)

CHAPTER 8 EXERCISES

I. THE INTERVIEW AS A TEST (text pp. 206-207)

1.   List six ways in which an interview resembles a test.

a. _____   d. _____

b. _____   e. _____

c. _____   f. _____

II. RECIPROCAL NATURE OF INTERVIEWING (text p. 208)

1.   Research findings have consistently indicated that participants influence each other in an interview. Summarize the findings of Akehurst and Vrij (1999), who studied criminal suspects being interviewed, and Heller (1971), who examined the phenomenon called "social facilitation".

a. *Akehurst and Vrij*: _____

_____

b. *Heller*:_____

_____

III. PRINCIPLES OF EFFECTIVE INTERVIEWING (text pp. 208-217)

A. The Proper Attitudes (text pp. 208-209)

1.   What have research findings demonstrated regarding a central influence on the degree to which one person influences another? _____

2.   Identify attitudes related to good interviewing skills: _____

_____

3. The most important factor in patients' evaluations of clinical interviews is their perception of the interviewer's feelings. What perceptions did Saccuzzo (1975) find were associated with patients':

a. *positive evaluations of sessions*? _____

b. *poor evaluations of sessions?* _____

B. Responses to Avoid (text pp. 209-210)

4.   Inappropriately phrased probing statements can inhibit interviewees. However, appropriately phrased probing statements or questions can elicit vital information from interviewees. In the table below, rephrase each probing statement/question so that it is more effective. (See Table 8-2 on text p. 210 for examples).

Ineffective Probing Statement	More Effective Probing Statement or Question
I see you were dismissed from your position at Company X. Why did you get fired?	
Why have you been so depressed lately?	
Why didn't you do something earlier about your child's behavior problems?	
Why would you say something so ridiculous?	

5.   Although judgmental and hostile statements are very ineffective in most interviews, they may serve a particular purpose in specific types of interviews.

a. *What purpose(s) might these statements serve in an interview?* _____

_____

_____

b. *Give a specific "real-world" example of an interview situation in which these types of statements might be used very deliberately to yield necessary information.* _____

_____

_____

_____

6.   What message(s) does a false reassurance (e.g., "Everything is okay, don't worry about it.") give to a person who has just revealed a concern or problem? _____

_____

_____

C. Effective Responses (text pp. 211-212)

7.   For what reasons are open-ended questions more effective than closed-ended questions? _____

_____

_____

8.   In the table below, rephrase the closed-ended questions to become more effective open-ended questions (see Table 8-3 on text p. 211 for examples).

Closed-Ended Questions	More Effective Open-Ended Questions
Do you have a good relationship with your parents?	
Will you be able to handle the stress of this job?	
Do you know what career opportunities are available for people with degrees in psychology?	
Have you ever used illegal drugs?	

D. Responses to Keep the Interaction Flowing (text pp. 212-215)

9.   What is the purpose of transitional phrases such as "I see" or "Go on"? _____

_____

10.   Verbatim playback, paraphrasing, and restatement are responses that encourage interviewees to elaborate. Imagine you are a professor on a graduate school admissions committee. Paraphrase or restate the comments below, made by a student interviewing for a position in the Ph.D. psychology program:
"I conducted a study for my Experimental Methods class and was a research assistant for one of the professors in the psychology department. I also presented a research paper at a student conference last April."

_____

_____

_____

11.   Now, give a summarizing or clarification response to the student's comments. _____

_____

_____

12.   What is the value of the empathy or understanding response? _____
_____
_____

E. Measuring Understanding (text pp. 215-217)

13.   Describe the characteristics of each level of empathy response.

Level One _____

Level Two _____

Level Three _____

Level Four _____

Level Five _____

14.   After reading through text pp. 215-217, skip to the exercise on the next page. The table shows an interaction between two friends, Michelle and Claire. Identify the following aspects of Claire's responses to Michelle's statements:

> → was the response effective (+) or ineffective (-)? Place a ✓ in the appropriate space.
>
> → what was the response type? (e.g., verbatim playback, judgment, etc.)
>
> → what was the response level? (1-5)
>
> → can you identify a more effective response?

IV. TYPES OF INTERVIEWS (text pp. 217-225)

A. Evaluation Interview (text pp. 217-218)

1.   Confrontations, which point out discrepancies or inconsistencies in interviewee's statements, can be an important tool in the evaluation, or therapeutic, interview. What three types of discrepancies might an evaluation interviewer point out or confront, according to Carkhuff (1969)?

a. _____

b. _____

c. _____

2.   Direct questioning, rather than open-ended facilitative techniques, is more effective in what situations and with which types of individuals? _____
_____
_____
_____

STATEMENTS	+	−	RESPONSE TYPE & LEVEL
			MORE EFFECTIVE RESPONSE
Michelle: I think my boyfriend is cheating on me.			
Claire: So, you suspect Lance is being unfaithful.			
Michelle: He is withdrawing from me. And yesterday I saw him in a car with a woman I didn't recognize. I haven't asked him about it yet, though.			
Claire: Maybe you are just paranoid.			
Michelle: I don't think so.			
Claire: One of my ex-boyfriends cheated on me two years ago. I decided certain people are simply jerks who can't be trusted.			
Michelle: I don't know what to do.			
Claire: Sounds like you are feeling very anxious about talking to Lance about your suspicions.			
Michelle: Yes, I am. And if we break up, I'll be so angry and disappointed.			
Claire: If that happens you'll be just fine, don't worry.			
Michelle: I think I'll talk to him about it tonight after dinner. I wonder how I should bring up the subject.			
Claire: Good question…So, do you think these shoes go with my outfit? Maybe I should have worn my leather sandals instead.			

B. Structured Clinical Interviews (text pp. 218-223)

3.   Describe the characteristics of the structured clinical interview. _____

_____

_____

4.   As opposed to their predecessors, more recent editions of the *Diagnostic and Statistical Manual of Mental Disorders (DSM)* are considerably more reliable with regard to psychiatric diagnoses. How was reliability of the DSM increased? _____

_____

5.   What is a primary strength and a primary limitation of structured interview techniques?
Strength: _____

_____

Limitation: _____

_____

C. Case History Interview (text pp. 223-224)

6.   What is the purpose of the case history interview? _____

_____

7.   Imagine that you are conducting a case history interview with George, a 50-year-old man. Identify four effectively phrased questions you would ask him in the first 30 minutes of the interview.

(1) _____

(2) _____

(3) _____

(4) _____

D. Mental Status Examination (text pp. 224-225)

8.   What is the purpose of the mental status examination (MSE)? _____

_____

_____

9.   Mental status examinations assess multiple aspects of a patient's functioning. In the table on the next page, identify pieces of information you could obtain through questions or observation that might help you evaluate each dimension listed. An example is provided to get you started.

MSE Dimension	Information to be gained
Appearance	*Is there evidence of adequate personal hygiene? Is clothing relatively clean and appropriate?*
General Behavior	
Emotion	
Intelligence	
Thought Processes	
Attention	
Sensory Experiences	

F. Developing Interviewing Skills (text p. 225)

10.   Describe three steps one might take to develop effective interviewing skills.

a. _____

b. _____

c. _____

V. SOURCES OF ERROR IN THE INTERVIEW (text pp. 225-230)

A. Interview Validity (text pp. 226-229)

1.   Imagine that you are interviewing applicants for a managerial position in a business. Identify three things about an applicant that might contribute to a "positive halo effect" and three things that might contribute to a "negative halo effect".

Positive halo effect   (1) _____

(2) _____

(3) _____

Negative halo effect   (1) _____

(2) _____

(3) _____

2.   The term "general standoutishness" (p. 226) refers to the tendency to form an opinion of someone based on one outstanding characteristic. Research on this tendency has examined the characteristics of personal appearance and culture/race. Summarize research findings on biases associated with these two characteristics.

Personal appearance: _____

_____

_____

_____

_____

Culture/Race: _____

_____

_____

_____

_____

3.   The predictive validity of interview data varies widely. Summarize findings on correlations between interview ratings and other outcome measures (such as tests and supervisor ratings). Then, briefly explain why the predictive validity of interview data might vary so much. _____

_____

_____

_____

_____

_____

B. Interview Reliability (text pp. 229-230)

4.   Discuss differences between the reliability of structured and unstructured interviews. _____

_____

_____

_____

_____

_____

Key Terms and Concepts to Know from Chapter Eight

Directive interview

Nondirective interview

Selection interview

Social facilitation

Interpersonal influence

Interpersonal attraction

Stress interview

Effective interviewer responses

Ineffective interviewer responses

Responses to keep interview flowing
- Transitional phrase
- Verbatim playback
- Paraphrasing and restatement
- Summarizing
- Clarification response
- Empathy and understanding

Measuring understanding statements (level 1-5 responses)

Evaluation interview

Structured clinical interview

Case history interview

Mental status exam

Interview validity

Halo effect

General "standoutishness"

Interview reliability

CHAPTER 8 PRACTICE QUIZ

1.   **Which of the following is NOT a similarity between an interview and a test?**

   a. both are used to make predictions about a person's behavior
   b. both can be structured or unstructured
   c. both can be evaluated in terms of reliability and validity
   d. both require face-to-face contact with an examiner

2.   **The more tense and nervous interviewers are, the more tense and nervous interviewees will be. This fact illustrates**

   a. the halo effect.
   b. social facilitation.
   c. general standoutishness.
   d. the stress interview.

3.   **Statements such as "Why did you do that?" and "Why did you lie to your friend?" are called _____ statements, and should be avoided in an interview.**

   a. probing
   b. falsely reassuring
   c. clarifying
   d. closed-ended

4.   **Which of the following response types is not essentially interchangeable with the interviewee's statements?**

   a. restatement
   b. verbatim playback
   c. paraphrasing
   d. clarification

5.   **Direct questions are often more effective than open-ended questions**

   a. with uncooperative interviewees.
   b. with more intelligent interviewees.
   c. at the beginning rather than at the end of the interview.
   d. in every interview situation.

6\. "You always worry too much. Everything will turn out just fine, you'll see." This is an example of a(n) _____ response.

- a. false reassurance
- b. verbatim playback
- c. understanding / empathy
- d. probing

7\. A central difference between the Level-one response and the Level-two response is that the latter response

- a. is interchangeable with the interviewee's statement.
- b. is superficially related to the interviewee's statement.
- c. is an interpretation of the interviewee's statement.
- d. does not acknowledge the interviewee's statement.

8\. The primary purpose of which type of interview is to diagnose psychosis, neurological damage, and other major psychiatric problems?

- a. case history interview
- b. therapeutic interview
- c. mental status examination
- d. employment interview

9\. Which of the following types of interviews is most reliable?

- a. case history interviews
- b. structured interviews
- c. semistructured evaluation interviews
- d. unstructured interviews

10\. Dr. Melvin conducted an interview with a new client, Marcus. During the interview, Marcus interrupted Dr. Melvin several times and seemed in a hurry to leave her office. In the next few weeks, Dr. Melvin had to work very hard to ensure that her initial impressions of Marcus would not bias her clinical judgment. This example best illustrates an attempt to counter:

- a. social facilitation.
- b. a level two response.
- c. the halo effect.
- d. interpersonal attraction.

Chapter 8: Interviewing Techniques

✍Student Workbook Assignment 8.1

⤙ Creating an Interview Schedule ⤚

◆ **DESCRIPTION OF THE ASSIGNMENT**

For this assignment, imagine that you are interviewing people in order to select a new roommate. Further imagine that you can ask only 10 questions during the interview. What questions will elicit the most useful information to help you make a selection?

◆ **DIRECTIONS**

➔ **Before beginning this assignment, make sure you have read Chapter 8.**

(1)   Write 10 effective interview questions for the purpose of selecting a new roommate. Be sure to pay attention to characteristics of good versus poor interview questions!

◄ CHAPTER 9: *Theories of Intelligence and the Binet Scales* ►

CHAPTER 9 EXERCISES

I.   THE PROBLEM OF DEFINING INTELLIGENCE (text pp. 234-236)

1.   When you say that someone you know is "smart" or "intelligent," what do you mean? In your opinion, what are the characteristics of an intelligent person? _____

_____

_____

_____

_____

131

2.   In the table below, write definitions of intelligence articulated by experts in the field. Do these definitions reflect your own conception of intelligence (from 1. on the previous page?)

Expert	Intelligence is:
Binet	
Spearman	
Freeman	
Das	
Gardner	
Sternberg	
Anderson	

3.   Describe the three research traditions that have been employed to study the nature of intelligence.

a. *psychometric tradition*:_____

_____

b. *information-processing tradition*: _____

_____

c. *cognitive tradition*: _____

_____

4.   In 1904, Alfred Binet was appointed by the French minister to a commission charged with what task?

_____

_____

II. BINET'S PRINCIPLES OF TEST CONSTRUCTION (text pp. 236-237)

1.   Binet believed intelligence expressed itself through what three facilities? _____

_____

A. Principle I: Age Differentiation (text pp. 236-237)

2.	What specific criteria did Binet use to identify age-differentiated tasks for his intelligence test?

_____

_____

3.	What is Binet's concept of "mental age?" _____

_____

4.	If a 10-year-old child completed a set of tasks that were appropriate for a 12-year-old child, what would be the 10-year-old child's mental age? _____

B. Principle II: General Mental Ability (text p. 237)

5.	Binet was interested in measuring *general mental ability*, or the sum of the combined elements of intelligence. What were two benefits of Binet's focus on general mental ability in the construction of his test?

a.	_____

_____

b.	_____

_____

III. SPEARMAN'S MODEL OF GENERAL MENTAL ABILITY (text pp. 237-239)

1.	What was Spearman's belief about the nature of intelligent behavior? _____

_____

_____

2.	Define both "positive manifold" and "factor analysis", and explain how Spearman used each as evidence in support of his notion of g.

a. *positive manifold*: _____

_____

b. How does positive manifold support g? _____

_____

c. *factor analysis*: _____

_____

d. How does factor analysis support g? _____

_____

A. Implications of General Mental Intelligence (*g*) (text p. 238)

3.   The Binet scale was developed under the assumption that a person's intelligence can best be represented by a single score *g* that reflects what? _____

B. The *gf-gc* Theory of Intelligence (text p. 239)

4.   A more recent theory of multiple intelligences is the *gf-gc* theory, which holds that there are two basic types of intelligence: fluid intelligence (*gf*) and crystallized intelligence (*gc*). Describe each type below.

        gf (fluid intelligence): _____

        _____

        gc (crystallized intelligence): _____

        _____

IV. THE EARLY BINET SCALES (text pp. 239-241)

A. The 1905 Binet-Simon Scale (text p.p. 239-240)

1.   Complete the following questions about the 1905 Binet Simon Scale.

1a. The scale consisted of 30 items increasing in difficulty. List two examples of items on the scale.

        1. _____

        2. _____

1b. Three levels of intellectual deficiency were designated. List and describe these three levels.

        1. _____

        2. _____

        3. _____

1c. Binet developed the first major test of intelligence. However, what were three shortcomings of the scale?

        1. _____

        2. _____

        3. _____

B. The 1908 Scale (text pp. 240-241)

2.   How did the 1908 *age scale* differ from the age differentiation concept employed in the 1905 scale?

_____

_____

3.   A limitation of both the 1905 and the 1908 Binet-Simon Scale was the use of a single score that reflected a very limited range of abilities. These abilities were: _____

4.   The primary improvement in the 1908 scale was the introduction of the "mental age" concept. Review the answers you provided for questions about mental age in Section I, Part A ("Principle I: Age Differentiation").

V. TERMAN'S STANFORD-BINET INTELLIGENCE SCALES (text pp. 242-246)

1.   In _____, Binet and Simon revised their intelligence test again to create a third version containing minor improvements over the second (1908) version.

A. The 1916 Stanford-Binet Intelligence Scale (text p. 242)

2.   In 1916, L.H. Terman developed the Stanford-Binet, an intelligence test based on the Binet-Simon scale that retained the principles of age differentiation, general mental ability and the age scale. Further, although Terman increased the size of the standardization sample, the sample was still far from adequate. Why?

_____

_____

B. The Intelligence Quotient (IQ) (text pp. 242-243)

3.   What was the formula used by Terman to derive the intelligence quotient (IQ)? (Be sure to spell out all components of the formula): _____

4.   In the table below, calculate the IQs of the subjects listed.

Subject	Mental Age	Chronological Age	Intelligence Quotient (IQ) equation
Sheila	19.5	19.5	IQ =
Christopher	14	10	IQ =
Benjamin	19.5	22	IQ =
Alicia	7	12	IQ =
Hannah	19.5	30	IQ =

5.   What was the maximum possible mental age a person could obtain on the Stanford-Binet? _____

6.   Explain why Sheila's, Benjamin's, and Hannah's IQ scores might have underestimated their "true" IQs.

_____

_____

_____

7.   Because of the potential problem of underestimating the IQs of people over a certain age, Terman placed a maximum limit on the chronological age that would be figured into the IQ equation.

a. What was this age? _____

b. How did Terman justify this maximum chronological age? _____

_____

C. The 1937 Scale (text pp. 244-245)

8.   The 1937 Stanford-Binet Scale made several improvements over its predecessor. In the table below, summarize these improvements.

Improvements in the 1937 Stanford-Binet Scale	
Aspect	**Description of improvement**
Age ranges	
Instructions	
Items	
Standardization sample	
Alternate forms	

9.   Two significant problems with the 1937 scale emerged. These problems pertained to (a) the reliability of the test and (b) differential variability in IQ scores. Describe each problem below -- make sure you understand *why* each is a problem.

a. *reliability*: _____

_____

b. *differential variability in IQ scores*: _____

_____

> **♀ Focused Example 9-1,** *Differential Variability in IQ Scores*
> This Focused Example examines in more detail the problem of differential variability of IQs in the 1937 version of the Stanford-Binet scales. Essentially, because the standard deviation of IQs varied considerably at different age levels, an IQ in one age range was not comparable to the same IQ in another age range. • If the standard deviation of IQs in the 6-year old group was 12.5 (and the mean was set at 100), what would be the IQ of a 6-year-old child who scored 1 standard deviation below the mean? • Now, if a 12-year-old child got that same IQ, approximately how far below the mean would his score fall if the standard deviation of IQs for 12-year-olds was 20? • What you should see in this example is that a 6-year-old and a 12-year-old with the very same IQs are not comparable in terms of where their scores fall in the distribution at their respective age levels.

D. The 1960 Stanford-Binet Revision and Deviation IQ (SB-LM) (text pp. 245-246)

10.   The 1960 revision of the Stanford-Binet scale (SB-LM) incorporated several improvements over its predecessors. For example, instructions for scoring and test administration were improved. Further, the age range was extended from 16 to 18 years. Also, tasks that met two criteria were selected for the SB-LM. What were these criteria? _____

_____

_____

11.   In the 1960 revision, the problem of differential variation in IQ scores was solved through the implementation of the *deviation IQ* concept. Complete the following statements related to this concept.

a. The deviation IQ was a standard score with a mean of _____ and a standard deviation of _____.

b. The deviation IQ was derived by examining the standard deviation of _____ for a representative sample of examinees at each chronological age level.

c. The deviation IQ could be compared across chronological age levels because an IQ at one age level (for example, an IQ of 90 at the 10-year-old age level) corresponded to the same _____ as the same IQ at another age level (for example, an IQ of 90 at the 18-year-old age level).

12.   Although the 1960 revision did not include a new standardization sample, a more representative sample of _____ children was obtained in 1972, and was thereafter used with the 1960 revision.

VI. THE MODERN BINET SCALES (text pp. 246-250)

A. Model for the Fourth and Fifth Editions of the Binet Scale (text p. 247)

1.   Whereas the earlier version of the Binet scale were based on _____ model of intelligence, the Fourth (1986) and Fifth (2003) editions incorporate the _____ theory of intelligence.

2.   Complete the diagram below that depicts the hierarchical model of intelligence on which the more recent versions of the Stanford-Binet are based.

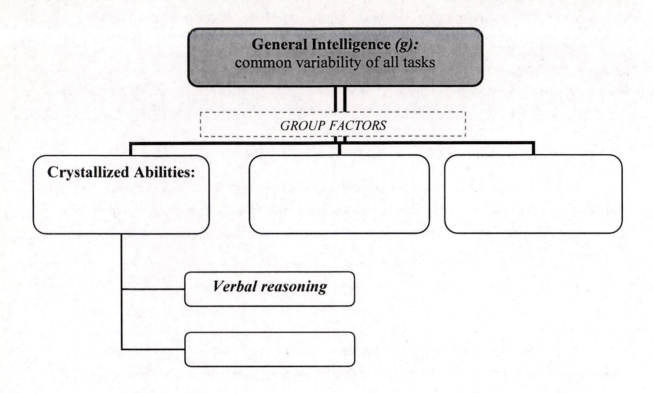

3.   The model of intelligence on which the modern Binet scales are based (depicted in the diagram above) stem from the work of _____ who argued for a multidimensional conception of intelligence comprised of independent factors, or " _____ ."

B. Characteristics of the 1986 Revision (text pp. 247-250)

4.   A major change in the 1986 revision was that the age-scale format was completely eliminated. What replaced the age-scale format? _____

_____

_____

C. Characteristics of the 2003 Fifth Edition (text pp. 250-251)

5.   Complete the table on the next page, which summarizes the content areas/factors and subtests (both verbal and nonverbal) on the 2003 Fifth Edition of the Stanford-Binet. Be sure to review Figure 9.9 on p. 249.

CONTENT AREAS /FACTORS AND SUBTESTS ON THE 2003 (FIFTH EDITION) STANFORD-BINET INTELLIGENCE SCALE		
Content Area / Factor	*Verbal Subtest*	*Nonverbal Subtest*
Fluid Reasoning (FR)	*Analogies*	*Matrices*

6.   Administration of the 2003 edition of the Stanford Binet begins with the examinee taking a verbal and a nonverbal "routing test" (or subtest). These routing tests contain items of _____ content that gradually increase in _____ .

7.   From the verbal and nonverbal routing tests, the administrator is able to ascertain the examinee's level of ability, which is called the _____ . The administrator can then give the examinee the remaining eight subtests, which are arranged in an age-scale format. Because items that are too easy are not given to the examinee, this procedure saves time.

8.   Define the following terms as they relate to the 2003 Fifth Edition of the Stanford-Binet:
a. *basal:* _____
_____
b. *ceiling*: _____
_____

9.   Scaled scores on each of the 10 Stanford-Binet subtests have a mean of _____ and a standard deviation of _____ .

10. Standard scores with a mean of _____ and a standard deviation of _____ are yielded for Nonverbal IQ (a composite of the 5 nonverbal subtest scores), Verbal IQ (a composite of the 5 verbal subtest scres), and Full Scale IQ (a composite of all 10 subtest scores), as well as each of the five factors.

D. Psychometric Properties of the 2003 Fifth Edition (text pp. 251-252)

E. Median Validity (text p. 252)

11.   In the table below, summarize the characteristics of the 2003 edition of the Stanford-Binet.

Characteristics of the 2003 (Fifth Edition) Stanford-Binet Scale	
Characteristic	*Description*
Age range	
Norms / Standardization Sample	
Reliability	*Internal consistency:*
	Test-Retest:
	Interscorer:
Validity	

Key Terms and Concepts to Know from Chapter Nine

Intelligence

Psychometric approach

Information-processing approach

Cognitive approach

Alfred Binet's definition of intelligence

Age differentiation

Mental age

General mental ability

Spearman's *g*

Positive manifold

Factor analysis

Gf-gc theory
- Fluid intelligence
- Crystallized intelligence

1905 Binet-Simon scale (characteristics and properties)

1908 Binet-Simon scale (characteristics and properties)

1916 Stanford-Binet Intelligence Scale (characteristics and properties)

Intelligence quotient (IQ)

1937 Stanford-Binet Intelligence Scale (characteristics and properties)

1960 Sanford-Binet revision (SB-LM;characteristics and properties)

Deviation IQ

Hierarchical model of intelligence employed in the 4th and 5th edition Binet scales

1986 Stanford-Binet scale (characteristics and properties)

2003 Stanford-Binet scale (characteristics and properties)

Start point, basal, and ceiling

CHAPTER 9 PRACTICE QUIZ

1.   **The concept of *g* refers to**

    a. the degree to which intelligence is genetically determined.
    b. the level of giftedness demonstrated by examinees on an intelligence test.
    c. the view that one general mental ability factor underlies all intelligent behavior.
    d. the notion that gradations of performance are reflected in intelligence test scores.

2.   **Which of the following concepts did Binet incorporate into the first two versions (1905 and 1908) of the Binet-Simon scale of intelligence?**

    a. intelligence quotient
    b. mental age
    c. crystallized intelligence
    d. deviation IQ

3.   **The standardization sample of the 1916 Stanford-Binet scale was inadequate in that**

    a. it was comprised exclusively of white children from California.
    b. it was obtained in France but was used in testing American children.
    c. it was comprised exclusively of children from rural areas.
    d. only children between the ages of 6 and 12 were represented.

4.   **If a 10-year-old child was found to have a mental age of 5 on the 1916 Stanford-Binet scale, the child's intelligent quotient (IQ) would be**

    a. 200.
    b. 150.
    c. 100.
    d. 50.

5.   **A central problem of the 1937 revision of the Stanford-Binet scale was that**

    a. each age group in the standardization sample was comprised of 30 or fewer children.
    b. the age range of examinees for whom the test was appropriate decreased significantly.
    c. the reliability coefficients were approximately the same across age groups.
    d. different age groups showed significant differences in the standard deviation of IQ scores.

6. _____ is a standard score with a mean of 100 and a standard deviation of 16 (later 15) that was first introduced in the 1960 revision of the Stanford-Binet.

    a. The intelligence quotient (IQ)
    b. Mental age (MA)
    c. The deviation IQ
    d. *g*

7. **The knowledge you have acquired through your academic studies would best be described in terms of**

    a. crystallized intelligence.
    b. *g.*
    c. IQ.
    d. fluid intelligence.

8. **The *gf-gc* theory of intelligence is**

    a. the basis of the original and all subsequent revisions of the Binet scales of intelligence.
    b. a hierarchical model on which only the later versions of the Stanford-Binet are based.
    c. a single-factor model introduced by Spearman and used as the basis of the 2003 revision of the Stanford-Binet.
    d. no longer a viable model of intelligence in contemporary times.

9. **Administration of the modern Stanford-Binet requires examiners to continue testing until**

    a. the examinee passes all items on the routing tests.
    b. the examinee fails all items on the routing tests.
    c. the examinee's basal level is reached.
    d. the examinee's ceiling is reached.

10. **Which of the following is <u>false</u> with regard to the psychometric properties of the 2003 (Fifth) edition of the Stanford-Binet?**

    a. Internal consistency reliabilities for the three IQs are all above .90.
    b. Test-retest reliabilities are strong, but vary according to age level and time interval.
    c. Interscorer agreement was relatively low with average coefficients of .50-.60.
    d. Adequate convergent validity with other intelligence tests has been established.

✍Student Workbook Assignment 9.1

⊶ Creating Your Own Subtests for an Intelligence Test ⊷

♦ DESCRIPTION OF THE ASSIGNMENT

Intelligence tests reflect the theory of intelligence favored by the test developer. In this assignment, you will identify a theory or definition of intelligence that appeals to you. Then you will create both a verbal and a nonverbal subtest for an intelligence test based on the theory or definition you chose.

♦ DIRECTIONS

→ **Before beginning this assignment, make sure you have read Chapter 9.**

(1) Select a definition of intelligence that appeals to you from text p. 234.

(2) Describe a verbal-type subtest and a performance (nonverbal)-type subtest that reflect the definition of intelligence you selected.

(3) Be sure to discuss the definition of intelligence on which your subtests are based, and the types of items or tasks presented to examinees on each subtest.

(4) Describe at least three specific examples of items from each subtest, including how they should be scored.

→ CHAPTER 10: *The Wechsler Intelligence Scales: WAIS-IV, WISC-IV, and WPPSI-III* ➤

CHAPTER 10 EXERCISES

I.   THE WECHSLER INTELLIGENCE SCALES (text pp. 257-259)

1.   David Wechsler objected to the _____ offered by the Binet scale because it did not reflect varied abilities associated with intelligence; further, Wechsler paid attention to _____ factors in the underlying theory of his scale, which Binet had essentially ignored.

2.   Wechsler criticized what he considered was the inappropriateness of the 1937 version of the Binet scale as a measure of adult intelligence. Summarize four of Wechsler's criticisms below.

a. _____

b. _____

c. _____

d. _____

A. Point and Performance Scale Concepts (text pp. 257-259)

3.   One of the two primary differences between the Wechsler and the original (pre-1986) Binet scales was that Wechsler's test used a *point scale* rather than an age scale. Describe the point scale concept below.

_____

_____

_____

4.   The other primary difference between the Wechsler and the Binet scales was that Wechsler's test included a *performance scale*, which provided a measure of nonverbal intelligence. Performance scale tasks required examinees to do something rather than simply answer questions. Below, summarize three ways in which the performance scale concept was a strength of the Wechsler scales.

a. _____

_____

b. _____

_____

c. _____

_____

II. FROM THE WECHSLER-BELLEVUE INTELLIGENCE SCALE TO THE WAIS-IV (text p. 259)

1.   Describe the characteristics of the first Wechsler-Bellevue scale's (inadequate) standardization sample.

_____

2.   The Wechsler-Bellevue scale was first published in 1939, and then was revised in _____ (WAIS), in _____ (WAIS-R), in _____ (WAIS-III), and again in _____ (WAIS-IV).

III. SCALES, SUBTESTS, AND INDEXES (text pp. 259-267)

1.   How did Wechsler define intelligence? _____

_____

_____

♪ *Carefully examine Table 10-1 (text p. 260) which presents the core subtests on the Wechsler. Also, look at Figure 10.6 (text p. 266), which shows which subtests comprise each of the four Index Scores. It will be important for you to know the subtests and their associated Indexes, as well as what major functions each subtest measures.*

A. A Closer Look at the Subtests (text pp. 260-265)

2.   In the table below and the next page, describe the task (or type of item) presented on each of the seven Verbal Scale subtests. Then identify both intellectual and non-intellectual factors that influence subtest scores. Underline the major function each subtest is designed to measure. Finally, identify the Index (VC, PR, WM, or PS) associated with each subtest.   An example (Digit Span) is completed for you.

◎ WECHSLER SUBTESTS ◎	
VOCABULARY (Index:)	
Task (or item type)	
Factors influencing scores	
SIMILARITIES (Index:)	
Task (or item type)	
Factors influencing scores	
ARITHMETIC (Index:)	
Task (or item type)	
Factors influencing scores	
DIGIT SPAN (Index: WM)	
Task (or item type)	*Repeat digits forward and backward.*
Factors influencing scores	*Short-term (immediate) auditory memory.* *Also, attention and test anxiety influence scores.*
INFORMATION (Index:)	
Task (or item type)	
Factors influencing scores	

COMPREHENSION (Supplemental test)	
Task (or item type)	
Factors influencing scores	

LETTER-NUMBER SEQUENCING (Supplemental test)	
Task (or item type)	
Factors influencing scores	

DIGIT-SYMBOL CODING (Index:)	
Task (or item type)	
Factors influencing scores	

BLOCK DESIGN (Index:)	
Task (or item type)	
Factors influencing scores	

MATRIX REASONING (Index:)	
Task (or item type)	
Factors influencing scores	

SYMBOL SEARCH (Index:)	
Task (or item type)	
Factors influencing scores	

B. From Raw Scores to Scaled and Index Scale Scores (text pp. 265-267)

3.   Raw scores on individual subtests are converted to standard scores with a mean of _____ and a standard deviation of _____ ; this raw-to-standard score conversion allows testers to compare scores on subtests, even though the subtests produce different maximum total scores.

4.   To create the subtest scales scores, WAIS-IV test developers used a statistical method called _____, which resulted in the creation of (age) reference-group _____ that allow testers to compare subtest scores across examinees.

5.   The four Index scales are derived by adding up the relevant _____ subtest scores; each Index score has a mean of _____ and a standard deviation of _____.

C. Index Scores (text p. 266)

6.   In the table below, write the names of the core subtests that comprise each of the four Index Scores (be sure to look at Figure 10-6 on p. 266). Then describe what each Index Score measures.

Index	Subtests	Measures
Verbal Comprehension		
Perceptual Reasoning		
Working Memory		
Processing Speed		

D. Full-Scale IQs / FSIQs (text p. 267)

8.   Like the Index scores, the FSIQ (a composite of all age-corrected Index scores) has a mean of _____ and a standard deviation of _____; the FSIQ is a measure of _____.

IV. INTERPRETIVE FEATURES OF THE WECHSLER TESTS (text pp. 267-270)

✦ *In Section IV, the text authors draw upon research and examples based on the Verbal IQ (VIQ) and the Performance IQ (PIQ), which were the two primary composite scales on the previous WAIS-III. Because of commonalities in subtests that comprise the composite scores, the WAIS-III's VIQ is somewhat analogous to a combination of the WAIS-IV's Verbal Comprehension Index and the Working Memory Index. The WAIS-III's PIQ is somewhat analogous to a combination of the WAIS-IV's Perceptual Reasoning Index and the Processing Speed Index.*

A. Index Comparisons (text pp. 267-268)

1. The meaning of an examinee's Verbal IQ can be better interpreted when it is compared with his or her Performance IQ. How might the following comparisons of Verbal IQ and Performance IQ scores be interpreted?

a. *Both the Verbal and the Performance IQ are low (between 50 and 60, for example)*: _____

_____

_____

b. *The Verbal IQ is low (e.g., 70) but the Performance IQ is much higher (e.g., 105)*: _____

_____

_____

2. Research findings on ethnicity and VIQ-PIQ comparisons indicate that it is inappropriate to make sweeping generalizations about the meaning of Index _____.

B. Pattern Analysis (text p. 268)

3. How might an examiner conduct a *pattern analysis* of scores on the Wechsler scales? _____

_____

_____

4. Research strongly suggests that pattern analysis must be done cautiously, perhaps to generate _____ that should be corroborated or refuted by other data sources.

C. Hypothetical Case Studies (text pp. 268-270)

✦ *Be sure to read through both hypothetical case studies, "A Drop in Grades" (pp. 268-269) and "A Slow Leaner," (pp. 269-270) carefully. Both case studies provide valuable insights into how Wechsler scale profiles might be interpreted in "real-world" practice. Note that these case studies are based on the WAIS-III, rather than the WAIS-IV, the essential lessons about profile interpretation apply to both the WAIS-III and the WAIS-IV.*

V. PSYCHOMETRIC PROPERTIES OF THE WECHSLER ADULT SCALE (text pp. 270-271)

A. Standardization (text p. 270), B. Reliability (text pp. 270-271) and C. Validity (text p. 271)

1.   In the table below, summarize research findings on the psychometric properties of the WAIS-IV.

WAIS IV Psychometric Property	Summary of Research Findings
STANDARDIZATION	
RELIABILITY	Split-half
	Test-retest
	Standard error of measurement (SEM)
VALIDITY	

VI. EVALUATION OF THE WECHSLER ADULT SCALES (text p. 271)

1.   Why should examiners be cautious about inferences made on the basis of pattern analyses of subtests on the WAIS-IV? _____

_____

_____

_____

VII. DOWNWARD EXTENSIONS OF THE WAIS-IV: THE WISC-IV AND THE WPPSI-III (text pp. 271-277)

A. The WISC-IV (text pp. 272-275)

1.   The Wechsler Intelligence Scale for Children-Fourth Edition (WISC-IV) measures intelligence in children age _____ years to _____ years, _____ months.

2.   Like the WAIS-IV, the WISC has abandoned the _____ dichotomy, and instead yields four major _____ which are summed to derive the Full Scale IQ.

3.   List the subtests that comprise each of the four indexes on the WISC-IV.
a. *Verbal Comprehension Index*: _____
b. *Perceptual Reasoning Index*: _____
c. *Processing Speed Index*: _____
d. *Working Memory Index*: _____

4.   Below, summarize some of the improvements made to the WISC-IV from the earlier WISC-III.

_____

_____

_____

_____

_____

5.   A strength of the WISC-IV is that *item bias* was examined empirically. Why is the use of item analysis and similar empirical methods superior to expert judgments of items? _____

_____

_____

_____

_____

6.   In the table below, summarize the listed characteristics of the WISC-IV.

WISC IV Characteristic	Summary / Description
STANDARDIZATION	
RAW SCORES & SCALED SCORES	
INTERPRETATION	
RELIABILITY	
VALIDITY	

B. The WPPSI-III (text pp. 275-277)

7.   The WPPSI is the Wechsler _____ and _____ Scale of Intelligence.

8.   Name and describe the only two subtests included on the WPPSI-R that were <u>not</u> on either the WAIS or the WISC.

a. _____

_____

b. _____

_____

9.   The WPPSI-III is designed for children age _____ years _____ months to age _____ years _____ months.

10.   Summarize reviews of the WPPSI's validity and usefulness: _____

_____

_____

Key Terms and Concepts to Know from Chapter Ten

Wechsler's view on intelligence tests

Point scale concept

Performance scale concept

Wechsler's definition of intelligence

Basic approach of the Wechsler scales

WAIS-IV Core Subtests

WAIS-IV Index scores

- Verbal comprehension

- Perceptual reasoning

- Working memory

- Processing speed

Full-Scale IQ

WAIS –III Verbal-Performance IQ comparisons

Pattern analysis

Standardization of the WAIS-IV

Reliability of the WAIS-IV

Validity of the WAIS-IV

WISC-IV
- Description, age range, etc.
- Subtests
- Item bias
- Standardization
- Raw scores/Scaled scores
- Interpretation
- Reliability of the WISC-IV
- Validity of the WISC-IV

WPPSI-III
- Description, age range, etc.
- Subtests
- Reliability of the WPPSI-III
- Validity of the WPPSI-III

CHAPTER 10 PRACTICE QUIZ

1.   **Wechsler's criticisms of the Binet scales related to**

    a. the Binet scale's use of a point scale rather than an age scale.
    b. the lack of validity of Binet scale items designed for children.
    c. the failure of Binet to include any speeded (or timed) items.
    d. the Binet scale's inadequate measurement of adult intelligence.

2.   **An examiner administering the WAIS-IV asks Julie a series of question such as "In what way are the sun and the moon alike?" The examiner is administering the _____ subtest.**

    a. Comprehension
    b. Similarities
    c. Vocabulary
    d. Information

3.   **On the WAIS-IV, Digit Span and Arithmetic comprise the _____ Index, whereas Block Design, Matrix Reasoning, and Visual Puzzles comprise the _____ Index.**

    a.   Working Memory; Perceptual Reasoning
    b.   Verbal Comprehension; Working Memory
    c.   Processing Speed; Perceptual Reasoning
    d.   Perceptual Reasoning; Verbal Comprehension

4.   **Which of the following Wechsler subtests is one of the most stable measures of general intelligence?**

    a. Digit Span
    b. Vocabulary
    c. Comprehension
    d. Information

5.   **Questions such as, "A man sells twelve apples at 25 cents apiece. How much money does he make?" might be found on the _____ subtest of the _____ scale of the WAIS-IV.**

    a. Arithmetic; Performance
    b. Digit Span; Performance
    c. Arithmetic; Verbal
    d. Digit Span; Verbal

6.   On all the Wechsler scales, subtest scores have a mean of _____ and a standard deviation of _____, whereas the Full Scale IQ has a mean of _____ and a standard deviation of _____.

    a. 10, 3; 100, 15
    b. 15, 5; 500, 100
    c. 100, 15; 10,3
    d. 10, 3; 50, 10

7.   Which of the following is <u>not</u> correct with regard to the psychometric properties of the WAIS-III?

    a. Test-retest reliabilities of the Verbal, Performance, and Full Scale IQs are all very strong.
    b. Test-retest reliabilities of the subtests are all very strong.
    c. The standard error of measurement (SEM) for the Full Scale and Verbal IQs are smaller than the SEM for the Performance IQ.
    d. Internal consistency reliabilities for the non-speeded subtests are very strong.

8.   The WISC-IV is designed for children between the ages of approximately

    a. 3 and 18.
    b. 5 and 18.
    c. 6 and 16.
    d. 3 and 12.

9.   A recent innovation in the WISC-IV is the use of _____ to identify item biases.

    a. opinions of experts in the field of intelligence testing
    b. judges who were trained to recognize bias
    c. content analysis
    d. statistical analysis

10.   Which of the following subtests is included on the WPPSI-III, but not on the WAIS-III or the WISC-IV?

    a. Object Assembly
    b. Coding
    c. Animal Pegs
    d. Symbol Search

☞Student Workbook Assignment 10.1

◄ Interpreting a Wechsler Profile ►

♦ DESCRIPTION OF THE ASSIGNMENT

In this assignment, you will examine a set of hypothetical Wechsler Adult Intelligence Scale (WAIS) subtest scores. Then you will describe the strengths and weaknesses you would expect to observe in the examinee during a typical day at work and school.

Read this important note! Learning to competently administer, score and interpret intelligence tests such as the Wechsler and Stanford-Binet Scales requires months (if not years) of supervised training at the graduate level. This assignment is not designed to teach you how to interpret tests. Therefore, completion of this assignment will not make you more qualified to administer, score, and/or interpret actual intelligence tests. Rather, the purpose of this assignment is to familiarize you with very basic concepts and procedures underlying the use of intelligence test scores.

♦ DIRECTIONS

➔ **Before beginning this assignment, make sure you have read Chapter 10.**

(1) Examine Dominic's WAIS-IV scores, presented below. Organize the subscales into the four Indexes.

(2) What appear to be Dominic's strongest skills or abilities (a) at the Index level? (b) at the subscale level?

(3) During a typical day at work or school, on what tasks does Dominic probably excel?

(4) What appear to be Dominic's weakest skills or abilities (a) at the Index level? (b) at the subscale level?

(5) During a typical day at work or school, what tasks are probably most challenging for Dominic?

(6) Based on Dominic's strengths and weaknesses, describe an optimal work and/or learning environment for him.

Examinee: Dominic G.
Age: 19
Occupation: Server at an elegant dining establishment
College major: Business/marketing

WECHSLER ADULT INTELLIGENCE SCALE (WAIS-IV)			
Subscale	*Scaled Score*	*Subscale*	*Scaled Score*
Information	13	Visual Puzzle	7
Arithmetic	13	Block Design	6
Similarities	11	Symbol Search	10
Vocabulary	14	Digit-Symbol Coding	9
Digit Span	12	Matrix Reasoning	7

◄ CHAPTER 11: *Other Individual Tests of Ability* ►
in Education and Special Education

Chapter 11 Outline

CHAPTER 11 EXERCISES

1.   Discuss the facts and outcome of the court case *Ford and Ford v. Long Beach Unified School District* (2002): _____

_____

_____

_____

_____

I. ALTERNATIVE INDIVIDUAL ABILITY TESTS COMPARED WITH THE BINET AND WECHSLER SCALES (text pp. 280-282)

1.   On pp. 280-281 (and Table 11-1 on p. 282), your text describes both advantages and disadvantages of alternative individual ability tests compared to the more established and researched Binet and Wechsler scales.

a. *What are three prominent <u>disadvantages</u> of alternative individual ability tests?*

      (1) _____

      (2) _____

      (3) _____

b. *What are three prominent <u>advantages</u> of alternative individual ability tests?*

      (1) _____

      (2) _____

      (3) _____

II. ALTERNATIVES COMPARED WITH ONE ANOTHER (text pp. 282-283)

1.   For what reasons might an examiner choose an alternative individual ability test over the more established ability tests such as the Wechsler and the Binet? _____

_____

_____

_____

_____

2.   On pp. 282-283 (and Table 11-2), your text describes ways in which alternative individual ability tests differ from one another. List (and give examples of) these differences below.

a. _____

b. _____

c. _____

d. _____

e. _____

f. _____

g. _____

h. _____

i. _____

III. SPECIFIC INDIVIDUAL ABILITY TESTS (text pp. 284-300)

1.   Early individual ability tests other than the Binet were designed for specific populations, produced a single score, and had nonverbal performance scales. Briefly describe the purpose of each of the early individual ability tests listed below.

a. *Seguin Form Board Test* (1800s): _____

_____

_____

b. *Healy-Fernald Test* (1911): _____

_____

_____

c. *Knox test battery* (1914): _____

_____

_____

A. Infant Scales (text pp. 284-291)

2.　　　Complete the table (on this and the next page) that summarizes characteristics of four scales of infant ability.　Identify the scale's age range, what it measures, type of scores, types of behaviors sampled, how the scale is used in research and/or practice, and strengths and limitations of the scale.

Brazelton Neonatal Assessment Scale (BNAS)	
Age range	
What is measured	
Type of scores	
Types of behaviors sampled	
How scale has been used in research or practice	
Strengths of the scale	
Limitations of the scale	
Gesell Developmental Schedules (GDS)	
Age range	
What is measured	
Type of scores	
Types of behaviors sampled	
How scale has been used in research or practice	
Strengths of the scale	
Limitations of the scale	

Bayley Scales of Infant Development-Third Edition (BSID-III)	
Age range	
What is measured	
Type of scores	
Types of behaviors sampled	
How scale has been used in research or practice	
Strengths of the scale	
Limitations of the scale	
Cattell Infant Intelligence Scale (CIIS)	
Age range	
What is measured	
Type of scores	
Types of behaviors sampled	
How scale has been used in research or practice	
Strengths of the scale	
Limitations of the scale	

B. Major Tests for Young Children (text pp. 291-296)

↳ *Questions B3. through B6. relate to the **McCarthy Scales of Children's Abilities (MSCA)**.*

3. The McCarthy scales measure ability in children ages _____ years to _____ years.

4. Complete the following statements related to types and meaning of scores on the McCarthy scales.

    a. Of the 18 scales, 15 are combined to yield a _____ (or GCI).

    b. The GCI is a standard score with a mean of _____ and a standard deviation of _____.

    c. The GCI is an index of _____

    _____

    d. The GCI is a composite of subtest scores on three scales. (Identify the subtests on each scale below)

    (1) *Verbal Scale*: _____

    _____

    (2) *Perceptual Performance Scale*: _____

    _____

    (3) *Quantitative Scale*: _____

    _____

5. Reliability coefficients for the GCI are strong, and concurrent validity data include correlations between the GCI and the Stanford-Binet IQ of _____ and the WPPSI Full-Scale IQ of _____.

6. For decades, the McCarthy scales have been used as a measure of ability in research studies. Below, List some of the questions researchers who have used the McCarthy scales have posed below.

a. (Jensen et al. 2010) _____

_____

b. (Freire et al, 2010) _____

_____

c. (Nordhov et al, 2010) _____

_____

d. (Hoekstra et al. 2010) _____

_____

e. (Nores & Barnett, 2010) _____

_____

f. (Hubbs-Tait, et al., 2002) _____

_____

g. (McGill-Evans & Harrison, 2001) _____

_____

🏃 *Questions B7. through B12. relate to the **Kaufman Assessment Battery for Children, 2nd Edition (KABC-II).***

7.   The KABC-II measures ability in children ages _____ years to _____ years.

8.   Based on the work of several prominent cognitive neuroscientists, the KABC-II attempts to distinguish two types of higher brain processes associated with problem-solving strategies: **sequential processing** and **simultaneous processing**. Define and give examples of each type of processing in the spaces provided.

Sequential   DEFINITION:_____

Processing   _____

            EXAMPLES _____

Simultaneous   DEFINITION _____

Processing   _____

            EXAMPLES _____

9.   Two major advantages of the KABC-II are that (a) in addition to the intelligence or ability score, it also offers an _____ score based on the KTEA-II, and (b) it has a _____ measure of ability that is useful in testing children who are "linguistically different" or handicapped.

10.   The KABC-II yields raw scores on all 18 subtests that can be converted to standard scores with a mean of _____ and a standard deviation of _____; global scales can also be converted to standard scores with a mean of _____ and a standard deviation of _____, as well as to percentiles and age-equivalent norms.

11.   Complete the following statements related to the validity of the KABC (not the more recent KABC-II):
   a. Factor analysis has supported the _____ distinction.
   b. Compared to the Binet and Wechsler, the KABC shows smaller differences in scores between _____ and white examinees.
   c. The KABC tends to underestimate the scores of _____ children.
   d. Some researchers have found that the KABC was biased against _____.

12.   In the table below, summarize strengths and criticisms of the KABC and KABC-II.

Strengths of the KABC and KABC-II	Criticisms of the KABC and KABC-II

C. General Individual Ability Tests for Handicapped and Special Populations (text pp. 296-300)

13.   Complete the table (below and on the next page) that summarizes characteristics of four alternative ability tests designed for handicapped and special populations. Identify the age range and special populations the test was designed for, what the test measures, tasks, and strengths and limitations of each test.

Columbia Mental Maturity Scale-Third Edition (CMMS)	
Age range and special population(s) test is designed for	
What the test measures	
Tasks (or types of items) presented to examinees	
Strengths/Advantages	
Limitations/Disadvantages	
Peabody Picture Vocabulary Test-Fourth Edition (PPVT-IV)	
Age range and special population s) test is designed for	
What the test measures	
Tasks (or types of items) presented to examinees	
Strengths/Advantages	
Limitations/Disadvantages	

Leiter International Performance Scale-Revised (LIPS-R)	
Age range and special population(s) test is designed for	
What the test measures	
Tasks (or types of items) presented to examinees	
Strengths/Advantages	
Limitations/Disadvantages	
Porteus Maze Test (PMT)	
Age range and special population(s) test is designed for	
What the test measures	
Tasks (or types of items) presented to examinees	
Strengths/Advantages	
Limitations/Disadvantages	

IV. TESTING LEARNING DISABILITIES (text pp. 300-309)

1.　　　What is a traditional definition of "learning disability?" _____

_____

_____

2.   Complete the following statements related to IDEA (20 U.S.C. 1400 et seq.).

a. IDEA stands for _____ with _____ _____ Act.

b. IDEA provides for: _____

c. To qualify for IDEA, a child must: _____

_____

3.   According to Novick and Arnold's book *Why is My Child Having Trouble at School?*, what are some

signs of a possible learning problem? _____

_____

✦ *Questions 4. and 5. relate to the **Illinois Test of Psycholinguistic Abilities (ITPA-3)**.*

4.   The ITPA is a test of learning disabilities based on the concept that a failure to respond correctly (e.g.,

in a classroom setting) can result from:

   (a) problems in the "input system," such as difficulty understanding the meaning of words

   (b) problems in the "information analysis system," such as difficulty understanding the relationship

   between two concepts

   (c) problems in the "response system," such as deficits in motor or verbal skills

The diagram below depicts the three-stage model on which the ITPA is based (see Figure 11-9 on p. 302). Each

of the first 10 subtests described in Table 11-4 on text p. 303 is designed to measure problems in a particular

stage. Examine the table and then use your critical thinking skills to identify TWO subtests associated with each

stage in the model.

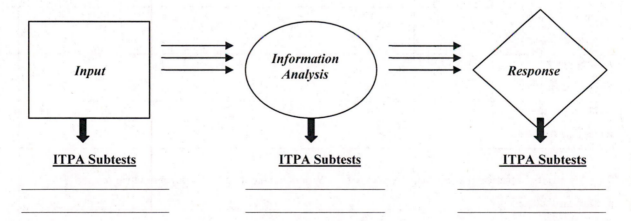

ITPA Subtests   **ITPA Subtests**   **ITPA Subtests**

_____   _____   _____

_____   _____   _____

5.   The ITPA-3 is designed for use with children between the ages of _____ and _____, and generates three

global composite scores _____

that can indicate "specific strengths and weaknesses among linguistic abilities" and "can be used to assess

linguistic delays," according to the test manual.

❦ Questions 6. through 9. relate to the **Woodcock-Johnson III.**

6.   The Woodcock-Johnson III is a respected measure of learning disabilities that assesses what aspects of

functioning? _____

_____

7.   The Woodcock Johnson-III evaluates the possibility of learning disabilities by comparing and

examining discrepancies between and within scores on the cognitive abilities battery and the achievement

battery. These comparisons are possible because both batteries were normed together (on the same

standardization samples).

a. What is an example of an *intra-ability discrepancy*? _____

_____

b. What is an example of an *ability-achievement discrepancy*? _____

_____

c. How is "major discrepancy" defined? _____

_____

8.   The Woodcock Johnson-III is comprised of a grand total of 42 subtests on four batteries. In the table

below, identify the number and examples of subtests on each of the four batteries.

Battery	Number of subtests	Examples of subtests
Cognitive Ability- Standard Battery		
Cognitive Ability – Extended Battery		
Achievement – Standard Battery		
Achievement – Extended Battery		

9.   Briefly describe the following aspects of the Woodcock-Johnson-III's psychometric properties.

a. standardization: _____

b. split-half reliability: _____

c. construct validity: _____

d. convergent validity: _____

e. criterion validity: _____

10.   What are the three conclusions drawn by the text authors on page 305 regarding learning disability tests?

One: _____

Two: _____

Three: _____

A. Visiographic Tests (text pp. 305-308)

11.   Visiographic tests require examinees to do what? _____.

12.   Tests designed to detect the presence of brain damage are based on the concept of *psychological deficit*. What does this concept mean in terms of the diagnosis of specific types or areas of brain damage? _____

_____

_____

13.   Describe the characteristics of each of three vislographic tests in the table below.

Benton Visual Retention Test (BVRT)	
Tasks (or types of items) presented to examinees	
Scoring	
Interpretation of scores/ Evidence of validity	
Bender Visual Motor Gestalt Test (BVMGT)	
Tasks (or types of items) presented to examinees	
Scoring	
Interpretation of scores/ Evidence of validity	
Memory-For-Designs Test (MFD)	
Tasks (or types of items presented to examinees	
Scoring	
Interpretation of scores/ Evidence of validity	

B. Creativity: Torrance Tests of Creative Thinking (TTCT) (text pp. 308-309)

14.   How is "creativity" defined? _____

_____

15.   The Torrance Tests of Creative Thinking (TTCT) measures aspects of creativity including *fluency, originality,* and *flexibility.* Describe how each aspect is measured on the TTCT.

a. *fluency*: _____

b. *originality*: _____

c. *flexibility*: _____

C. Individual Achievement Tests: Wide Range Achievement Test-4 (text p. 309)

16.   Examination of discrepancies between scores on intelligence and achievement tests can reveal important information about examinees. Identify one hypothesis about the meaning of each of the two discrepancies listed below.

a. *High intelligence test score / Low achievement test score*: _____

_____

b. *Low intelligence test score / High achievement test score*: _____

_____

17.   The Wide Range Achievement Test-4 (WRAT-4) is an individual achievement test which assesses grade-level functioning in _____, _____, and _____ among children age 5 and older.

18.   Although the WRAT was revised in 1993, it continued to be criticized for its failure to accurately evaluate _____ ability; although quick and simple to administer and score, the "jury is still out" on the extent to which the test is psychometrically sound.

Key Terms, Concepts, and Tests to Know from Chapter Eleven

Ford and Ford v. Long Beach Unified School District (2002)

Seguin Form Board Test

Healy-Fernald Test

Brazelton Neonatal Assessment Scale (BNAS)

Gessell Developmental Schedules (GDS)
- Developmental quotient

Bayley Scales of Infant Development- Third Edition (BSID-III)

Cattell Infant Intelligence Scale (CIIS)

McCarthy Scales of Children's Abilities (MSCA)
- General cognitive index (GCI)

Kaufman Assessment Battery for Children, Second Edition (KABC-II)
- Sequential-simultaneous distinction

Columbia Mental Maturity Scale-Third Edition (CMMS)

Peabody Picture Vocabulary Test-Fourth Edition (PPVT-IV)

Leiter International Performance Scale-Revised (LIPS-R)

Porteus Maze Test (PMT)

Learning disability

Individuals with Disabilities Act (IDEA)

Illinois Test of Psycholinguistic Abilities (ITPA-3)
- Three-stage information processing model

Woodcock-Johnson III

Visiographic tests

Benton Visual Retention Test-Fifth Edition (BVRT-V)

Bender Visual Motor Gestalt Test (BVMGT)

Memory for Designs (MFD) Test

Creativity

Torrance Tests of Creative Thinking (TTCT)

Wide-Range Achievement Test-4 (WRAT-4)

CHAPTER 11 PRACTICE QUIZ

1. Which of the following is <u>not</u> an advantage of many alternative individual ability tests over the Wechsler and Binet scales?

    a. nonverbal test administration is possible
    b. less influenced by scholastic achievement
    c. stronger standardization samples
    d. better at assessing people with sensory deficits

2. Which of the following scales of intelligence in infants and young children employs a developmental quotient (DQ) which is evaluated by assessing the presence or absence of behavior associated with maturation?

    a. Brazelton Neonatal Assessment Scale (BNAS)
    b. Gessell Developmental Schedules (GDS)
    c. Bayley Scales of Infant Development- 3rd Edition (BSID-III)
    d. Cattell Infant Intelligence Scale (CIIS)

3. Which of the following scales is a measure of ability in children that has been employed in studies of early intervention of at-risk children, the effects of mothers' smoking and exposure to lead on children's abilities, and cognitive abilities among Mexican-American children?

    a. Kaufman Assessment Battery for Children-2nd Edition (KABC-II)
    b. Leiter International Performance Scale-Revised (LIPS-R)
    c. Wide Range Achievement Test-4 (WRAT-4)
    d. McCarthy Scales of Children's Abilities (MSCA)

4. The Illinois Test of Psycholinguistic Abilities (ITPA-3) is based on the notion that learning problems can occur as a result of problems in any one of three stages of information processing, including

    a. encoding, storage, and retrieval.
    b. sensation, perception, and action.
    c. input, information analysis, and response.
    d. stimulus, response, modification.

5. Which of the following tests provides both an ability/intelligence score and a corresponding achievement score?

    a. Kaufman Assessment Battery for Children-2nd Edition (KABC-II)
    b. Leiter International Performance Scale-Revised (LIPS-R)
    c. Illinois Test of Psycholinguistic Abilities (ITPA)
    d. McCarthy Scales of Children's Abilities (MSCA)

6.   **The Columbia Mental Maturity Scale-3ʳᵈ edition (CMMS) is a measure of**

a. intellectual functioning among individuals with sensory, physical, or language deficits.
b. nonintellectual factors such as motivation and anxiety that influence intelligence test performance.
c. cognitive and achievement deficits associated with learning disabilities among children.
d. mild, moderate, severe, and profound levels of mental retardation.

7.   **Which of the following tests is an individual scale of achievement that purports to measure reading, spelling and arithmetic?**

a. Kaufman Assessment Battery for Children-2ⁿᵈ Edition (KABC-II)
b. Leiter International Performance Scale-Revised (LIPS-R)
c. Wide Range Achievement Test-4 (WRAT-4)
d. McCarthy Scales of Children's Abilities (MSCA)

8.   **Which of the following is <u>not</u> an example of a visiographic test?**

a. Benton Visual Retention Test
b. Peabody Picture Vocabulary Test
c. Bender Visual Motor Gestalt Test
d. Memory-for-Designs Test

9.   **Which of the following factors is <u>not</u> measured by the Torrance Test of Creativity?**

a. flexibility
b. originality
c. fluency
d. spontaneity

10.   **IDEA provides for**

a. free intelligence testing for low income and disadvantaged children.
b. access to achievement test preparation programs for all children.
c. free, daily, private tutoring for children with learning disabilities.
d. free and appropriate special education services for all learning disabled children.

✍**Student Workbook Assignment 11.1**

⊸ Creating a Measure of Creativity ⊶

♦ **DESCRIPTION OF THE ASSIGNMENT**

In this assignment, you will describe a creative measure of creativity.

♦ **DIRECTIONS**

➔ **Before beginning this assignment, make sure you have read Chapter 11.**

(1) In creating your measure of creativity, you will use the definition of creativity found on text p. 308: *Creativity is the ability to be original, to combine known facts in new ways, or to find new relationships between known facts.*

(2) Describe the types of items or tasks on your measure of creativity.

(3) Give at least three examples of items, including how they would be scored.

(4) Describe how the test should be administered.

◄ CHAPTER 12: *Standardized Tests in Education, Civil Service, and the Military* ►

Chapter 12 Outline

I.   Comparison of Group and Individual Ability Tests (text pp. 313-315)

    A.   Advantages of Individual Tests (text p. 314)

    B.   Advantages of Group Tests (text pp. 314-315)

II.   Overview of Group Tests (text pp. 315-316)

    A.   Characteristics of Group Tests (text p. 315)

    B.   Selecting Group Tests (text pp. 315-316)

    C.   Using Group Tests (text p. 316)

III.   Group Tests in the Schools: Kindergarten Through 12th Grade (text pp. 317-322)

    A.   Achievement Tests Versus Aptitude Tests (text pp. 317-318)

    B.   Group Achievement Tests (text pp. 318-320)

    C.   Group Tests of Mental Abilities (Intelligence) (text pp. 320-322)

IV.   College Entrance Tests (text pp. 322-326)

    A.   The SAT Reasoning Test (text pp. 323-324)

    B.   Cooperative School and College Ability Tests (text pp. 324-325)

    C.   The American College Test (text pp. 325-326)

V.   Graduate and Professional School Entrance Tests (text pp. 326-333)

    A.   Graduate Record Examination Aptitude Test (text pp. 326-330)

    B.   Miller Analogies Test (text pp. 330-331)

    C.   Law School Admission Test (text pp. 331-333)

VI.   Nonverbal Group Ability Tests (text pp. 333-339)

    A.   Raven Progressive Matrices (text pp. 333-336)

    B.   Goodenough-Harris Drawing Test (text pp. 336-337)

    C.   The Culture Fair Intelligence Test (text p. 337)

    D.   Standardized Tests Used in the U.S. Civil Service System (text pp. 337-338)

    E.   Standardized Tests in the U.S. Military: The Armed Services Vocational Aptitude Battery (text pp. 338-339)

CHAPTER 12 EXERCISES

I. COMPARISON OF GROUP AND INDIVIDUAL ABILITY TESTS (text pp. 313-315)

1.   The text states (on p. 313) that compared to low scores on individual ability tests, low scores on group tests are often difficult to interpret. Why might this be the case? _____

_____

_____

179

A. Advantages of Individual Tests (text p. 314)

2. One of the primary advantages of individual ability tests is that significant information about the examinee beyond test scores can be gathered. Give two examples of such information.

a. _____

b. _____

B. Advantages of Group Tests (text pp. 314-315)

3. List three distinct advantages of group ability tests.

a. _____

b. _____

c. _____

II. OVERVIEW OF GROUP TESTS (text pp. 315-316)

A. Characteristics of Group Tests (text p. 315)
B. Selecting Group Tests (text pp. 315-316)

1. If you took a group test, it would probably be a _____ or perhaps a computer-administered test consisting primarily of _____ items (although some items might require a free response).

C. Using Group Tests (text p. 316)

2. Because the results of group tests are used much more frequently than are results from individual tests, it is important for consumers of group tests to consider several suggestions presented by the text authors. In the spaces provided, briefly explain *why* each suggestion is important to consider.

a. *Use results with caution, because*: _____

_____

_____

b. *Be especially suspicious of low scores, because*: _____

_____

_____

c. *Consider wide discrepancies a warning signal, because*: _____

_____

_____

d. *When in doubt, refer, because:* _____

_____

_____

III. GROUP TESTS IN THE SCHOOLS: KINDERGARTEN THROUGH 12TH GRADE (text pp. 317-322)

A. Achievement Tests Versus Aptitude Tests (text pp. 317-318)

1.   Complete the following statements related to achievement, aptitude and intelligence tests.

a. **Achievement tests** measure what a person has already _____ through instruction or training, and are evaluated primarily on the basis of _____-related evidence for validity.

b. **Aptitude tests** measure an individual's _____ for learning in the future, so it makes sense that these tests are evaluated on the basis of _____-related evidence for validity

c. **Intelligence tests** are similar to aptitude tests in that they predict _____ performance, but unlike aptitude tests, they predict _____ rather than specifically (e.g., in science or math.)

B. Group Achievement Tests (text pp. 318-320)

2.   Summarize the central characteristics of the Stanford Achievement Test (SAT) and the Metropolitan Achievement Test (MAT) in the table below.

Stanford Achievement Test (SAT)	
Age or grade range	
What the test measures	
Psychometric properties (standardization, reliability, validity, etc.)	
Metropolitan Achievement test (MAT)	
Age or grade range	
What the test measures	
Psychometric properties (standardization, reliability, validity, etc.)	

C. Group Tests of Mental Abilities (Intelligence) (text pp. 320-322)

3.   Summarize the characteristics of three group tests of intelligence in the table below.

Kuhlman-Anderson Test – Eighth Edition (KAT)	
Age or grade range	
Standardization, norms, special populations	
Types of items/ item content	
Scores yielded	
Psychometric properties	
Strengths	
Weaknesses	
Hemnon-Nelson Test (HN-T)	
Age or grade range	
Standardization, norms, special populations	
Types of items/ item content	
Scores yielded	
Psychometric properties	
Strengths	
Weaknesses	
Cognitive Abilities Test (COGAT)	
Age or grade range	
Standardization, norms, special populations	
Types of items/ item content	
Scores yielded	
Psychometric properties	
Strengths	
Weaknesses	

IV. COLLEGE ENTRANCE TESTS (text pp. 322-326)

A. The SAT Reasoning Test (text pp. 323-326)

1.   In use since the year _____, the Scholastic Reasoning Test (SAT-I) is the most widely used of the college entrance tests.

2.   When compared to the original norms developed in 1941 (with the mean set at _____ for each of the two sections), modern SAT examinees tended to score about _____ points to _____ points lower on both the Verbal and the Math sections of the test; national averages in the 1980s and 1990s were about _____ on the SAT-V and about _____ on the SAT-M.

3.   What historic event occurred in June, 1994? _____

_____

_____

_____

4.   The current version of the SAT has three scored section, each scored between _____ and _____ points; the theoretical maximum number of points is now _____ instead of the original 1600.

5.   The most recent version of the SAT is _____ minutes longer than the original version (requiring an administration time of 3 hours and 45 minutes).

a.   The longer time span probably *rewards* test takers possessing which characteristics? _____

_____

b.   The longer time span may *disadvantage* which test takers? _____

_____

6.   Briefly describe the characteristics of the three scored section of the most recent version of the SAT.

a. Critical reading: _____

_____

b. Writing: _____

_____

c. Math: _____

_____

7.   A weakness of the SAT is that the test is not a good predictor of college grades among students who score in the _____ ranges, perhaps because many other factors predict college success. List examples of these factors. _____

_____

8.   The overall validity of the SAT for predicting first-year college GPA is good, with a median coefficient of about _____, indicating that approximately _____% of the variation in GPA can be predicted by SAT scores.

9.   Which groups of examinees tend to score relatively lower on the original SAT? _____
_____

B. Cooperative School and College Ability Tests (text pp. 324-325)

10.   The Cooperative School and College Ability Tests (SCAT), which was developed in the year _____ and has not been updated since, measures school-learned abilities as well as the potential to: _____
_____.

11.   Some researchers have criticized the SCAT on the basis of the _____ of its standardization sample, the lack of documentation of its psychometric properties, and its failure to provide empirical support for the assertion that previous success in school (as measured by the SCAT) can predict future success.

C. The American College Test (text pp. 325-326)

12.   The American College Test (ACT) was updated in the year _____, and is especially useful for which group? _____

13.   The ACT yields both a composite score as well as content scores in which areas? _____
_____

14.   Scores on the ACT can range from 1 to 36; among students aspiring to go to college, the mean ACT score is _____ with a standard deviation of _____.

15.   The predictive validity of the ACT is very similar to that of the _____, and the correlation between the two tests is _____.

V. GRADUATE & PROFESSIONAL SCHOOL ENTRANCE TESTS (text pp. 326-333)

A. Graduate Record Examination Aptitude Test (text pp. 326-330)

1.   The Graduate Record Examination Aptitude Test (GRE) consists of a General test that yields a
_____ score (GRE-V), a _____ (GRE-Q), and an
_____ score (GRE-A).

2.   The format of both the GRE-V and the GRE-Q sections is multiple-choice, whereas the GRE-A section consists of: _____.

3.   The GRE also contains an advanced test that measures achievement in at least 20 _____.

4.   The GRE underwent a major revision in 2011. List changes to the GRE. _____
_____
_____

5.   The mean of both the GRE-V and GRE-Q sections is _____, with a standard deviation of _____.

6.   Describe the areas covered on the:
        a. GRE-V _____
        b. GRE-Q _____

7.   Summarize results of studies examining the extent to which the GRE predicts performance in graduate school (including the over- and under-prediction of success among certain groups of examinees).

_____
_____
_____
_____
_____

8.   How might *grade inflation* and *restriction of range* affect validity coefficients found in studies of the GRE? _____
_____
_____
_____

9.   Over the last several decades, there has been an overall decline in _____ scores on the GRE, with a corresponding rise in _____ and _____ scores. What is one explanation for this pattern? _____
_____

B. Miller Analogies Test (text pp. 330-331)

10.   Unlike the GRE, the Miller Analogies Test (MAT) consists entirely of _____ items in which examinees must identify logical _____ for 100 analogy problems.

11.	Like the GRE, the MAT has not demonstrated much evidence for _____ validity, over-predicts success of _____-year old examinees, and under-predicts success of _____-year old examinees.

C. Law School Admission Test (text pp. 331-333)

12.	The Law School Admissions Test (LSAT) does not require examinees to have specific knowledge in any one area, so students in any major can take the LSAT without _____.

13.	Under extreme time pressure, LSAT examinees complete what three types of problems?

a. _____

b. _____

c. _____

14.	Admission into law school is based very heavily on a weighted composite of what two variables?

_____

15.	The LSAT has excellent psychometric properties, including _____ coefficients in the .90s, good predictive validity for _____ in law school, and outstanding content validity in the sense that skills tested on the LSAT: _____

_____.

16.	Despite its widespread use, the LSAT (and the SAT) has been questioned with regard to possible racial and gender bias. What did Jay Rosner of the Princeton Review Foundation report about LSAT test items?

_____

_____

17.	Rosner, and others, define a "biased item" as an item that is more likely to be answered correctly by one group (e.g., non-minorities, males) than by another groups (e.g., minorities, females). Do you agree with Rosner's definition? Explain your answer. _____

_____

_____

_____

VI. NONVERBAL GROUP ABILITY TESTS (text pp. 333-339)

🕭 *Before you complete questions related to text material on nonverbal group ability tests, go ahead and try your hand at a few nonverbal ability test items! Three examples appear in Figures 12-6 and 12-7 on text p. 334, and two more sample items are on the next Workbook page.*

Sample Matrices-Type Item 1:   YOUR ANSWER: _____

1   2   3

4   5   6

Sample Matrices-Type Item 2:   YOUR ANSWER: _____

1

2

3

4

Sample matrices-type items created by the author.

A. Raven Progressive Matrices (text pp. 333-336)
B. Goodenough-Harris Drawing Test (text pp. 336-337)
C. The Culture Fair Intelligence Test (text p. 337)

1.   Complete the table below which summarizes characteristics of three nonverbal ability tests.

Raven Progressive Matrices	
Age, ability, and skill range	
Types of items (or tasks)	
Psychometric properties (e.g., standardization, reliability, validity)	
Strengths & special features	
Weaknesses & limitations	
Goodenough-Harris Drawing Test	
Age, ability, and skill range	
Types of items (or tasks)	
Psychometric properties (e.g., standardization, reliability, validity)	
Strengths & special features	
Weaknesses & limitations	
The Culture Fair Intelligence Test	
Age, ability, and skill range	
Types of items (or tasks)	
Psychometric properties (e.g., standardization, reliability, validity)	
Strengths & special features	
Weaknesses & limitations	

D. Standardized Tests Used in the U.S. Civil Service System (text pp. 337-338)

2.   The General Aptitude Battery (GATB) is a group ability test designed by the U.S. Employment Service for use in making decisions about _____.

3.   What abilities and aptitudes does the GATB measure? _____

_____

_____

_____

4.   One criticism of the GATB is that it is outdated, since it was standardized in the year _____ on a sample of working adults between the ages of _____ and _____ whose mean education level was _____ years.

5.   Describe the GATB's controversial use of *within-group norms* prior to the passage of the Civil Rights Act of 1991 (which now forbids the use of these norms in employment decisions). _____

_____

_____

_____

E. Standardized Tests in the U.S. Military: The Armed Services Vocational Aptitude Battery (text pp. 338-339)

6.   The Armed Services Vocational Aptitude Battery (ASVAB) is a multiple aptitude battery designed for the Department of _____ for use with students in grade 11 and above; it can be used in educations settings or in the military to help identify people who qualify for entry into the military and assign them to military _____ programs.

7.   The ASVAB consists of 10 subtests. List them. _____

_____

_____

_____

8.   Unlike the GATB, the ASVAB has excellent psychometric properties. Describe them below.

_____

_____

_____

_____

Key Concepts, Terms, and Tests to Know from Chapter Twelve

Group tests

Individual tests

Achievement tests

Aptitude tests

Stanford Achievement Test

Metropolitan Achievement Test (MAT)

Kuhlmann-Anderson Test (KAT)-Eighth edition

Hemnon-Nelson Test (HM-T)

Cognitive Abilities Test (COGAT)

SAT Reasoning Test

Cooperative School and College Ability Tests (SCAT)

American College Tests (ACT)

Graduate Record Examination Aptitude Test

Miller Analogies Test

Law School Admission Test (LSAT)

Raven Progressive Matrices (RPM)

Goodenough-Harris Drawing Test (G-HDT)

Culture Fair Intelligence Test

General Aptitude Test Battery (GATB)

Armed Services Vocational Aptitude Battery (ASVAB)

CHAPTER 12 PRACTICE QUIZ

1.   **Which of the following is considered an advantage of group ability tests over individual ability tests?**

   a. They allow the examiner to closely observe the examinee's behavior in a standardized setting.
   b. They have more objective and reliable scoring procedures.
   c. They provide considerable information about examinees beyond the test score.
   d. They require a high level of skill and training to administer.

2.   **Which of the following is not a group test of intelligence?**

   a. The Cognitive Abilities Test (COGAT)
   b. The Hemnon-Nelson Test (H-NT)
   c. Miller Analogies Test (MAT)
   d. Kuhlman-Anderson Test (KAT)

3.   **The current version of the SAT Reasoning Test was first administered in**

   a. 1994.
   b. 2000.
   c. 2005.
   d. 2007.

4.   **Which of the following is not true of the most recent version of the SAT?**

   a. It is 45 minutes shorter than the original SAT
   b. The verbal section of the SAT emphasizes reading comprehension.
   c. The test may disadvantage students with learning disabilities such as ADHD.
   d.   The writing section consists of both an essay and multiple choice questions.

5.   **For which group of students does the SAT and other college entrance tests have difficulty predicting college grades?**

   a. Students who score in the lower ranges
   b. Students who score in the middle ranges
   c. Students who score in the higher ranges
   d. All students

6.   In 2002, the _____ of the Graduate Record Examination Test (GRE) was (were) changed from a multiple-choice to an essay format.

    a.   Analytical Reasoning section
    b.   Subject Tests
    c.   Verbal section
    d.   Quantitative section

7.   Both the SAT and the GRE have standard mean scores of _____ and standard deviations of _____.

    a.   40; 2
    b.   50; 10
    c.   100; 15
    d.   500; 100

8.   Which of the following is true with regard to the psychometric properties of the GRE?

    a.   Test-retest and internal consistency reliabilities are less than adequate.
    b.   Predictive validity regarding first-year graduate school grades is less than adequate.
    c.   The achievement of older students is over-predicted.
    d.   The achievement of younger students is under-predicted.

9.   The Law School Admissions Test (LSAT) contains all of the following types of problems except

    a.   reading comprehension.
    b.   analytical reasoning.
    c.   ethical reasoning.
    d.   logical reasoning.

10.   Lucy is being administered a nonverbal ability test consisting of a series of designs or patterns with missing parts. She must select the part that fits the design or completes the pattern from as many as eight choices. Lucy is being administered

    a. the Raven Progressive Matrices (RPM).
    b. the Armed Services Vocational Aptitude Battery (ASVAB).
    c. The General Aptitude Test Battery (GATB).
    d. the Goodenough-Harris Drawing Test.

✍Student Workbook Assignment 12.1

⊶ Constructing and Testing Your Own Matrices ⊷

♦ **DESCRIPTION OF THE ASSIGNMENT**

As you know, matrices are among the most common types of items found on non-verbal ability measures. In this assignment, you will create and pilot-test your own matrices.

♦ **DIRECTIONS**

→ **Before beginning this assignment, make sure you have read Chapter 12.**

(1) Create at least three matrices that might be seen on a non-verbal ability test. Examples of matrices can be found on text p. 326 and in this Workbook chapter. Your matrices should differ in difficulty level: one should be fairly easy, one should be moderately challenging, and the third should be very challenging.

(2) Describe your matrices by identifying the rule(s) that determine the correct answer for each matrix sequence or pattern.

(3) Conduct a pilot test of your matrices. Administer the matrices to 10 different people. Record (a) how long it took each subject to respond to each item, and (b) whether the correct answer was selected.

(3) Describe the results of your study, including (a) whether the rules you identified for the matrices seemed to hold up or need revision, and (b) whether the matrices progressed in difficulty as intended.

⫷ CHAPTER 13: *Applications in Clinical and Counseling Settings* ⫸

Chapter 13 Outline

I.   Strategies of Structured Personality Test Construction (text pp. 343-346)

      A.   Deductive Strategies (text p. 344)

      B.   Empirical Strategies (text pp. 344-346)

      C.   Criteria Used in Selecting Tests for Discussion (text p. 346)

II.   The Logical-Content Strategy (text pp. 346-348)

      A.   Woodworth Personal Data Sheet (text pp. 346-347)

      B.   Early Multidimensional Logical-Content Scales (text p. 347)

      C.   Mooney Problem Checklist (text p. 347)

      D.   Criticisms of the Logical-Content Approach (text p. 348)

III.   The Criterion-Group Strategy (text pp. 348-360)

      A.   Minnesota Multiphasic Personality Inventory (text pp. 348-359)

      B.   California Psychological Inventory-Third Edition (text pp. 359-360)

IV.   The Factor Analytic Strategy (text pp. 360-364)

      A.   Guilford's Pioneer Efforts (text p. 361)

      B.   Cattell's Contribution (text pp. 361-364)

      C.   Problems with the Factor Analytic Strategy (text p. 364)

V.   The Theoretical Strategy (text pp. 364-369)

      A.   Edwards Personal Preference Schedule (text pp. 364-366)

      B.   Personality Research Form and Jackson Personality Inventory (text p. 366-368)

      C.   Self-Concept (text pp. 368-369)

VI.   Combination Strategies (text pp. 369-373)

      A.   Positive Personality Measurement and the NEO-PI-3 (text pp. 369-370)

      B.   The NEO Personality Inventory-Three (NEO-PI-3) (text pp. 370-373)

VII: Frequently Used Measures of Positive Personality Traits (text pp. 373-379)

      A.   Rosenberg Self-Esteem Scale (text pp. 373-374)

      B.   General Self-Efficacy Scale (text p. 374)

      C.   Ego Resiliency Scale Revised (text p. 374)

      D.   Dispositional Resilience Scale (text p. 374)

      E.   Hope Scale (text p. 375)

      F.   Life Orientation Test-Revised (LOT-R) (text p. 375)

      G.   Satisfaction with Life Scale (text pp. 376)

      H.   Positive and Negative Affect Schedule (text p. 376)

      I.   Coping Intervention for Stressful Situations (text p. 377)

      J.   Core Self-Evaluations (text p. 377)

VIII.   Future of Positive Personality Research (text pp. 378-379)

CHAPTER 13 EXERCISES

1.   Define the following terms related to *personality* and *personality testing*.

a. *personality:* _____

_____

b. *personality traits:* _____

c. *personality types:* _____

d. *personality states:* _____

e. *self-concept:* _____

f. *structured (objective) personality assessment*: _____

_____

g. *projective personality assessment*: _____

_____

2.   What prompted the development of the first self-report questionnaire of personality? _____

_____

_____

_____

I. STRATEGIES OF STRUCTURED PERSONALITY TEST CONSTRUCTION (text pp. 343-346)

A. Deductive Strategies (text p. 344)

1.   The deductive strategy of test development called the *logical-content strategy* is also known as the content approach, the intuitive approach, and the rational approach. How are tests developed with the logical-content strategy? _____

_____

_____

_____

_____

2.   The *theoretical strategy* is another type of deductive strategy of test development. How are tests developed with the theoretical strategy? _____

_____

_____

_____

B. Empirical Strategies (text pp. 344-346)

3.   How are empirical strategies different from deductive strategies in their approach to test development?

_____

_____

_____

_____

4.   The first step in the *criterion-group strategy* of test development involves identifying a criterion group of interest to the test developer (e.g., individuals with a particular diagnosis or people working in a specific occupation). From this first step, how are items ultimately selected? _____

_____

_____

_____

_____

5.   Face validity of items is not a consideration in the criterion-group strategy of test development. What does this mean? _____

_____

_____

6.   What is *cross-validation* and why is it necessary? _____

_____

_____

_____

_____

⚑ **For a review of factor analysis, see Chapter 3 of the text (pp. 91-93) and the Workbook (p. 45).**

7.   A second type of empirical strategy of test development is the *factor-analytic* strategy. In this strategy, test-developers begin with a large data set consisting of inter-correlations between a large number of items. Then this data set is factor analyzed.

a. What is the purpose of this factor analysis? _____

_____

b. How do test developers identify labels, or names, for the factors? _____

_____

_____

C. Criteria Used in Selecting Tests for Discussion (text p. 346)

8.   There are literally hundreds of personality tests published in the United States today; only a select few are described in Chapter 13. What four criteria were used by the authors to decide which tests would be included in your text?

a. _____

b. _____

c. _____

d. _____

II. THE LOGICAL CONTENT STRATEGY (text pp. 346-348)

A. Woodworth Personal Data Sheet (text pp. 346-347)

1.   What was the purpose of the Woodworth Personal Data Sheet? _____

_____

2.   The Woodworth consisted of 116 items that could be answered "yes" or "no." Answer the following questions about this test.

a. What was the source of items? _____

b. What is an example of an item? _____

c. The single score yielded by the test was a measure of what? _____

d. Describe how test developers minimized the number of *false positives* (i.e., examinees who would be in an "at-risk" group based on the test, but who would later be cleared by a psychiatric interview) on the Woodworth:

_____

_____

_____

e. How were decisions made about which items/symptoms would be included on the test? _____

_____

_____

_____

B. Early Multidimensional Logical-Content Scales (text p. 347)

3.   Other than the items on the scales, in what important way(s) were the Bell Adjustment Inventory and the Bernreuter Personality Inventory different from, and probably better than, the Woodworth? _____

_____

_____

_____

C. Mooney Problem Checklist (text p. 347)

4.   Unlike the Woodworth Personal Data Sheet, the Mooney Problem Checklist is still in use today. In what way are these two tests similar? _____

_____

D. Criticisms of the Logical-Content Approach (text p. 348)

5.   The logical-content approach to test development assumes that one can interpret test results at face value. If the face validity of test responses is assumed, what *other* assumptions must one make about the person taking the test? _____

_____

_____

_____

6.   Read over the assumptions you listed above. To what extent do you think some or all of these assumptions are accurate or realistic? Explain. _____

_____

_____

III. THE CRITERION GROUP STRATEGY (text pp. 348-360)

A. Minnesota Multiphasic Personality Inventory (text pp. 348-359)

1. Complete the following statements about the MMPI.

    a. MMPI items are statements to which examinees respond with _____ or _____.

    b. The *validity scales* on the MMPI reveal an examinee's approach to the test. One approach might be to deliberately endorse many pathological items in an attempt to "_____". Another approach might be to avoid or deny any pathological items in an attempt to "_____".

    c. The *clinical scales* on the MMPI were designed to identify _____.

    d. The *content scales* are related to specific content areas such as _____.

    e. Raw scores on the MMPI are converted to _____, with a mean of _____ and a standard deviation of _____.

    f. The purpose of the MMPI is to aid in the diagnosis or assessment of _____.

    g. The MMPI requires a _____-grade reading level, whereas the MMPI-2 requires a _____-grade reading level.

2.   The original MMPI was developed according to the criterion-group (also called the contrasted-group) method. After selecting 504 items from a pool of over 1000, Hathaway and McKinley identified eight criterion groups, each with about 50 patients. They also identified a control group of about 700 people. Describe each criterion group (look at text pp. 350-351, including Table 13-1) and the control group in the table below.

CRITERION GROUP	DESCRIPTION
Hypochondriacs	
Depressives	
Hysterics	
Psychopathic deviates	
Paranoids	
Psychasthenics	
Schizophrenics	
Hypomanics	
CONTROL GROUP	

3.   The authors used the criterion-group strategy to decide which items would go onto which scale(s). Then, they conducted a cross-validation study on the eight scales. Describe the purpose of this study:

_____

_____

_____

4.   Two scales were added to the eight existing clinical scales. Name and describe each below.

Name of scale   *Description of scale*

_____   _____

                                         _____

_____   _____

                                         _____

5.   The three validity scales were designed to assess an examinee's approach to taking the test (e.g., whether they were honest or not). In the table below, describe each validity scale and give an example of an item on that scale. (Be sure to read text pp. 352-353, including Table 13-2).

Validity Scale	Description of Scale	Example of Item
L Scale (Lie scale, a.k.a. the "fake good" scale)		
K Scale (Defensiveness scale)		
F Scale (Infrequency scale, a.k.a. the "fake bad" scale)		

6.   On the original MMPI, a T-score of _____ (or _____ standard deviations above the mean) and above is considered clinically significant, whereas on the MMPI-2, a T-score of _____ (or _____ standard deviations above the mean) and above is considered significant.

7.   Paul Meehl, a respected clinical researcher, suggested that rather than interpreting single-scale elevations, users of the MMPI should examine particular patterns of scores on the test. What pattern should be examined first and foremost, according to Meehl? _____

> ✎ How did Meehl's criterion-group strategy used in the *validation* of the MMPI differ from the criterion-group strategy used in the *development* of the MMPI? ✎
>
> As opposed to the criterion-group strategy used in the initial development of the MMPI, Meehl's criterion-group approach to *validating* the MMPI did not focus on whether items or scales could distinguish a particular psychiatric patient group from a normal control group. Rather, the latter approach used patterns of scores on the MMPI to define the criterion groups. For example, one criterion group might consist of individuals with a 49/94 two-point code and another might be people with a 68/86 pattern. The characteristics of these homogeneous groups (i.e., groups of people who have the same score pattern) are then examined in various ways. So, rather than asking, "does this particular scale distinguish between people with schizophrenia and other people?" Meehl's strategy asked, "in what ways do people with this particular score pattern differ from others?" Because it was known that single scale elevations did not directly translate into psychiatric diagnoses (e.g., an elevation on the Depression scale did not necessarily mean the person was clinically depressed), Meehl recommended that to avoid misinterpretation, scales should be identified by their number rather than the name it was originally given (e.g., "Scale 2" instead of "Depression Scale"). In practice, however, both the numbers and the names (or their abbreviations) are used in reference to individual scales on the MMPI.

8.   After reading material on interpreting the MMPI (text pp. 353-355 and Table 13-3), complete the following exercise which asks you to identify the clinical scales associated with interpretive statements made about an examinee's MMPI results.

Patty C. is a 41-year-old female who was referred for psychological testing at State Psychiatric Hospital. In the table below, you will see a number of interpretive statements based on Patty's scores on the clinical scales of the Minnesota Multiphasic Personality Inventory. Your task is to read each statement and decide which scale it refers to. Then, write Patty's two-point MMPI code at the bottom of the table.

MMPI Clinical Scale (Number and name)	MMPI T Score	INTERPRETIVE STATEMENT
	90	Patty seems to feel mistreated and picked on, and may be very angry and resentful. She is probably argumentative and suspicious of others' motives. It is very possible that delusions of persecution or grandeur are present.
	75	Patty seems to feel a fairly high level of sadness and pessimism. She might brood a lot, or feel excessive, inappropriate guilt.
	45	Patty does not appear to have many concerns about her body functions; she does not complain of physical symptoms such as general fatigue or sleep problems.
	65	Patty is moderately uncomfortable in social situations. She does not participate in many social activities, and may be described by others as cold and aloof.
	80	Patty appears to be fearful, anxious, and insecure. Obsessive thinking could be present. She ruminates over failures and is indecisive.
	55	Patty is not highly immature, suggestible or naive. She does not seem to use her physical symptoms as a way to avoid or deny conflicts or problems in her life.
	80	Patty tends to have a fairly high energy and activity level. She is likely to be impulsive and may have difficulty controlling her mood swings.
	100	Confusion and disorientation, and possibly unusual sensory experiences, could be common experiences for Patty. She probably feels isolated, misunderstood, and unaccepted by her peers.
	40	Patty's pattern of responses is typical of female examinees, showing fairly conventional and traditional feminine interest patterns.
	65	Patty seems to show signs of aggressiveness and irresponsibility. She is probably rebellious and has difficulty with authority figures.

Patty's two-point code on the MMPI would be:

9.   As described on p. 355, MMPI patterns are often given numerical codes based on Welsh's (1948) system. Write Patty C.'s pattern of MMPI scores as a Welsh code in the space below.

10. One goal of the MMPI revision process during the 1980's was to create a separate form for adolescents (called the MMPI-A). Complete the table below, which summarizes other changes to the MMPI that eventually led to publication of the MMPI-2 in 1989.

Change made	Description of change
Number of items	
How items were written	
Cutoff for clinically significant scale elevations	
Norms	
Validity scales	
Content Scales	

11. Regarding psychometric properties of the MMPI and MMPI-2, reliability appears to be generally adequate overall when compared to similar tests. On the other hand, there are some points of concern regarding other psychometric properties. Describe *why* the following two characteristics of the MMPI and MMPI-2 are problematic.

a. *item overlap/intercorrelations among clinical scales*: _____
_____

_____

b. *imbalance in the way items are keyed:* _____
_____

_____

12. Two identical MMPI profiles can mean different things depending on the demographic characteristics of the examinees. What demographic characteristics appear to be related to MMPI and MMPI-2 scales?
_____

_____

13.   Thousands of validity studies have been conducted on the MMPI and MMPI-2, showing that distinct score patterns are related to numerous psychiatric diagnoses/problems and critical life events/situations. List some of these diagnoses and events. _____

_____

_____

_____

_____

C. California Psychological Inventory-Third Edition (text pp. 359-360)

14.   Unlike the MMPI and MMPI-2, the California Psychological Inventory (CPI) evaluates personality in _____ individuals.

15.   Read the brief descriptions of four individuals presented below. Identify with a ✓ whether you think each individual would obtain a high (H) or a low (L) composite score on the CPI scales grouped into Classes I through IV (as described on text pp. 359-360).

Description	California Psychological Inventory							
	Class I		Class II		Class III		Class IV	
	H	L	H	L	H	L	H	L
Darryl is a private person who enjoys reading and other solitary activities. He feels anxious in social situations and is often confused about how to respond to others. He is not very spontaneous. Darryl's closest friend describes him as a capable and dependable guy who is "honest to a fault."								
Hanh loves to go out with her friends and meet new people. She is respected as an excellent listener who gives good advice. Hanh is very intelligent person who doesn't hide her opinions; she enjoys a good argument. She gets herself into trouble by spending too much money on things she doesn't need.								
Paul has a tendency to be arrogant and overly competitive. He often acts without considering potential consequences, and as a result, has been arrested several times for shoplifting and driving after consuming a lot of alcohol. He also fails to pay his bills on time, so his credit rating is terrible.								
Sharla is an organized person who uses her time efficiently. She has a few close friends, but prefers to spend her free time writing a novel she hopes to publish. Sharla also volunteers two days a week at a local homeless shelter. Although she is a very accomplished person, she lacks self-confidence.								

16.   In what ways is the CPI similar to the MMPI? _____

_____

_____

_____

_____

_____

IV. THE FACTOR ANALYTIC STRATEGY (text pp. 360-364)

Go back to Chapter 3 pp. 91-93 and review factor analysis. Factor analysis is also covered on p. 45 of the Student Workbook. In short, factor analysis allows test developers to identify the minimum number of factors (e.g., that will form scales on a test) that can explain the most variation in scores.

A. Guilford's Pioneer Efforts (text p. 361)

1. Guilford and his colleagues used factor analysis to find the main ______________________________ underlying all personality tests; items that correlated highly with the resulting factors could be used in a new test of personality.

2. Although no longer used today, the first major structured personality test to be developed through the factor analytic strategy was the Guilford-Zimmerman Temperament Survey, which consisted of 10 personality dimensions, each measured by 30 items. What were the 10 dimensions? ______________________________

____

____

B. Cattell's Contribution (text pp. 361-364)

3. Cattell formed a list of 171 trait adjectives, asked college students to rate their friends on these adjectives, and then factor analyzed the data. Describe what Cattell did next that ultimately led to creation of the Sixteen Personality Factor Questionnaire (16PF). ______________________________

____

____

____

____

4. Complete the following table which shows the nine norm groups for the 16PF.

	Gender		
Groups	Males; Adults		Combined males & females; Adults
		Females; College students	
	Males; High school seniors		

5. The median short-term test-retest reliability coefficient is ________ for the 16 source traits, but long-term test-retest reliability is significantly lower.

6. Despite the attempt to identify distinct factors, the 16 source traits are intercorrelated, with some correlations as high as ________; therefore, four ______________________ factors (combining the 16 source traits) have been identified for which scores can be derived.

7.	Examine the 16PF scores of 21-year-old James, a college junior, presented in the table below. Refer to Table 13-4 on text p. 362 to describe James' personality traits. For example, on Factor H, James obtained a sten of 9 which is a relatively high score. Looking at Table 13-4, you can see that James' Factor H score suggests he is uninhibited and does not get intimidated or stressed out very easily. (Note: You will notice that James did not obtain any middle-ground scores on the 16PF, which would be unusual in an actual profile.) After you write a couple notes about James based on each Factor score, answer three questions about your impressions of him that *integrate* your interpretations of individual Factor scores.

Factor	James' sten score	Notes
A	3	
B	10	
C	8	
E	8	
F	8	
G	3	
H	9	*Uninhibited; does not get intimidated or stressed out very easily*
I	3	
L	8	
M	8	
N	2	
O	3	
Q1	10	
Q2	9	
Q3	2	
Q4	8	
What are James strengths, in your opinion? What does he do well?		
What are James limitations, in your opinion? What does he struggle with?		
If you met James, what do you think he would be like?		

C. Problems with the Factor Analytic Strategy (text p. 364)

8.	Factor analysis tends to identify sources of _____ variance at the expense of _____ variance; this problem leads to potentially important factors being missed.

V. THE THEORETICAL STRATEGY (text pp. 364-369)

1.   Some test developers use major theories of personality to construct their tests. How is the validity of a test based on a theory supported? _____

_____

A. Edwards Personal Preference Schedule (text pp. 364-366)

2.   The Edwards Personal Preference Schedule (EPPS) is based on Murray's theory of human needs. Below, define each of the three examples of Murray's needs presented in the text on p. 356.
   a. need for achievement: _____
   b. need for deference: _____
   c. need for exhibition: _____

3.   Edwards found a clever way to deal with examinees' tendencies to respond to items in a socially desirable manner. He started by rating each item on the EPPS in terms of social desirability. What did he do next that reduced the problem of socially desirable response styles? _____

_____

_____

_____

4.   The EPPS provides another check for validity in the form of a _____ scale with 15 pairs of statements repeated in identical form (to identify whether examinees answered the same way both times).

✁ What are ipsative scores? ✁

The Edwards Personal Preference Schedule (EPPS) is somewhat unique in that it produces *ipsative scores* which reflect the relative strengths of needs within the examinee (rather than comparing the strength of one examinee's needs to the strengths of other examinees' needs).

Items on the EPPS are made up of two statements, each reflecting a different need. Examinees must choose the statement reflecting the need that is strongest relative to the other. For example, one item on the EPPS might pit a statement reflecting the need for achievement against a statement reflecting the need for order. Even if the examinee has a high need both for achievement *and* for order, he or she must choose the need that is paramount. Therefore, as the test progresses and pairs of different needs are pitted against one another, the *ipsative scores* emerge as a picture of the examinee's unique pattern of relative needs. In this way, the individual examinee provides his or her own frame of reference in terms of determining relative strengths of needs.

---

5.   What are two central criticisms of the EPPS? _____

_____

_____

_____

B. Personality Research Form and Jackson Personality Inventory (text pp. 366-368)

6. Regarding their theoretical foundations, in what ways are the Personality Research Form (PRF) and the Jackson Personality Inventory (JPI):

a. *similar to the EPPS?* _____

b. *different from the EPPS?* _____

_____

_____

7. The creators of the PRF and JPI wanted to create homogenous (independent, unique) scales on their measures. Explain how the test developers chose items to include on the measures' specific scales.

_____

_____

_____

_____

_____

_____

8. To assess validity, the PRF and the JPI have an infrequency scale similar to the _____ scale on the MMPI and a _____ scale similar to the K scale on the MMPI.

9. The PRF is intended for _____ purposes, whereas the JPI is intended for use with _____ individuals to assess aspects of personality such as interpersonal, cognitive and value orientations (see Table 13-5 on p. 368 for specific traits measured).

C. Self-Concept (text pp. 368-369)

10. Describe the typical measure of self-concept that employs a checklist format. _____

_____

_____

_____

11. Describe the Q-sort technique used by Rogers to evaluate self-concept. _____

_____

_____

_____

_____

VI. COMBINATION STRATEGIES (text pp. 369-373)

A. Positive Personality Measurement and the NEO-PI-3 (text pp. 369-370)

1. What do you think are two reasons it is useful or even necessary to measure "negative" personality characteristics or psychopathology? _____

_____

_____

_____

2. What do you think are two reasons it is useful or even necessary to measure "positive" personality characteristics? _____

_____

_____

_____

B. The NEO Personality Inventory-Three (NEO-PI-3) (text pp. 370-373)

3. Using both empirical (factor analysis) and theoretical strategies, the authors of the NEO Personality Inventory –Revised (NEO-PI-R) identified three domains of personality, each with six facets. In the table below, describe each domain and its facets.

Domain	Domain description	Facets of domain
N – Neuroticism		
E—Extroversion		
O—Openness		

4. Both internal consistency and test-retest reliabilities for the three NEO-PI-R domains are in the high _____ to the low _____; predictive and concurrent validity studies show coefficients in the _____.

5.　　　Research with the NEO-PI-R has provided support for the *five-factor model*, which is believed to describe the independent dimensions of human personality.　Identify the factor from the model that matches each description below.

Factor Description　　　　　　　　　　　　　　　　　　　　　**Factor**

a. *responsible vs. irresponsible; organized vs. disorganized; careful vs. impulsive; hard-working vs. lazy*

_____

b. *imaginative vs. unimaginative; creative vs. concrete; conventional vs. original; curious vs. close-minded*

_____

c. *sociable vs. withdrawn; talkative vs. quiet; assertive vs. timid; inhibited vs. spontaneous*

_____

d. *helpful vs. uncooperative; good-natured vs. unpleasant; trusting vs. suspicious*

_____

e. *calm vs. anxious; emotionally stable vs. moody; secure vs. insecure; self-confident vs. self-doubting*

_____

6.　　　Conscientiousness, made up of the achievement and dependability facets, is central to theories of positive personality traits. Research findings show that Conscientiousness is positively associated with what variables? _____

_____

7.　　　Neuroticism seems to be negatively associated with the variables listed in 6. above, while Openness is correlated with _____ _____, and success in specific job settings (along with Extroversion and Agreeableness).

8.　　　Summarize research findings on the question of whether the "big five" dimensions of personality can be applied across cultures. _____

_____

_____

_____

_____

_____

_____

VII: FREQUENTLY USED MEASURES OF POSITIVE PERSONALITY TRAITS
(text pp. 373-379)

In the table below, summarize characteristics of 10 measures of positive personality traits presented in the text.

Scale Name	Construct measured	Item Types/Examples	Psychometric properties
Rosenberg Self-Esteem Scale (text pp. 373-374)		10 items rated on a 4-point Likert scale; (examples of items not provided)	
General Self-Efficacy Scale (text p. 374)			Generally adequate internal consistency; positively correlated w/ favorable emotions, optimism, self-esteem, etc.
Ego Resiliency Scale (text p. 374)		14 items rated on a 4-point Likert scale; "I get over my anger at someone reasonable quickly."	
Dispositional Resilience Scale (text p. 374)	*Hardiness:* the ability to view stressful situations as meaningful, changeable, and challenging.		
Hope Scale (text p. 375)			Adequate internal consistency & test-retest reliability; predicts college graduation, healthy adjustment, good problem-solving skills, good health
Life Orientation Test-Revised (LOT-R) (text p. 375)			
Satisfaction with Life Scale (text pp. 376)	Life satisfaction among many groups, including minorities, cancer patients, the elderly, college students, etc.		
Positive & Negative Affect Schedule (text p. 376)			Good internal consistency and test-retest reliability; convergent validity (correlates w/ measures of psychological distress).
Coping Intervention for Stressful Situations (text p. 377)		48 items rated on a 5-point Likert scale; items focus on responses to specific stressful situations	
Core Self-Evaluations (text p. 377)	Core personality construct consisting of self-esteem, self-efficacy, neuroticism, and locus of control		

VIII. FUTURE OF POSITIVE PERSONALITY RESEARCH (text pp. 378-379)

1.   Three primary questions have been raised regarding the measurement of positive personality traits. Summarize research findings addressing each question, below.

Question 1: *Are the various tests of different positive personality traits really measuring unique constructs, or are they all related to a single underlying construct?*

Research findings: _____

_____

_____

_____

_____

_____

_____

Question 2: *Are positive personality traits independent constructs, or are we simply measuring the <u>absence</u> of negative personality traits?*

Research findings: _____

_____

_____

_____

_____

_____

_____

Question 3: *Does the presence of positive personality traits diminish the impact of negative personality traits? And if so, to what extent?*

Research findings: _____

_____

_____

_____

_____

_____

_____

Concepts, Terms, and Tests to Know From Chapter Thirteen

Personality

Personality traits

Personality types

Personality states

Self-concept

Self-report questionnaires

Structured method of personality assessment

Projective method of personality assessment

Deductive strategy
- Logical-content strategy
- Theoretical strategy

Empirical strategy
- Criterion-group strategy
- Factor analytic strategy

Woodworth Personal Data Sheet

Mooney Problem Checklist

Minnesota Multiphasic Personality Inventory (MMPI)
- Fake bad
- Fake good
- Content scales
- MF scale
- Si scale
- validity scales (L, K, F)
- two-point code
- VRIN
- TRIN
- Response style

California Psychological Inventory (CPI)
- Class I scales
- Class II scales
- Class III scales
- Class IV scales

J.R. Guilford

Guilford-Zimmerman Temperament Survey

R.B. Cattell

Surface traits

Source traits

Sixteen Personality Factor Questionnaire (16 PF)

Edwards Personal Preference Schedule (EPPS)
- Ipsative score

Personality Research Form

Jackson Personality Inventory

Self concept

Carl Rogers' theory of self

Q-sort technique

Hardiness

Self-efficacy

NEO Personality Inventory-Three (NEO-PI-3)
- The five-factor model of personality
- Extraversion
- Neuroticism
- Conscientiousness
- Agreeableness
- Openness to Experience

Rosenberg Self-Esteem Scale

General Self-Efficacy Scale (GSE)

Ego Resiliency Scale

Dispositional Resilience Scale (DRS)

Hope Scale

Life Orientation Test-Revised (LOT-R)

Satisfaction with Life Scale (SWLS)

Positive and Negative Affect Schedule (PANAS)

Coping Intervention for Stressful Situations (CISS)

Core Self-Evaluations

CHAPTER 13 PRACTICE QUIZ

1.   Dr. Bunny found that the test item, "I would rather eat jelly beans on Monday than on Tuesday," successfully discriminated between people with schizophrenia and other psychiatric patients. If Dr. Bunny keeps the item on her Schizophrenia Test for this reason alone, she is probably using the _____ strategy of test construction.

   a. criterion-group
   b. logical content
   c. theoretical
   d. factor analytic

2.   Raw scores on the California Psychological Inventory (CPI) are converted into standard scores called _____ that have a mean of _____.

   a. T-scores; 10
   b. Z- scores; 0
   c. Sten scores; 50
   d. T-scores; 50

3.   Jim was given a battery of tests, including the MMPI, in order to help determine whether he is competent to stand trial for attempted murder. Jim wants to avoid the trial as long as possible, because he believes the prosecutor's case against him is very strong. In other words, Jim is very invested in being found **incompetent** to stand trial due to severe psychological problems. Given this information, you might expect to see an elevation on which scale of the MMPI?

   a. the L scale
   b. the K scale
   c. the F scale
   d. the Si scale

4. Currently, interpretations of the MMPI are based on

   a. examination of single scale elevations.
   b. comparisons of MMPI profiles with MMPI-2 profiles.
   c. subjective judgments by experienced clinicians.
   d. analysis of patterns of elevations across two or more scales.

5.   Cattell developed this personality test by first identifying all the adjectives that describe personality traits and then using statistical analyses to arrive at basic dimensions that accounted for all the trait variables. This test is

   a. the 16PF.
   b. the CPI.
   c. the NEO-PI-R.
   d. the EPPS.

6.	**Which of the following statements is FALSE with regard to the Woodworth Personal Data Sheet?**

a. It yielded several clinical scores and a "fake bad" score .
b. It was a mass screening test (administered to groups rather than individuals one at a time).
c. It was used to identify military recruits likely to break down in combat.
d. It was the first personality inventory ever developed.

7.	**The _____ is a personality test that yields ipsative scores.**

a. 16PF
b. CPI
c. NEO-PI-3
d. EPPS

8.	**Which of the following is a problem of <u>both</u> the CPI and MMPI?**

a.	very low test-retest reliability coefficients
b.	high inter-correlations among the subscales
c.	lack of standardized scoring procedures
d.	very few empirical studies documenting criterion validity

9.	**Frank is a loner who does not like to socialize with others. Frank is highly anxious in social situations because he is very insecure about his appearance and personality. Based on this information, Frank's NEO-PI-3 profile would probably show a high score on _____ and a low score on _____.**

a. neuroticism; extroversion
b. conscientiousness; agreeableness
c extroversion; openness
d. agreeableness; neuroticism

10.	**Research on the measurement of positive personality traits has found that**

a. various measures of different positive personality traits are measuring a single construct.
b. positive and negative affect are two separate and unique constructs.
c. the presence of positive affect does not appear to minimize the effects of negative affect.
d. measures of positive personality traits are more reliable than measures of negative personality traits.

✍Student Workbook Assignment 13.1

⊶ Describing the Personality Test File of Lindy M. ⊷

♦ **DESCRIPTION OF THE ASSIGNMENT**

In this assignment, you will examine and interpret a hypothetical examinee's scores on both the MMPI-2 and the 16PF. Your task will be to integrate and describe findings from both tests in the context of information about the examinee.

Read this important note! Learning to competently administer, score and interpret structured personality tests such as the MMPI-2 and16PF requires months (if not years) of supervised training at the graduate level. This assignment is not designed to teach you how to interpret these structured tests. Therefore, completion of this assignment will not make you more qualified to administer, score, and/or interpret actual MMPI or 16PF test profiles. Rather, the purpose of this assignment is to familiarize you with very basic concepts and procedures underlying the use of structured personality tests.

♦ **DIRECTIONS**

➔ **Before beginning this assignment, make sure you have read Chapter 13.**

(1) Read the information about Lindy's background, presented below.

(2) Use information presented on text pp. 350-355 to identify the outstanding characteristics of Lindy's MMPI-2 profile.

(3) Use information presented on text pp. 361-363 to identify outstanding characteristics of Lindy's 16PF profile.

(4) Write a short (3-4 paragraph) description of Lindy's personality that <u>integrates</u> information from both tests and the case background.

Brief Case Background

Lindy M. is a 20-year old college student at a large university. She does well academically and holds a 3.65 grade point average. However, Lindy's mid-term grades this semester consisted of two Cs, three Ds, and one F. She and her boyfriend of two years ended their relationship several months ago; since the break-up, Lindy has had difficulty concentrating on her classes. Lindy reports that her relationships with her mother and younger sister are very good, but that her relationship with her father is somewhat strained. In particular, Lindy's father feels that Lindy spends too much money and does not work hard enough in school. Lindy disagrees with her father's assessment. Sometimes she feels very angry at her father, but does not know how to share her feelings with him in a way he will understand or accept. Lindy hopes to graduate with a business major and later pursue an MBA.

Lindy M.'s 16PF and MMPI-2 Score Profiles

16PF	
Factor	**Standard Ten (STEN) Score**
A	8
B:	7
C	2
E	3
F	6
G	9
H	2
I	9
L	3
M	7
N	2
O	9
Q_1	2
Q_2	3
Q_3	10
Q_4	7

Minnesota Multiphasic Personality Inventory-2	
Validity Scale	**T Score**
L	55
K	68
F	55
Clinical Scale	**T Score**
1	62
2	72
3	70
4	40
5	42
6	58
7	75
8	60
9	55
0	32

◄ CHAPTER 14: *Projective Personality Tests* ►

Chapter 14 Outline

CHAPTER 14 EXERCISES

I. THE PROJECTIVE HYPOTHESIS (text pp. 383-384)

1.　　　What is the **projective hypothesis?** _____

_____

_____

❧ This section of the text explains that the very same response to an ambiguous stimulus may have several possible meanings, depending on the characteristics of people who respond. Furthermore, users of projective tests often disagree about the types or levels of inference that should guide interpretations of examinees' responses. An interpretation might reflect a low level of inference, and be relatively straightforward or literal. On the other end of the spectrum, an interpretation might reflect a high level of inference with regard to an examinee's intrapsychic needs, conflicts, or motivations.

For example, an examinee says the ambiguous stimulus in the bottom left of this page looks like a gun. A low-inference interpretation might be that the examinee is able to accurately perceive the shape of the stimulus (it *does* have a gun-like shape). The interpretation that the examinee has actually had experiences with guns reflects a somewhat higher degree of inference. A much higher level of inference is involved in the interpretation that the examinee's response indicates violent impulses, or an unconscious wish to harm himself.

As with all tests, evidence of the validity of projective tests must include demonstrations that scores, and interpretations of scores, have meaning and utility. As you will discover in this chapter, more than any other type of test, projective tests have been challenged by researchers on the grounds of questionable validity.

II. THE RORSCHACH INKBLOT TEST (text pp. 384-399)

✦ *As stated in your text, the Rorschach Inkblot Test continues to be one of the most widely used tests in clinical settings, despite intense criticism by researchers and psychometricians. Keep this point in mind as you complete the exercises in this section.*

A. Historical Antecedents (text pp. 384-385)

1. Although not the first to consider the potential value of using inkblots to study personality, Herman Rorschach is credited with the idea that inkblots could be used to identify _____ in his 1921 book, *Psychodiagnostik*.

2. It may be more accurate to refer to the Rorschach as a <u>group</u> of tests that employ a common set of inkblot stimuli, since numerous individuals have developed and published unique systems of administering, scoring, and interpreting the test. List five of these individual "experts". _____

_____

_____

B. Stimuli, Administration, and Interpretation (text pp. 401-404)

3. The Rorschach Inkblot Test consists of 10 cards with bilaterally symmetrical inkblots on them: five cards are _____, two are _____, and three contain inkblots of various pastel shades.

4. Why is the examiner deliberately vague and non-directive when administering the Rorschach? _____

_____

_____

_____

5. During the _____ phase of Rorschach administration, the examiner gives the stimulus cards one by one to the examinee and asks, "What might this be?"

6. What does the examiner record during this first phase of Rorschach administration? _____

_____

_____

7. The second phase is called the _____ phase, in which the examiner shows examinees the cards again and asks for clarification about the initial responses in order to score them.

8.   This exercise summarizes material on scoring and interpreting Rorschach responses, which is covered on text pp. 385-391 and Table 14-1 on p. 390.   In the table below, describe how Rorschach examiners score five dimensions of responses.   Then, read through a hypothetical response to a fabricated Rorschach stimulus.   Take a guess about what part of the examinee's response might be relevant to each scored dimension.   (Note: Learning how to score and interpret a Rorschach takes months or even years of supervised graduate-level training.   This exercise is designed to familiarize you with very basic aspects of scoring, only.)

Dimension	Description	Examples of possible scores	Relevant part of sample response
Location	Where on the blot was the percept seen? Was the whole blot used or just a small part of it?	Whole (W); Common Detail (D); Unusual Detail (Dd)	
Determinant			
Form quality			
Content			
Popular (frequency)			

(sample inkblot stimulus created by the author)

Sample Response

Free association phase
To me this looks like a magical horse that is reaching out to clobber someone with its hoof.

Inquiry phase
I can see the horse right here on this side of the card (indicates circled area).

It looks like a horse because of its shape, and I can tell it's clobbering someone because this leg just looks like its moving.

221

9.　　　Rorschach experts such as Exner suggest that scoring categories can be summarized as frequencies or percentages to yield quantitative (as opposed to qualitative) information. Regarding *location*, for example, normal subjects usually produce a balance of W, D, and Dd responses. What might it mean if there is substantial deviation from this normal balance of location responses? _____

_____

_____

10.　　　With regard to *determinants*, some Rorschach experts believe that movement responses (M, FM, m) are related to _____ activity and impulses, and to the control and expression of _____ impulses.

11.　　　*Cooperative movement* responses might provide information about an examinee's attitudes toward how people _____ .

12.　　　Qualitative interpretation of Rorschach responses involves examination of the content and sequence of responses. Describe and give an example of the *confabulatory response,* which, if made frequently, might indicate the presence of a psychologically disordered state. _____

_____

_____

_____

C. Psychometric Properties (text pp. 391-399)

13.　　　What is "blind analysis" of the Rorschach? _____

_____

_____

14.　　　Summarize the three reasons given in the text for why blind analyses conducted by "Rorschach virtuosos" were so compelling and convincing (but perhaps not very accurate or reliable).

a. _____

_____

b. _____

_____

c. _____

_____

15.　　　Developed by Exner, the _____ _____ for scoring the Rorschach is the most widely taught and accepted method today.

16. Text pp. 393-399 present central criticisms related to the psychometric properties of the Rorschach. In the table below, summarize criticisms in the areas listed. First, describe in general terms the criticism or problem identified. Then give at least one specific example that illustrates the criticism or problem.

Area	General description of criticism or problem	Specific example
Norms		
Overpathologizing		
Unreliable scoring		
Lack of relationship to psychological diagnosis		
Lack of incremental validity		
The problem of "R"		

17. Evaluating the Rorschach is difficult because there is no universally accepted or standardized method of _____ or scoring. It is not surprising, then, that research findings on the psychometric properties of the Rorschach have been very inconsistent.

III. AN ALTERNATIVE INKBLOT TEST: THE HOLTZMAN (text p. 399)

1. The Holtzman Inkblot Test was designed to address some of the criticisms of the Rorschach. Complete the following statements about this test.

a. The examinee is given_____ per card.

b. Administration and scoring procedures are _____ and described.

c. A(n) _____ form of the test was created that correlates with the original.

d. Interscorer and split-half reliabilities are comparable to those of _____ tests.

2.   The Holtzman consists of 45 stimulus cards. How are responses scored? _____

_____

_____

3.   What accounts for the Holtzman Inkblot Test's relative unpopularity? _____

_____

_____

IV. THE THEMATIC APPERCEPTION TEST (text pp. 400-405)

1.   List three ways in which the Thematic Apperception Test is different from the Rorschach (*other* than the obvious difference of test stimuli).

a. _____

b. _____

c. _____

2.   The TAT is based on Henry Murray's theory that revolves around 28 specific _____.

3.   According to research findings, what variables are related to the need for achievement as measured by the TAT? _____

_____

A. Stimuli, Administration, and Interpretation (text pp. 401-404)

4.   Compared to the Rorschach, the TAT is more _____ and less _____.

5.   Describe TAT stimuli. _____

_____

_____

6.   Like the Rorschach, standardization of _____ and _____ are poor.

7.   Describe directions given to examinees and administration of TAT stimuli._____

_____

_____

_____

_____

_____

8. What is the purpose of recording an examinee's reaction time? _____

_____

_____

9. Most clinicians who use the TAT do not use a scoring system; rather, they rely on their clinical

_____ and _____ to score and interpret the test.

10. In the table below, describe aspects of TAT interpretation. Then, try to identify each aspect in the sample response provided. (<u>Note</u>: As is the case with any projective test, learning how to interpret the TAT requires lengthy formal training. This exercise is designed to help you study and remember general aspects of interpreting the TAT, only. The image shown below is a TAT-like stimulus, it is <u>not</u> an actual TAT stimulus.)

Aspect	Description	Relevant part of TAT response
Hero		
Needs		
Press		
Themes		
Outcomes		

Sample TAT Response

This young man just had a conversation with his mother. It went badly. He had asked her if he could borrow just a little money from her because he lost his job. She got angry and then started to cry. She made him feel very weak, as though he were not an adult, but a child. The man is angry and resentful, but doesn't want to show it. His mother might completely cut him off financially if he says what he really feels. She's just like all women in his life – manipulative and cold-hearted. The man decides to wait until his mother goes to sleep, then he plans to sneak into her room and steal some money. That night, he tries to carry out his plan. However, his mother wakes up and confronts him. She throws him out of the house. Later on, the man feels horrible about what he did, and tries to apologize to his mother. She will not forgive him. Inside, the man knows he doesn't deserve her forgiveness. He thinks he is just a screw-up who will never amount to anything.

11.   Table 14-4 on text p. 403 lists a number of assumptions underlying the TAT. The primary assumption is essentially a restatement of the _____ discussed earlier. Read and consider these assumptions carefully, because their validity has been generally supported by empirical research.

B. Psychometric Properties (text pp. 404-405)

12.   As with the Rorschach, administration, scoring, and interpretation procedures for the TAT are _____, so research findings on the psychometric properties of this test have been very inconsistent.

13.   Although studies of specific TAT variables such as _____ have revealed adequate reliabilities, both test-retest and split-half reliabilities are generally quite low.

14.   Although experts agree the TAT has shown evidence of _____-related validity, _____-related validity evidence has been difficult to document.

15.   A recent meta-analysis conducted by Spangler (1992) found average correlations between the TAT and various criteria to be only _____ to _____.

V. ALTERNATIVE APPERCEPTION PROCEDURES (text p. 405)

1.   The photo essay collection entitled _____ is the basis of a newly developed thematic apperception test called the _____TAT.

2.   The Children's Apperception Test (CAT) was developed for children ages _____ through _____, and uses _____ figures as stimuli.

3.   The Tell Me a Story Test (TEMAS) was designed specifically for _____ children, and holds promise as a multicultural projective test for minority children.

4.   Both the Gerontological Apperception Test and the Senior Apperception Test use stimuli showing what? _____

_____

_____

_____

VI. NON-PICTORIAL PROJECTIVE PROCEDURES (text pp. 405-408)

1.   Summarize characteristics of non-pictorial projective tests in the table below.

Word Association Test (text p. 406)	
Names of tests	*Word Association Test*
Description of test type and items/stimuli	
Strengths	
Limitations	

Sentence Completion Tasks (text pp. 406-407)	
Names of tests	
Description of test type and items/stimuli	
Strengths	
Limitations	

Figure Drawing Tests (text pp. 407-408)	
Names of tests	
Description of test type and items/stimuli	
Strengths	
Limitations	

Key Concepts, Terms, and Tests to Know from Chapter Fourteen

Projective hypothesis

The Rorschach Inkblot Test
- location
- determinant
- form quality
- content
- frequency of occurrence

The Holtzmann Inkblot Test

The Thematic Apperception Test (TAT)
- Hero
- needs
- press
- themes
- outcomes

Word Association Test

Rotter Incomplete Sentence Blank

Draw-A-Person Test

House-Tree-Person Test

Kinetic Family Drawing Test

CHAPTER 14 PRACTICE QUIZ

1.   **The projective hypothesis suggests that:**

a. we tend to project negative feelings about ourselves onto other people in order to elevate our sense of self-worth
b. personality tests should be validated by forming hypotheses about the relation of test scores to external behavior, and making projections about expected correlations
c. when we interpret ambiguous stimuli, we project our own thoughts, needs, and conflicts onto those stimuli
d. behavior is determined in part by projecting ourselves into the future and attempting to accomplish tasks that will allow us to reach future goals

2.   **One of the primary reasons it is difficult to evaluate the overall psychometric properties (reliability and validity) of the Rorschach is**

a. because there are several ways to score and interpret the Rorschach, published research findings on the test are difficult to compare.
b. users of the Rorschach are almost exclusively clinical practitioners, so very little scholarly research is published on the test.
c. reliability and validity are not relevant to the Rorschach, since it is a projective test.
d. although reliability and validity evidence for the Rorschach has been gathered, it is generally published only in doctoral dissertations rather than academic journals.

3.   **The Rorschach Inkblot Test consists of _____ stimulus cards.**

a.   5
b.   10
c.   12
d.   30

4.   **Which of the following questions would be asked of an examinee during the inquiry phase of a Rorschach examination?**

a. What might this be?
b. Can you see a bat or a butterfly?
c. What made it look like a mountain lion?
d. Are you finished with this card?

5.   **The Thematic Apperception Test was developed by**

a. Exner.
b. Freud.
c. Holtzman.
d. Murray.

6.   Sharon is taking the Rorschach Inkblot Test. When shown one of the cards, Sharon says "This whole thing, it looks like one huge butterfly." Sharon's response can easily be scores in terms of its

      a.   location and determinant.
      b.   content and location.
      c.   determinant and content.
      d.   determinant and form quality.

7.   In the interpretation of the Thematic Apperception Test, *press* refers to

      a.   environmental forces.
      b.   internal conflicts.
      c.   physiological needs.
      d.   unrealistic demands.

8.   With regard to a central criticism of the Rorschach, the problem of "R" refers to the fact that

      a.   reliability of the test is very low.
      b.   examinees can give as many responses as they wish.
      c.   examinees often cannot remember their responses during the inquiry phase.
      d.   revised versions of the test do not show adequate psychometric properties.

9.   Which of the following characteristics describes the Thematic Apperception Test (TAT), but not the Rorschach Inkblot Test?

      a.   It was well-received by the scientific community
      b.   It was oversold with extravagant claims
      c.   It was advertised as a diagnostic instrument
      d.   It is used primarily in clinical settings

10.   Which of the following is <u>not</u> an example of a nonpictorial projective procedure?

      a.   the Holtzman Inkblot Test
      b.   the Kinetic Family Drawing
      c.   the Rotter Incomplete Sentence Blank
      d.   the House-Tree-Person Test

✍**Student Workbook Assignment 14.1**

⊶ Interpreting a Pictorial-Type Projective Test Response ⊷

♦ **INTRODUCTION TO THE ASSIGNMENT**

This assignment encourages you to think about the projective hypothesis, the basis of projective personality test construction and interpretation.

Read this important note! Learning to competently administer, score and interpret projective tests such as the Rorschach Inkblot Test and the Thematic Apperception Test requires months (if not years) of supervised training at the graduate level. This assignment is not designed to teach you how to interpret pictorial-type projective tests. Therefore, completion of this assignment will not make you more qualified to administer, score, and/or interpret actual projective tests. Rather, the purpose of this assignment is to familiarize you with very basic concepts and procedures underlying the use of projective tests. The projective-type stimulus presented in this assignment is not an actual stimulus from a test, but was created specifically for the Workbook.

♦ **DIRECTIONS**

➔ **Before beginning this assignment, make sure you have read Chapter 14.**

(1) Read the response to the pictorial-type projective stimulus shown. The response was given by a 20-year old female. Then answer the following questions.

    (a) What is the projective hypothesis? What information would you need about the examinee to determine whether his/her response reflected (or supported) the **projective hypothesis**?

    (b) Who appears to be the **hero(s)** in this response? What **needs** seem to be expressed in this response?

    (c) As you know, examiners never make interpretations based on a single response to a projective stimulus. However, examiners might begin to formulate hypotheses (to be explored through further testing) about an examinee's experiences, conflicts, feelings, and desires as he/she progresses through the test. Identify two **hypotheses** you might want to explore based on this individual's response.

This girl is looking at a group of students who are talking and laughing on the university campus. She is wishing she could be part of the group. She wonders if she should approach them and introduce herself, but is nervous…what if they have no interest in getting to know her? Ever since she transferred from another college, this girl has felt very lonely. Finally, she gathers up her courage and walks over to the students. It turns out that she has a lot in common with them, and over the next year, the girl develops friendships with each of them. The girl feels very happy that she finally has a social group at her new school.

231

⊷ CHAPTER 15: *Computers and Basic Psychological Science in Testing* ⊶

Chapter 15 Outline

I. Cognitive-Behavioral Assessment Procedures (text pp. 413-425)

     A. The Rationale for Cognitive-Behavioral Assessment (text pp. 413-414)

     B. Procedures Based on Operant Conditioning (text pp. 415-417)

     C. Self-Report Techniques (text pp. 417-421)

     D. Kanfer and Saslow's Functional Approach (text pp. 421-422)

     E. The Dysfunctional Attitude Scale (text pp. 422-423)

     F. Irrational Beliefs Test (text p. 423)

     G. Irrational Beliefs Inventory (pp. 423-424)

     H. Cognitive Functional Analysis (text pp. 424-425)

II. Psychophysiological Procedures (text pp. 425-427)

     A. Physiological Variables with Treatment Implications (text p. 426)

     B. Evaluation of Psychophysiological Techniques (text pp. 426-427)

III. Computers and Psychological Testing (text pp. 427-439)

     A. Computer Assisted Interview (text pp. 428-429)

     B. Computer Administered Tests (text pp. 429-430)

     C. Computer Diagnosis, Scoring, and Reporting of Results (text pp. 430-431)

     D. Internet Usage for Psychological Testing (text pp. 431-432)

     E. The Computerization of Cognitive-Behavioral Assessment (text pp. 432-434)

     F. Tests Possible Only with Computer (text pp. 434-435)

     G. Computer Adaptive Testing (text pp. 435-436)

     H. Psychophysical and Signal Detection Procedures (text pp. 436-439)

CHAPTER 15 EXERCISES

I. COGNITIVE-BEHAVIORAL ASSESSMENT PROCEDURES (text pp. 413-425)

A. The Rationale for Cognitive-Behavioral Assessment (text pp. 413-414)

1.   Complete the following table which compares traditional testing approaches and cognitive-behavioral testing approaches. For each, identify assumptions about symptoms, and the focus of assessment and treatment.

Model	Assumptions about symptoms	Focus of assessment	Focus of treatment
Traditional (medical) model			
Cognitive-Behavioral model			

B. Procedures Based on Operant Conditioning (text pp. 415-417)

2.   Complete the following figure (based on Table 15-3), which depicts the steps involved in cognitive-behavioral assessment based on operant conditioning.

Step 1

Identify critical behaviors

Step 2

Step 3

If excesses...

Step 4

If deficits...

C. Self-Report Techniques (text pp. 417-421)

3.   Identify two potential problems with behavioral observations.

a. _____

b. _____

4.   What do researchers assume about self-report data? _____

_____

_____

5.   Traditional self-report assessment procedures focus on personality traits as a primary determinant of behavior. What is the focus of cognitive-behavioral assessment strategies? _____

_____

6.   What is the content of items on the Fear Survey Schedule (FSS), a self-report measure frequently used in cognitive-behavioral self-report procedures? _____

_____

_____

7.   Self-report assertiveness measures are also commonly employed in cognitive-behavioral procedures. Describe a typical item on these measures. _____

_____

_____

8.   Self-report batteries consist of three types of scales. Describe these below.

Primary scales _____

Secondary scales _____

Tertiary scales _____

234

9.   What problems are associated with cognitive-behavioral self-report techniques? _____

_____

_____

D. Kanfer and Saslow's Functional Approach (text pp. 421-422)

10.   What is an important assumption of the functional (behavior-analytic) approach to assessment with regard to disordered behavior? _____

_____

11.   Define (and give an example of):

behavioral excess: _____

behavioral deficit. _____

E. The Dysfunctional Attitude Scale (text pp. 422-423)

12.   According to Beck's Cognitive Model of Psychopathology, in what way do *schemas*, or cognitive frameworks, shape the way we perceive ourselves, others, and the world around us? _____

_____

_____

_____

13.   A functional or adaptive schema might include the beliefs that we are worthy of love and respect, that other people are trustworthy, and that the world is a relatively safe place. Can you think of an example of a dysfunctional schema that might predispose people to engage in unhealthy or pathological behavior?

_____

_____

14.   How do Beck and his colleagues evaluate the extent to which a person's schemas are functional or dysfunctional? _____

_____

_____

_____

F. Irrational Beliefs Test (text p. 423)

15.   According to the cognitive perspective, "reality" is often not the primary determinant of behavior. What is? _____

_____

16.   The Irrational Beliefs Test (IBT) consists of _____ items that measure irrational beliefs (such as, "If I am to be happy, I must be well-liked by every person in my life").

17.   The reliability of the IBT is generally adequate, and although validity documentation is weak, IBT scores do seem to be related to both _____ and _____.

G. Irrational Beliefs Inventory (IBI) (text pp. 423-424)

18.   The Irrational Beliefs Test (IBI) is a _____ - item scale that improves on the weaknesses of the IBT since it measures _____ rather than the negative consequences (i.e., negative affect) associated with those beliefs.

19.   The IBI consists of what five subscales? _____

_____

H. Cognitive Functional Analysis (text pp. 424-425)

20.   What is the underlying premise of *cognitive-functional analysis*? _____

_____

_____

Read the following case of Richard, and then complete the cognitive-functional analysis that follows.

Richard is a 28-year-old male who is struggling with an alcohol dependency. Richard has been able quit drinking for short periods of time, and occasionally for up to two months, but always relapses into a pattern of self-destructive, weekend-long binges. The sequence of events that characterize Richard's relapses are fairly consistent. After he has been sober for about a week, Richard begins to feel he has more control over his drinking. He tells himself he can handle going to a bar with friends, and that he will drink club soda instead of alcohol. Richard usually takes his first drink about two hours after he arrives at the bar. He tells himself that he has been "good" for several weeks and deserves a reward. He thinks about how stressful work has been, and decides he will have one drink just to relax. Because Richard never tells his friends that he has stopped drinking alcohol, they unknowingly contribute to his relapse by buying him drinks. Richard accepts these drinks because he "doesn't want to offend his friends." As he drinks, Richard finds himself relaxing and having more fun. He thinks, "What's wrong with having a few drinks? Everyone else can drink, why can't I?" Furthermore, Richard's usual shyness seems to fade when he consumes alcohol. It is not uncommon for Richard to initiate conversation with an attractive woman he meets at the bar, which is something he would never do while sober. Unfortunately, Richard's "few drinks with friends" usually turns into a binge episode that lasts for days. And the cycle of quitting and relapsing begins again.

✦ *Before completing this exercise, make sure you have read "Cognitive Functional Analysis" on text pp. 424-425.*

21.   Identify both the environmental and the cognitive factors that **precede** Richard's drinking behavior (these can be viewed a "triggers" for the behavioral sequence).

Environmental antecedents: _____

_____

_____

Cognitive antecedents: _____

_____

_____

22.   Identify both the environmental and the cognitive factors that are **consequences of** Richard's drinking behavior (these can be viewed as factors that maintain the behavior).

Environmental consequence: _____

_____

_____

Cognitive consequences: _____

_____

_____

23.   If you were designing an intervention based on a cognitive-functional analysis, what specific suggestions would you give Richard regarding modifications in his environment and cognitions? _____

_____

_____

_____

24.   Describe two **self-monitoring** procedures you might incorporate into the intervention. _____

_____

_____

_____

II. PSYCHOPHYSIOLOGICAL PROCEDURES (text pp. 425-427)

1.   What is the "fundamental tenet" of psychophysiological measurement, according to Haynes (1991)?

_____

_____

A. Physiological Variables with Treatment Implications (text p. 426)

2.   What measurable physiological changes are associated with fear responses? _____

_____

3.   Describe how the *penile transducer* is used to objectively study sexual responses in men. _____

_____

_____

_____

B. Evaluation of Psychophysiological Techniques (text pp. 426-427)

4.   Summarize the findings of two studies that examined the relationship between measurable physiological processes and cognitive processes.

a. _____

_____

b. _____

_____

5.   One of the most serious potential problems in psychophysiological assessment relates to *artifacts*. (Note: An artifact is an extraneous variable the researcher is not interested in examining, but that nevertheless influences the results of investigations or assessments. Artifacts, like biases, threaten the validity of assessment data when they go unrecognized.)   What is another problem in psychophysiological assessment? _____

_____

_____

III. COMPUTERS AND PSYCHOLOGICAL TESTING (text pp. 427-439)

1.   What are the two primary ways computers are used in testing?

a. _____

b. _____

2.   Who (or what) was *Eliza*? _____

_____

_____

_____

A. Computer Assisted Interview (text pp. 428-429)

3.   How have computer-assisted interviews been used? _____

_____

4.　　Some researchers have found that the validity of computer-assisted interviews is actually *better than* that of paper-and-pencil forms. What are some possible explanations for this finding? _____

_____

_____

_____

_____

B. Computer Administered Tests (text pp. 429-430)

5.　　Traditional tests such as the MMPI and Big Five Personality tests yield similar results or profiles when administered by computer or by paper and pencil. What types of tests seem to show different results when administered by computer? _____

_____

6.　　Identify two benefits and two drawbacks of computer-administered tests.

Benefits: _____

Drawbacks: _____

C. Computer Diagnosis, Scoring, and Reporting of Results (text pp. 430-431)

7.　　Research has generally supported the reliability and usefulness of computer-generated test scores (of both structured and _____ tests), diagnoses, and narrative evaluations.

8.　　In educational testing, computerized _____ scoring has a long history, beginning with _____ (PEG) in 1966.

9.　　How do computer-scoring instruments such as IEA and the "E-rater" assess and score written work?

_____

_____

_____

_____

D. Internet Usage for Psychological Testing (text pp. 431-432)

10.　　Identify two research findings *specifically* related to comparisons between traditional paper-and-pencil psychological tests and Internet/Web-based tests.

a. _____

b. _____

E. The Computerization of Cognitive-Behavioral Assessment (text pp. 432-434)

11.   What are seven applications of computers to cognitive-behavioral assessment (Farrell, 1992)?

1. _____   5. _____

2. _____   6. _____

3. _____   7. _____

4. _____

12.   Computer-based cognitive-behavioral treatments have been found effective for evaluating and treating what problems and disorders? _____

_____

_____

_____

13.   How were palmtop computers used in the successful treatment of panic disorder?_____

_____

_____

_____

_____

F. Tests Possible Only with Computer (text pp. 434-435)

14.   Increasingly, the use of computer-generated virtual reality programs in the treatment of phobias is viewed not only as a legitimate treatment strategy, but as an *ideal* treatment strategy for these disorders. Why?

_____

_____

_____

_____

G. Computer Adaptive Testing (text pp. 435-436)

15.   In computer-adaptive testing, each item completed by the examinee is used to update the computer's estimation of the examinee's _____, and this estimation directs the next (and the next, and the next) item the examinee is exposed to.

16.   Computer-adaptive tests typically take less time to complete than traditional fixed-item tests. Why?

_____

_____

240

17.   Discuss "the most frequently debated drawback" of computer-adaptive testing. _____

_____

_____

_____

18. What are examples of frequently used computer adapted tests? _____

H. Psychophysical and Signal Detection Procedures (text pp. 436-439)

19.   Saccuzzo and his colleagues found that _____ may be related to speed of
information processing in the nervous system.

20.   Speed of information processing can be measured by identifying how long it takes a person to recognize
a stimulus they have *very* briefly been exposed to. The rate of _____ of information – from
initial presentation to _____ memory storage to the higher brain centers – is the speed of
information processing.

21.   Using signal detection procedures, Saccuzzo demonstrated that compared to both normal control
subjects and neurotic subjects, subjects with schizophrenia needed a longer _____ between the
presentation of an informational stimulus and a non-informational stimulus in order to correctly identify the first,
informational stimulus. This result indicated to the researchers that information was traveling more
_____ through the nervous systems of schizophrenics.

22.   Signal detection procedures and the _____ masking paradigm have also
been used to examine the relation of information processing speed to intelligence by comparing average-IQ
subjects and _____ subjects.

23.   List some advantages of signal detection approaches over other procedures: _____

_____

_____

_____

_____

_____

Key Concepts, Terms, and Tests to Know from Chapter Fifteen

Cognitive-Behavioral assessment

Operant conditioning

Behavioral deficits and excesses

Self-report technique

Fear Survey Schedule (FSS)

Self-report battery

Functional (behavioral-analytic) approach to assessment

Beck's cognitive model

Schema

Dysfunctional Attitude Scale (DAS)

Irrational Beliefs Test (IBT)

Irrational beliefs Inventory (IBI)

Cognitive functional analysis

Self-monitoring devices

"Eliza"

Computer-assisted interview

Project Essay Grade

Intelligent essay Assessor

"E-Rater"

Virtual reality programs

Computer-adaptive testing

Signal detection procedure

CHAPTER 15 PRACTICE QUIZ

1.   Traditional assessment and treatment models focus more on _____, whereas cognitive-behavioral assessment and treatment models target _____.

        a. environmental causes of problems; psychological causes of problems
        b. underlying causes of symptoms; the symptoms themselves
        c. psychological causes of problems; environmental causes of problems
        d. the symptoms themselves;   underlying causes of symptoms

2.   Cognitive-behavioral assessment involves the evaluation of the frequency, intensity, and duration of identified (problematic) critical responses. This evaluation establishes

        a. possible reasons why the response occurs.
        b. the value of an intervention.
        c. the baseline for the response.
        d. the goal of an intervention.

3.   Seven-year-old Candace throws a temper tantrum whenever she is asked to eat vegetables. According to Kanfer and Saslow's model, Candace is exhibiting

        a. a behavioral deficit.
        b. a psychological disorder.
        c. immature behavior.
        d. a behavioral excess.

4.   Which of the following is <u>not</u> a problem with most cognitive-behavioral self-report measures and procedures?

        a. there are too few of them available
        b. they are subject to response biases
        c. they lack evidence of reliability and validity
        d. the assume responses have face validity

5.   Which of the following might be an item on the Dysfunctional Attitudes Scale (DAS) or the Irrational Beliefs Test (IBT)?

        a. "I prefer to take my time on a project rather than rush through it."
        b. "I get upset when someone tries to take advantage of me."
        c. "If I am not involved in a romantic relationship it means I am unlovable."
        d. "Sometimes I think about changing my career focus."

6.　According to Beck, _____ are cognitive frameworks that organize prior experience, guide the interpretations of new experiences, and shape expectancies and predictions.

　　a. behavioral deficits
　　b. schemas
　　c. behavioral excesses
　　d. psychological disorders

7.　Which of the following strategies is used to assess blood pressure, skin conductance, papillary dilations, and erectile responses?

　　a. cognitive-functional analysis
　　b. self-monitoring procedures
　　c. psychophysiological techniques
　　d. signal detection strategies

8.　Through the use of signal detection procedures, Saccuzzo and his colleagues discovered that information processing speed was slower among _____ than control subjects.

　　a. intelligent subjects
　　b. subjects with schizophrenia
　　c. neurotic subjects
　　d. subjects with children

9.　Which of the following is true about the use of computers in psychological testing?

　　a. Computer-assisted interviews are typically less valid than traditionally-administered interviews.
　　b. Computers have never been used to provide therapeutic support to clients.
　　c. Computer-scored projective personality tests have demonstrated adequate validity.
　　d. Computers have not been able to successfully score written essays.

10.　Computer-adaptive tests

　　a. adjust to individual examinees' responses to test items.
　　b. are typically less precise and efficient than fixed-item tests.
　　c. take longer to complete than the same tests presented in a traditional format.
　　d. allow test-takers to go back and change previously answered questions.

✍Student Workbook Assignment 15.1

◄ Cognitive-Behavioral Assessment and Treatment: The Case of Lisa T. ►

♦ DESCRIPTION OF THE ASSIGNMENT

This assignment is a fun and interesting way to review and apply material on cognitive-behavioral assessment procedures presented in Chapter 15.

♦ DIRECTIONS

➜ **Before beginning this assignment, make sure you have read Chapter 15.**

(1) Imagine you are a cognitive-behavioral therapist in your university's counseling center. A young woman named Lisa T. is a new client.

(2) Read through Lisa's case materials (a case summary and critical events journal) presented below and on the next page.

(3) Address the following questions

(a) Describe differences between both the rationale and emphases of a traditional approach to assessment and a cognitive-behavioral assessment approach in this case.

(b) What are other types of behavioral self-report techniques that would be useful in your assessment of Lisa?

(c) As a cognitive-behavioral therapist, how will you conceptualize Lisa's presenting problem? (Note: Remember that cognitive-behavioral assessment approaches view situation-specific behavioral excesses or deficits *per se* as the focus of treatment rather than as a symptom of an underlying problem.)

(d) Assuming the daily entries in Lisa's critical events journal are similar to her entry for Monday, what is the approximate baseline rate of the problematic behavior (critical event)?

(e) Can you identify any patterns or themes in the environmental or cognitive circumstances that seem to precede, or act as "triggers" for, the problematic behavior/critical event?

(f) Can you identify any patterns or themes in the environmental or cognitive circumstances that follow, maintain, or reinforce the problematic behavior/critical event?

(g) Describe at least one cognitive-behavioral intervention that follows directly from your assessment of Lisa. How would you measure whether the intervention was successful?

CASE: Lisa T. (initial session)

Lisa T. is an intelligent, high-achieving 18-year old college sophomore. She has come to you, a cognitive-behavioral therapist in the university counseling center, because in the last six months she has experienced bouts of anxiety and what she describes as "anger issues." Lisa's primary concern is that because of her moodiness, relationships with family members, friends, and her boyfriend Randy have suffered. Your first therapy session with Lisa focuses on assessment. After gathering information about Lisa's family, medical, academic, and social history, you ask her to keep a "critical events journal" in the next week. In the journal, Lisa will keep track of the circumstances surrounding critical events (defined as events in which she feels her moodiness has threatened her relationships), including thoughts and feelings immediately preceding the critical events, and what happened immediately after the critical events. As a cognitive-behavioral therapist, you know the first step in intervention or treatment is to identify the specific environmental and cognitive circumstances that might trigger and maintain (or reinforce) maladaptive behavior.

		CRITICAL EVENTS JOURNAL		
		Date: *Monday, April 22*		
Day and time	Events (including thoughts & mood state) *preceding* behavioral response	Thoughts & self-statements immediately *preceding* behavioral response	My behavioral response	Events & thoughts *following* behavioral response
Monday, 11:55 a.m.	I was in a hurry to get some lunch before my 12:20 class. I hadn't eaten any breakfast and I was starving. In the cafeteria, a guy that is in one of my classes (but that I haven't really met) gave me a strange look as I was waiting in line to pay for my food.	*Thoughts:* He thinks I'm unattractive. Maybe he thinks I'm fat and shouldn't be eating lunch. *Self-statements:* "I'm a fat, ugly slob." "I'm a loser - I can't imagine why anyone would find me attractive"	Said "what's your problem, s____-head?" (I used a derogatory term).	He looked really surprised. I felt bad, so I took my lunch and ate it on the way to class. I saw the guy later and said I was sorry. He said "no big deal." I felt okay after that.
Monday, 2:15 p.m.	I locked my keys in the car. I knew I would be late for my therapy appointment and that made me upset. I called campus security to unlock my door, and it took them 20 minutes to show up.	*Thoughts:* I'm going to be late for my therapy appointment again. The security guy probably thinks because I'm a lowly student, I don't have anyplace I need to be anyway. *Self-statements:* "I'm an idiot." "I always screw up."	I said something sarcastic to the security officer when he finally showed up. Something along the lines of, "so I guess people like me really get in the way of those two hour coffee and donut breaks, huh?"	The security guy didn't really respond to what I said. Maybe he didn't hear me. I felt more calm and relaxed after I was sarcastic to the security officer, maybe because I was letting off some steam. I also felt a little guilty, though.
Monday 6:30 p.m.	Was feeling keyed-up and restless, but I don't know why. Called my friend Julia to ask if she wanted to see a movie. She made a bunch of excuses about why she couldn't go.	*Thoughts:* Julia doesn't like me. She's lying about having to study for a big exam tomorrow. *Self-statements:* "I'm not a fun, likeable person."	Begged Julia to go with me in a mocking voice as if to say, "Do you ACTUALLY think I care whether you go with me or not?"	She seemed hurt by my tone, but she called back an hour later and said she'd go to the movie with me tomorrow if I wanted. I felt relieved after that.

⊷ CHAPTER 16: *Testing in Counseling Psychology* ⊷

Chapter 16 Outline

I. Measuring Interests (text pp. 442-456)

      A. The Strong Vocational Interest Blank (text pp. 443-444)

      B. The Strong-Campbell Interest Inventory (text pp. 444-446)

      C. The Campbell Interest and Skill Survey (text pp. 446-447)

      D. The Reemergence of the Strong Interest Inventory (text pp. 447-448)

      E. The Kuder Occupational Interest Survey (text pp.448-452)

      F. The Jackson Vocational Interest Survey (text pp. 452-453)

      G. The Career Assessment Inventory (text p. 453)

      H. The Self-Directed Search (text pp. 453-454)

      I. Eliminating Gender Bias in Interest Measurement (text pp. 454-456)

      J. Aptitudes and Interests (text p. 456)

II. Measuring Personal Characteristics for Job Placement (text pp. 456-458)

      A. Trait Factor Approach: Osipow's Vocational Dimensions (text p. 456-457)

      B. Are There Stable Personality Traits? (text pp. 457-458)

CHAPTER 16 EXERCISES

I. MEASURING INTERESTS (text pp. 442-456)

1. The first interest inventory, the _____ Interest Inventory, was published in 1921.

2. Currently, there are over _____ interest inventories in use; the most widely used inventories are the _____ Vocational Interest Blank and the _____ Preference Survey.

A. The Strong Vocational Interest Blank (text pp. 443-444)

3. What similarities did Strong and his colleagues notice about people in the same line of work?

_____

_____

4. Describe the *criterion-group approach* on which the Strong Vocational Interest Blank (SVIB) is based.

_____

_____

_____

5.   Complete the following statements about the revised 1966 version of the SVIB.

a. Items related to _____ occupations for men and _____ occupations for women.

b. Items were weighted according to the frequency with which particular interests occurred in specific

_____ groups versus the _____.

c. The SVIB used standard scores with a mean of _____ and a standard deviation of _____.

d. Each occupational criterion group contained about _____ people.

e. Both short-term and long-term test-retest reliability coefficients were adequate, and validity data indicated the

SVIB predicted _____ well.

f. Studies showed that patterns of interest remained _____ over long periods of time.

g. Research on the SVIB indicated that interest patterns are fairly well established by age _____.

h. In the late 1960s and early 1970s, the SVIB was criticized for _____ bias and the lack of a

_____ associated with the test.

B. The Strong-Campbell Interest Inventory (text pp. 444-446)

6.   Campbell published a new version of the SVIB in 1974, called the _____

Interest Inventory (SCII).

7.   How were criticisms of the SVIB addressed in the revised SCII? _____

_____

_____

_____

8.   Examine Table 16-1 on text p. 445, which shows Holland's six personality types. In the figure below, write the name of each type on the space provided, and add a short note describing it underneath.

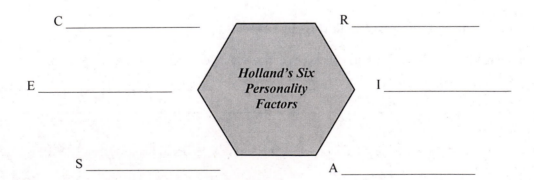

9.   In the table below, summarize the information provided by each of four sets of SCII scores.

Set of Scores	Information Provided
1—*General themes*	
2—*Administrative index*	
3—*Basic Interests*	
4—*Occupations*	

10.   The latest version of the SCII was published in _____.

11.   Describe changes to the latest revision of the SCII. _____

_____

_____

C. The Campbell Interest and Skill Survey (text pp. 446-447)

12.   After a lengthy legal dispute, Stanford University received the rights to publish the _____,
and Campbell received the rights to most of the cumulative work on the inventory, which he drew upon to
publish the _____ (CISS) in 1992.

13.   The CISS assesses examinees' interest in _____ academic and occupational topics, as well as
the degree of _____ examinees possess in 120 occupations.

14.   Like the SVIB, the CISS is based on _____ theory and uses standard scores with a
mean of _____ and a standard deviation of _____.

D. The Reemergence of the Strong Interest Inventory (pp. 447-448)

15.   The new Strong Interest Inventory (SII) was published in 2007. Complete the following statements describing the SII.

a.   Responses are given in a five-choice, _____-type format.

b.   Basic Interest Scales include _____*content scales* representing modern work life and workplaces.

c.   The SII contains 244 *occupational scales*, with greater focus on careers in business and _____ for both men and women.

d. New _____ groups include greater diversity.

 Be sure to review Psychological Testing in Everyday Life Box 16-1 *(pp. 450-451) which focuses on the SII.*

E. The Kuder Occupational Interest Survey (text pp.448-452)

16.   Describe the format and content of items on the Kuder Occupational Interest Survey (KOIS).

_____

_____

17.   Similar to the SCII and CISS, the KOIS examines the similarity between an examinee's _____ and those of _____.

18.   The KOIS offers separate norms for men and women, separate scales for _____, and new scales emphasizing nontraditional occupations for men and women.

19.   In the table below, summarize the information provided in each section of the KOIS.

KOIS section	Information provided
1—*Dependability of results*	
2—*Interest patterns (compared to normative samples)*	
3—*Interest patterns (compared to occupational groups)*	
4—*Interest patterns (compared to college majors)*	

21.   Complete the following statements regarding research on the KOIS.

a. Both short-term and long-term _____ are high.

b. Predictive validity, especially for the _____ scales, was strong.

c. Compared to high school students who did not receive their KOIS results, those who did receive their results reported greater confidence in _____.

d. _____ seem to have greater self-efficacy about succeeding in mechanical and physical work, whereas _____ have greater self-efficacy when working with people.

e. Studies using the KOIS have shown that _____ are quite stable over time.

F. The Jackson Vocational Interest Survey (text pp. 452-453)
G. The Career Assessment Inventory (text p. 453)
H. The Self-Directed Search (text pp. 453-454)

22.   In the table below, summarize characteristics of other interest inventories. A few cells are completed to get you started.

Name of career test	Purpose	Scores/scales yielded by test	Strengths (+) & criticisms (-)
The Jackson Vocational Interest Survey (VIS)			(+) recently revised; strong reliability; accurately predicts academic majors; no gender bias (-) none identified
Career Assessment Inventory (CAI)			
Self-Directed Search (SDS)		Self-scored; yields 6 summary interest scores reflecting Holland's theory (RIASEC)	

I. Eliminating Gender Bias in Interest Measurement (text pp. 454-456)

23.   What was the conclusion of the Commission on Sex Bias in Measurement regarding interest inventories? _____

_____

_____

24.   What is one argument in favor of interest inventories providing separate norms for men and women?

_____

_____

25.   What were the results of Budany and Hansen's (2011) meta-analysis of changes in college students' vocational interests between 1976 and 2004? _____

_____

_____

J. Aptitudes and Interests (text p. 456)

26. What is the most important point of this very brief section? _____

_____

II. MEASURING PERSONAL CHARACTERISTICS FOR JOB PLACEMENT (text pp. 456-458)

A. Trait Factor Approach: Osipow's Vocational Dimensions (text pp. 456-457)

1.   Osipow's approach to career guidance is consistent with _____ theory of personality, and uses batteries of _____ to learn as much about a person's traits as possible.

2.   What are two criticisms of Osipow's approach to career guidance?
a. _____
b. _____

B. Are There Stable Personality Traits? (text p. 457)

3. All approaches to occupational interest assessment assume that interests are relatively stable personality traits; however, Mischel and others have criticized the assumption that personality is stable over time and across situations. Explain why, according to the text authors, "[c]areer assessments may be a good exception to Mischel's criticism" (p. 457). _____

_____

_____

4. Attribution theory considers how people understand the _____ of events in their lives, and examines three sources: persons, _____ (things or some aspect of the environment), and _____ (situations).

5. Attribution researchers have found that people tend to describe their *own* behavior in terms of _____, but explain the behavior of *others* in terms of _____.

Concepts, Terms, and Tests to Know from Chapter Sixteen

Strong Vocational Interest Blank (SVIB)

Strong-Campbell Interest Inventory (SCII)

Holland's theory of vocational choice

The Campbell Interest and Skill Survey (CISS)

Strong Interest Inventory (SII)

Kuder Occupational Interest Survey (KOIS)

Self-efficacy

Jackson Vocational Interest Inventory (JVIS)

Career Assessment Inventory (CAI)

Self-Directed Search (SDS)

Commission on Sex Bias in Measurement

Osipow's assessment approach

Mischel's criticisms of trait theories

Attribution theory

CHAPTER 16 PRACTICE QUIZ

1.   The Strong Vocational Interest Blank (SVIB) was developed through the _____ approach.

    a. logical content
    b. theoretical
    c. criterion-group
    d. factor-analytic

2.   Which of the following was a criticism of the Strong Vocational Interest Blank (SVIB)?

    a. It was based too heavily on a theory of career choice.
    b. The scales were gender biased.
    c. Test-retest reliabilities were unacceptably low.
    d. Interest patterns fluctuated considerably over time.

3.   The Strong Campbell Interest Inventory (SCII)

    a. incorporates Holland's theory of vocational choice.
    b. provides scales for college majors.
    c. is designed specifically for nonprofessionally oriented adults.
    d. includes a self-efficacy scale.

4.   Which of the following is the correct sequence in which these interest inventories were developed?

    a. SVIB → CISS → SCII
    b. CISS → SVIB → SCII
    c. SCII → CISS → SVIB
    d. SVIB → SCII → CISS

5.   Types such as Realistic, Investigative, and Conventional are associated with _____ career-related theory.

    a. Super's
    b. Holland's
    c. Strong's
    d. Osipow's

6.   Which of the following is <u>false</u> regarding the Kuder Occupational Interest Survey (KOIS)?

    a. It is currently the most widely used interest inventory.
    b. It provides separate norms for men and women.
    c. It has a scale for college majors.
    d. Nontraditional occupations for men and women are included on the scale.

7.   Which of the following interest inventories is designed for individuals with limited or no college education?

    a. The Jackson Vocational Interest Survey
    b. The Strong Campbell Interest Inventory
    c. The Career Assessment Inventory
    d. The California Occupational Preference Survey

8.   The Commission of Sex Bias in Measurement concluded that career interest inventories:

    a. contributed to policies that guided men and women into gender-typed careers.
    b. have been successful in eliminating gender bias in their measurement of vocational interests.
    c. should provide separate norms for men and women.
    d. all of the above

9.   Attribution theory suggests that people:

    a. attribute their own career choices to their family background.
    b. attempt to find out as much about the personality traits of others as possible.
    c. wonder what causes events in other people's lives, but not in their own lives.
    d. explain the causes of events in their own lives in terms of situational factors, not personality traits.

10.   Which of the following interest inventories does not require the test-taker to meet with a test administrator?

    a. Kuder Occupational Interest Inventory
    b. Self-Directed Search
    c. Career Assessment Inventory
    d. Jackson Vocational Interest Inventory

Student Workbook Assignment 16.1

⊷ The Assertive Job-Hunting Questionnaire ⊷

♦ DESCRIPTION OF THE ASSIGNMENT

The Assertive Job-Hunting Questionnaire (Becker, Brown, LaFitte, Magruder, Murff, & Phillips, 1980) is a 25-item self-report measure of one's job-seeking style. Specifically, it assesses an individual's tendency to pursue jobs in an assertive vs. a passive fashion.

♦ DIRECTIONS

➜ **Before beginning this assignment, make sure you have read Chapter 16.**

(1) Complete the Assertive Job-Hunting Questionnaire on the next page.

(2) Score and interpret the Questionnaire using the following guidelines:

SCORING THE SCALE

To score this scale, you have to begin by reversing your responses on 18 of the items. On these items, convert the response you entered as follows: 1 = 6, 2 = 5, 3 = 4, 4 = 3, 5 = 2, and 6 = 1. The items to be reversed are 1, 2, 4, 5, 7, 8, 10, 11, 12, 14, 15, 17, 19, 20, 22, 23, 24, and 25. After making your reversals, add up the numbers that you have recorded for the 25 items on the scale.

INTERPRETING YOUR SCORES

High scores (117-150) suggests a very assertive approach to pursuing jobs.
Intermediate scores (95-116) indicates a somewhat assertive approach to pursuing jobs.
Low scores (0-94) indicates a passive approach to pursuing jobs.

(3) Answer the following questions.

    a. Do you believe your score on the Assertive Job-Hunting Questionnaire accurately reflects your approach to seeking jobs? Give examples from your own life that support your answer.

    b. Based on your scores, do you intend to change anything about your approach to job-hunting? Why or why not?

Assertive Job-Hunting Survey

INSTRUCTIONS: This inventory is designed to provide information about the way in which you look for a job. Picture yourself in each of these job-hunting situations and indicate how likely it is that you would respond in the described manner. If you have never job-hunted before, answer according to how you would try to find a job. Please record your responses in the spaces to the left of the items. Use the following key for your responses:

1	2	3	4	5	6
Very unlikely	Somewhat unlikely	Slightly unlikely	Slightly likely	Somewhat likely	Very likely

_____ 1. When asked to indicate my experiences for a position, I would mention only my paid work experience.

_____ 2. If I heard someone talking about an interesting job opening, I'd be reluctant to ask for more information unless I knew the person.

_____ 3. I would ask an employer who did not have an opening if he knew of other employers who might have job openings.

_____ 4. I downplay my qualifications so that an employer won't think I'm more qualified than I really am.

_____ 5. I would rather use an employment agency to find a job than apply to employers directly.

_____ 6. Before an interview, I would contact an employee of the organization to learn more about that organization.

_____ 7. I hesitate to ask questions when I'm being interviewed for a job.

_____ 8. I avoid contacting potential employers by phone or in person because I feel that they are too busy to talk to me.

_____ 9. If an interviewer were very late for my interview, I would leave or arrange for another appointment.

_____ 10. I believe an experienced employment counselor would have a better idea of what jobs I should apply for than I would have.

_____ 11. If a secretary told me that a potential employer was too busy to see me, I would stop trying to contact that employer.

_____ 12. Getting the job I want is largely a matter of luck.

_____ 13. I'd directly contact the person for whom I would be working, rather than the personnel department of an organization.

_____ 14. I am reluctant to ask professors or supervisors to write letters of recommendation for me.

_____ 15. I would not apply for a job unless I had all the qualifications listed on the published job description.

_____ 16. I would ask an employer for a second interviewer if I felt the first one went poorly.

_____ 17. I am reluctant to contact an organization about employment unless I know there is a job opening.

_____ 18. If I didn't get a job, I would call the employer and ask how I could improve my chances for a similar position.

_____ 19. I feel uncomfortable asking my friends for job leads.

_____ 20. With the job market as tight as it is, I had better take whatever job I can get.

_____ 21. If the personnel office refused to refer me for an interview, I would directly contact the person I wanted to work for, if I felt qualified for the position.

_____ 22. I would rather interview with the recruiters who came to the college campus than contact the employers directly.

_____ 23. If an interviewer says "I'll contact you if there are any openings," I feel there's nothing else I can do.

_____ 24. I'd check out available job openings before deciding what kind of job I'd like to have.

_____ 25. I am reluctant to contact someone I don't know for information about career fields in which I am interested.

From Becker, H. A. (1980). The Assertive Job-Hunting Survey. *Measurement and Evaluation in Guidance, 13*, 43-48. In Weiten, W. (2000) *Personal Explorations Workbook for Weiten and Lloyd's Psychology Applied to Modern Life*, (pp. 49-50). Belmont, CA: Wadsworth.

Student Workbook Assignment 16.2

◄ Researching Careers ►

♦ DESCRIPTION OF THE ASSIGNMENT

An important role of the counseling psychologist is to help clients identify and research careers that match their interests and skills. This assignment asks you to identify and gather information on a specific career of interest to you.

♦ DIRECTIONS

➔ **Before beginning this assignment, make sure you have read Chapter 16.**

(1) Identify a specific occupation or career you are interested in learning more about.

(2) Conduct research on the occupation or career. If your school has a career center, make use of it! Most career centers have a wealth of both print and online resources related to specific occupations (e.g., the U.S. Department of Labor's *Occupational Outlook Handbook*). Or visit online websites that provide detailed information about careers and career searches. Simply enter the key word "careers" in your search engine.

(3) Your write-up should include:

> *Occupational Information*: Definition of the occupation; description of work activities; work settings, etc.

> *Education and Training*: Educational requirements; specific occupational training required; personal qualifications; skills required, etc.

> *Income and Benefits*: Entry-level income; average income (mean and median); top earning potential; benefits provided, etc.

> *Outlook:* Employment outlook (both nationally and in your region); outlook for job security; outlook for advancement, etc.

> *Other Job Satisfaction Variables*: Community, collegiality and social benefits; intellectual or creative stimulation; variety and flexibility; independence and autonomy; prestige and status; contribution to others; leisure and vacation, etc.

➤ CHAPTER 17: *Testing in Health Psychology and Health Care* ➤

CHAPTER 17 EXERCISES

I. NEUROPSYCHOLOGICAL ASSESSMENT (text pp. 462-481)

A. Clinical Neuropsychology (text pp. 462-467)

1.   Define *clinical neuropsychology* _____

_____

_____

_____

2.   In what ways are neuropsychology and the following fields similar?

a. *neurology*: _____

b. *psychiatry*: _____

c. *psychometrics*: _____

3.   In what ways does neuropsychology differ from the fields mentioned in 2.? _____

_____

_____

4.   In the recent past, brain diseases could only be studied by examining the brains of people who had died; currently, neuropsychologists can use _____ (or brain scanning) to study these diseases.

5.   Use material from text p. 463 to answer the following question: "Now that we have advanced brain scanning techniques like CTs, MRIs, and fMRISs, why do we still need clinical neuropsychological tests of function and behavior to identify brain lesions or tumors? What is the benefit of these tests?"

_____

_____

_____

_____

_____

_____

6.   The roots of clinical neuropsychology can be traced to Broca and Wernicke, who discovered in the 19th century that _____ was localized in the _____ hemisphere of the brain. Later, Brodmann developed the first functional map of the _____, while others developed methods for associating _____ with different areas of the brain and used psychological tests to estimate areas of brain damage.

7.   List four of the multiple areas of specialization in neuropsychology.

a. _____

b. _____

c. _____

d. _____

8.   Neuropsychologists study specific problems in both short-term and long-term memory. Describe each type of memory below.

Short-term memory _____

_____

Long-term memory _____

_____

9.   Performance on neuropsychological tests is linked to specific problems, such as visuospatial skill deficits in patients with _____ dementia, long-term memory deficits (retrograde amnesia) in patients with _____ disease, and difficulty recalling more _____ events in patients with Alzheimer's disease.

10.   In a study comparing recently detoxified alcoholics, former alcoholics who had not used alcohol for 18 months, and non-alcoholic controls subjects, the recently detoxed alcoholics scored lower on which memory-related measures? _____

11.   Neuropsychological studies have located control of language among right-handed individuals, as well as _____ of left-handed individuals, in the _____ hemisphere.

12.   What kinds of deficits are seen in individuals with Wernicke's aphasia? _____

_____

_____

⚑ *Be sure to examine Table 17-1 on text p. 467, which identifies neuropsychological deficits associated with damage to the right and the left hemispheres.*

B. Developmental Neuropsychology (text pp. 467-471)

13.   What is the value of performing repeated neuropsychological evaluations on a child undergoing prolonged medical treatment or with a serious medical illness? _____

_____

14.   One problem with neuropsychological assessment of children is that brain injuries may be missed until the child reaches an age where he/she faces material in school that reveals a deficit. What is a second problem?

_____

_____

_____

15.   Neuropsychological tests for children include measures of general development and _____ functioning (such as Child Behavior Checklist) and measures of _____ and executive function (such as The Trail Making Tests).

16.   List some executive functions: _____

_____

_____

17.   Mirsky and colleagues have identified four factors of mental processing that can be related to specific regions in the brain.   Identify and describe each of these factors in the table below.

Mental processing factor	Description

18.   Neuropsychological problems appear in learning disabilities such as _____, a specific reading disorder characterized by difficulties in decoding _____; this learning disability affects about 4% of school-aged children and _____% of learning disabled children.

19.   Neuropsychological tests have been used to determine malingering, or _____ illness.

20.   What is a CRI? _____

_____

_____

⚡ Focused Example 17-2, *Neuropsychological Consequences of Football Head Injuries*
This Focused Example discusses an issue that has received great attention in the media in recent years: the occurrence and consequences of concussions experienced by football players, especially those in the NFL. Make sure you can answer the following questions: ● What is a concussion? ● What are the neurological results of violent shaking of the brain? ● How common are concussions in the NFL? ● NFL players who sustained concussions appear to be at significantly higher risk for what problems?

---

21.   Clinical neuropsychologists also study the cognitive effects of early brain lesions. In one study, researchers found that high-risk infants experience persistent problems in what areas by the time they are five years old? _____

22. Summarize three specific ways (identified on text p. 471) in which developmental neuropsychologists work to understand brain-behavior relationships in children.
(a) _____

(b) _____

(c) _____

🍂 Be sure to read page 471 and examine Figure 17-4 on p. 472, both of which describe a seven-step model that is used by neuropsychologists to formulate a child's rehabilitation plan.

C. Adult Neuropsychology (text pp. 471-477)

*Questions 23. through 26. relate to the **Halstead-Reitan Neuropsychological Battery**, one of the most widely used approaches to assessing the consequences of brain injury among adults and children.*

23.   In addition to tests contained in the Halstead-Reitan battery, examinees are typically administered both the _____ and the _____.

24.   Use Table 17-2 on text p. 474 to complete the table below. Identify (a) the component of the Halstead-Reitan Neuropsychological Battery, (b) the task the examinee must complete, and (c) the ability or skill measured. [* means the test is a related procedure often administered along with the Halstead-Reitan battery.]

Component	Task	Ability or skill measured
	Examinee must identify whether pairs of rhythm beats are the same or different	
*		Speed; visual scanning; ability to process information in sequence
Speech-sounds perception test		
		Motor speed and left-right hand preference
	Learning experiment	
*	Examinee gets touch, visual, and auditory information on one side of the body and then on the other side	
* Strength of grip test		
	Examinee puts blocks with different shapes into the correct holes with the same shape	

25.   Validity studies have shown that performance on specific subtests of the Halstead-Reitan battery is associated with dysfunction in one of the two _____ of the brain; for example, difficulty on the right side of the body is associated with dysfunction in the _____ side of the brain.

26.   What is one criticism of the Halstead-Reitan battery? _____

_____

Questions 27. through 30. relate to the **Luria-Nebraska Neuropsychological Battery**, *another frequently-used assessment battery.*

27.   Define and give an example of Luria's concept of *pluripotentiality.*_____

_____

_____

28.   When Golden (at the University of Nebraska) developed a _____
version of Luria's test, it became known as the Luria-Nebraska Neuropsychological Battery.

29.   The Luria-Nebraska battery has _____ items that can be administered in about _____ hours.

30.   Use Table 17-3 on text p. 476 to complete the table below. Identify (a) the component of the Luria-Nebraska Battery, (b) the task the examinee must complete, and (c) the ability or skill measured.

Test	Task	Ability or skill measured
	Blindfolded examinees identify shapes and letters drawn on the backs of their hands, common objects, where they've been touched	
Reading		
		Arithmetic
Expressive speech		
	Examinees listen to spoken phonemes, words, and sentences	
Motor functions		
		Rhythm and pitch skills
	Items similar to those on an intelligence test	
		Visual and spatial skills
Memory		

.D. California Verbal Learning Test (text pp. 477-480)

31.   The California Verbal Learning Test (CVLT) is designed to identify different _____,

processes, and _____ that are associated with specific deficits.

32.   What variables does the CVLT assess? _____

_____

_____

33.   Unlike those who are simply highly anxious, adults with limited learning capacity may show several

patterns of responses on the CVLT. Describe two of these patterns.

a. _____

b. _____

34.   The CVLT has been used to compare patients with Alzheimer's disease, Korsakoff's syndrome, and
Huntington's disease. In the table below, describe these conditions and summarize patterns of CVLT scores
associated with each.

Condition	Description	CVLT score patterns
Alzheimer's disease		
Korsakoff's syndrome		
Huntington's disease		

35.   A children's version of the CVLT (the CVLT-C) is used to evaluate what problems? _____

_____

_____

_____

36.   The CVLT was standardized on a large _____ sample, and has shown strong

reliability and validity (e.g., correlations between .32 and .40 with the WISC-R vocabulary subtest).

E. Automated Neuropsychological Testing (text pp. 480-481)

37. The Automated Neuropsychological Metrics (ANAM) test system provides computerized interpretation of neuropsychological tests.

a. The ANAM was developed by the U.S. Department of Defense. For what purpose? _____

_____

b. The ANAM is now used in clinical populations, such as patients with what conditions? _____

_____

c. The ANAM includes a variety of tasks. What are examples? _____

_____

II. ANXIETY AND STRESS ASSESSMENT (text pp. 481-485)

A. Stress and Anxiety (text pp. 481-482)

1. Define each of the three components of psychological stress shown below. Then try to identify a specific example from *your* life that illustrates each component.

Components of Psychological Stress

Frustration   *Conflict*   *Pressure*

Definition

_____   _____   _____

_____   _____   _____

_____   _____   _____

_____   _____   _____

Example

_____   _____   _____

_____   _____   _____

_____   _____   _____

_____   _____   _____

2. What are the characteristics of *anxiety*? _____

_____

_____

B. The State-Trait Anxiety Inventory (text pp. 482-483)

3.   Define the following terms.

State anxiety: _____

Trait anxiety: _____

4.   Complete the following statements about the State-Trait Anxiety Inventory (STAI).

a. The STAI consists of a _____ item A-Trait scale and a similar A-State scale.

b. Test-retest reliability for the trait scale ranges from _____ to _____; as expected, the state scale shows much lower test-retest reliability because state anxiety *should* be _____ over time.

c. _____ validity has been demonstrated through strong correlations between the STAI and other measures of anxiety, such as the Taylor Manifest Anxiety Scale and the IPAT Anxiety Scale.

5.   Describe the findings of a study showing that the two scales of the STAI measure different aspects of anxiety (i.e., that there is *discriminant* evidence for the construct validity of the STAI). _____

_____

_____

_____

_____

6.   Factor analyses have also supported the two-factor structure of the STAI, in samples of people with serious _____ and of _____ workers.

C. Measures of Coping (text pp. 483-484)

7.   List the seven subscales on the Ways of Coping Scale. _____

_____

_____

8.   Describe two categories of strategies for dealing with stressful situations.

Problem-focused strategies:_____

_____

Emotion-focused strategies: _____

_____

9.   List the three categories of items on the Coping Inventory.

a. _____

b. _____

c. _____

E. Ecological Momentary Assessment (text pp. 484–485)

10.   Describe the method known as Ecological Momentary Assessment (EMA), including what, how, and where data are collected: _____

_____

_____

_____

11.   What variables have been measured with EMA? _____

_____

_____

III. QUALITY OF LIFE ASSESSMENT (text pp. 485–496)

1.   Identify six factors, conditions, or events you think significantly impact most people's quality of life. _____

_____

_____

A. What is Health-Related Quality of Life? (text p. 486)

2.   How does the World Health Organization (WHO) define *health status*? _____

_____

_____

3.   Describe the two major approaches to quality-of-life assessment.

Psychometric approach: _____

_____

_____

Decision-theory approach: _____

_____

_____

_____

B. Common Methods for Measuring Quality of Life (text pp. 486–489)

4.   The most commonly used quality-of-life measure is the _____ _____

_____ _____ _____ (SF-36).

5.   The SF-36 includes 8 health concepts. What are they? _____

_____

_____

6.   Describe the two parts of the Nottingham Health Profile.

(1) _____

_____

_____

(2) _____

_____

_____

➤ *Due to rising costs of health care, interest in the cost-effectiveness of health care programs has grown. Quality-of-life data can be used in* **equations** *that quantify the benefits of health care interventions in terms of quality-adjusted life-years (QALYs).*

7.   What are the steps involved in obtaining quality-adjusted life-years (pp. 488-489)?

(1) First, patients are classified according to objective levels of functioning in terms of _____

_____

(2) Next, each individual is: _____

_____

(3) To score different levels of wellness, observable health states are placed onto a preference continuum, with

_____

(4) Finally, _____

C. mHealth and New Mobile Technologies (text pp. 489-490)

8.   What is mHealth? _____

_____

_____

9. The three major categories of mHealth technologies used to transmit health data/information are:

        (a) _____

        (b) _____

        (c) _____

10.   The value of mHealth devices is that they provide potentially continuous data streams that capture

health information in the context of _____.

11.   Describe a way in which mHealth could revolutionize each of the following

(a) *Measurement of behavioral and environmental exposures in everyday life*: _____

_____

(b) *Medical diagnosis*: _____

_____

(c) *Treatment and disease management*: _____

_____

D. NIH Toolbox (text pp. 490-492)

12.   The National Institutes of Health (NIH) is in the process of creating an NIH "Toolbox" that can be used for standardized assessment of neurological and behavioral function. What is the purpose of this effort?

_____

_____

13.   Still under construction, the NIH Toolbox at this time consists of measures of what four areas of function (see also Table 17.4 on pp. 491-492)? _____

E. The 2015 Medical College Admissions Test MCAT) (text pp. 492-496)

14.   The Medical College Admissions Test (MCAT) currently takes 5 ½ hours to complete and consists of tests of: _____.

15.   Starting in 2015, the MCAT will include a new test section on the _____
_____ foundations of behavior; this new section of the MCAT will take _____
minutes to complete and consists of stimulus paragraphs followed by about _____ multiple-choice questions.

16.   Based on a preliminary draft, the five core content areas in the new section of the MCAT are:

(1) _____

(2) _____

(3) _____

(4) _____

(5) _____

17.   The significance of behavioral factors to health are shown by statistical models indicating that between _____% and _____% of the increased life expectancy in the U.S. since 1970 is attributable to modifications in risk factors for coronary heart disease, including _____.

Concepts, Terms, and Tests to Know from Chapter Seventeen

Clinical neuropsychology

Neuropsychological assessment

Developmental neuropsychology

Executive function

- Focus execute

- Sustain

- Encode

- Shift

Dyslexia

Halstead-Reitan Neuropsychological Battery

Luria-Nebraska Neuropsychological Battery
- pluripotentiality

California Verbal Learning Test (CVLT)

Automated Neuropsychological Metrics (ANAM)

Psychological stress
- Frustration
- Conflict
- Pressure

Anxiety

State anxiety

Trait anxiety

State-Trait Anxiety Inventory (STAI)

Ways of Coping Scale

Coping Inventory

Ecological momentary assessment (EMA)

Quality of life assessment

Sickness Impact Profile (SIP)

SF-36

Nottingham Health Profile (NHP)

QALYs

mHealth

NIH Toolbox

MCAT

CHAPTER 17 PRACTICE QUIZ

1.   Which of the following is **not** an example of an executive function that might be assessed on a neuropsychological test?

        a. forming a realistic goals
        b. paying attention to relevant information
        c. taking specific action to complete a task
        d. planning how to get something done

2.   Which of the following is the most likely outcome for Bradley, a right-handed man who suffered a massive stroke in the left hemisphere of his brain?

        a. He will experience spatial orientation problems.
        b. He will experience long-term memory problems.
        c. His vision will be impaired.
        d. He will experience language problems.

3.   Which of the following tests in the Halstead-Reitan Neuropsychological Battery is used to measure motor speed and right-left hand preference?

        a. tactual test
        b. rhythm test
        c. finger oscillation test
        d. trail-making test

4.   Which of the following measures strategies, processes, and errors made on learning tasks that are associated with specific neurological deficits?

        a. the Halstead-Reitan Neuropsychological Battery
        b. the Luria-Nebraska Neuropsychological Battery
        c. the Wechsler Memory Scale
        d. the California Verbal Learning Test

5.   The concept of *pluripotentiality* is associated with

        a. the Halstead-Reitan Neuropsychological Battery
        b. the Luria-Nebraska Neuropsychological Battery
        c. the Wechsler Memory Scale
        d. the California Verbal Learning Test

6.   The _____ component of psychological stress occurs when an individual feels that he/she is being prevented from attaining an important goal.

   a. conflict
   b. emotionality
   c. frustration
   d. pressure

7.   Use of computer technology to collect data from subjects about their moment-to-moment heart rate and blood pressure in their own environments is an example of:

   a. quality of life assessment.
   b. neuropsychological assessment.
   c. ecological momentary assessment.
   d. decision theory assessment.

8.   Approaches to quality-of-life assessment based on decision theory

   a. give weights to different dimensions of health to arrive at a single measure of health status.
   b. focus on cognitive aspects of health-risk and health-protective behavior.
   c. provide separate measures for many aspects of quality of life.
   d. have not generated quality of life measures useful to medical professionals.

9.   Craig is clinically obese and has just been diagnosed with diabetes. As part of his treatment plan, Craig takes pictures of his meals on his smartphone and then uses an app that calculates portion size and recommends how much he should eat. This is an example of

   a. quality of life assessment.
   b. mHealth.
   c. ecological momentary assessment.
   d. decision theory assessment.

10.   The Medical College Admissions test (MCAT) will introduce in 2015 a new test section focused on:

   a. empathy and bedside manner
   b. ability to understand and work with data spreadsheets for billing
   c. spiritual and religious concepts
   d. behavioral and social sciences

⚞Student Workbook Assignment 17.1

⚺ Creating an "A List" Neuropsychological Screening Test ⚻

♦ **DESCRIPTION OF THE ASSIGNMENT**

On the next page, you will see a list of neurological deficits whose names begin with the letter A. Some of these terms you may have encountered in other classes (e.g., *amnesia* in Abnormal Psychology, *agnosia* and *apraxia* in Physiological Psychology), but the majority will likely be new to you. This assignment asks you to create a test to detect the possible presence of one of the deficits on the "A List."

♦ **DIRECTIONS**

➜ **Before beginning this assignment, make sure you have read Chapter 17.**

(1) Examine the "A List" of Neurological Deficits table presented on the next page. Identify a deficit that is interesting to you. (<u>Note:</u> You might want to gather more information about the deficit from a textbook or online resource.)

(2) Create and describe a test that could be used to screen for the presence of the deficit you chose. Be sure to identify any stimuli, tools, objects, or instruments necessary for the test.

(3) Describe at least three examples of items or tasks. Also, discuss how the items/tasks would be scored.

(3) Describe in sufficient detail how your screening test would be administered.

(4) Describe the overall pattern of test results you would expect if the examinee had the neurological deficit your measure was designed to screen for.

The "A List" of Neurological Deficits

Acalculia: Inability to perform mathematical operations.

Agnosia: Partial or complete inability to recognize sensory stimuli, unexplainable by a defect in elementary sensation or by a reduced level of alertness.

Agraphia: Decline or loss of the ability to write.

Akathesia: Condition of motor restlessness, ranging from a feeling of inner disquiet to an inability to sit or lie quietly.

Akinesia: Absence or poverty of movement.

Alexia: Inability to read.

Allesthesia: Sensation of touch experienced at a point remote from the place touched.

Amblyopia: Dimness of vision without obvious impairment of the eye itself.

Amnesia: Partial or total loss of memory.

Amusia: Inability to produce (motor) or comprehend (sensory) musical sounds.

Anarthria: Incoordination of the musculature of the mouth, resulting in speechlessness.

Anomia: Difficulty in finding words, especially those naming objects.

Anopia: Loss of vision.

Anosmia: Absence of the sense of smell.

Anosognosia: Loss of ability to recognize or to acknowledge an illness or bodily defect; usually associated with right parietal lesions.

Aphagia: Inability to eat or chew.

Aphasia: Defect or loss of power of expression by speech, writing, or signs, or of comprehending spoken or written language due to injury or disease of the brain.

Apraxia: Inability to make voluntary movements, in the absence of paralysis or other motor or sensory impairment, especially an inability to make proper use of an object.

Aprosodia: Condition in which there is a loss of production or comprehension of the meaning of different tones of voice.

Asomatognosia: Loss of knowledge or sense of awareness of one's own body and bodily condition; may occur on one or both sides of the body; most commonly results from damage to the right parietal lobe.

Astereognosis: Inability, with no defect of elementary tactile sensation, to recognize familiar objects by touch.

Asymbolia: Inability to employ a conventional sign to stand for another object or event.

Ataxia: Failure of muscular coordination; any of various irregularities of muscular action.

Autotopagnosia: Inability to localize and name the parts of one's own body; for example, finger agnosia.

Definitions of terms from Kolb, B. & Wishaw, I. (1996). *Fundamentals of Human Neuropsychology.* New York, NY: W.H. Freeman & Co.

⤙ CHAPTER 18: *Testing in Industrial and Business Settings* ⤛

CHAPTER 18 EXERCISES

I. PERSONNEL PSYCHOLOGY: THE SELECTION OF EMPLOYEES (text pp. 500-501)

1.   Two major areas of industrial/organizational (I/O) psychology are personnel psychology and organizational psychology. Describe the emphasis of each area below.

personnel psychology _____

_____

organizational psychology _____

_____

A. Employment Interview (text pp. 500-501)

2.   Reviewers of research on employment interviews recommend a(n) _____ interview format because they are more reliable and valid.

3.   List negative factors that commonly lead to the rejection of job applicants. _____

_____

_____

4.   List positive factors, including factors related to making a good first impression, associated with acceptance of job applicants. _____

_____

_____

_____

II.   BASE RATES AND HIT RATES (text pp. 501-518)

5.   A _____ score is typically used when a test is utilized to make a dichotomous decision (e.g., acceptable candidate/unacceptable candidate).

6.   The table below is adapted from Table 18-1 on text p. 502. Write "Hit" in the cells indicating the test has made the correct prediction. Write "Miss" in cells indicating the test has made an incorrect prediction.

Decision on the basis of cutting score

		Hire	Don't hire
Job Performance (Criterion)	**Success on the job**		
	Failure on the job		

7.   Define the following terms.

a. *hit rate*: _____

_____

b. *base rate*: _____

_____

c. *false negative*: _____

_____

d. *false positive*: _____

_____

8.   Come up with an original example (one not in the text) of a situation in which a *false negative* would be more costly than a false positive. _____

_____

_____

9.　　　Now come up with an original example of a situation in which a *false positive* would be more costly than a false negative. _____

_____

_____

_____

↳ *Be sure to carefully read the medical example presented on text pp. 503-504, and Tables 18-2 and 18-3.*

A. Taylor-Russell Tables (text pp. 505-511)

↳ *Before completing this section of the Workbook, make sure you have read through pp. 505-511 on use of the Taylor-Russell tables. Pay special attention to the "real-life example using the data from the Yale Ph.D. program in psychology" beginning on text p. 509, because it is similar to the Workbook exercise presented below and on the next page.*

10.　　　Taylor-Russell tables are useful in evaluating the validity of a test with regard to the amount of information the test provides over and above base rate information. In this exercise, you will use the Taylor Russell tables to find the likelihood that an applicant to graduate school selected on the basis of his/her score on a measure used by a particular program will actually succeed.

　　　Descriptions of three hypothetical graduate programs are presented on the next page. Each program description includes the percentage of applicants admitted to the program (the *selection ratio*) and the validity coefficient of the primary measure used by the program to help make selection decisions. Your task is to use the Taylor-Russell Table on text p. 508 to evaluate the validity of the measures used by the four graduate programs in relation to the amount of information they contribute beyond the base rate (i.e., to evaluate incremental validity). For this exercise, the *base rate* is set at 60% for convenience only.

Directions:

(1) In the Taylor-Russell Table on text p. 508, find the row representing the validity of the measure used by Graduate Program A.

(2) Find the column in the Table representing the Graduate Program's selection ratio.

(3) Go across the row and down the column in the Table to find the estimate of the percentage of people who could be expected to succeed when selected on the basis of the measure. Look for this in the "Percentage Successful Using Test to Select Applicants" column in the Summary Table on the next page.

(4) Subtract the base rate of success from the success rate with the measure. Then look for this number and the incremental increase using the measure in the Summary Table.

(5) Now, *you* complete steps (1) through (4) for Graduate Programs B-D.

(6) Answer the questions that follow the Summary Table.

♦ ♦ ♦ Descriptions of Graduate Programs A-D ♦ ♦ ♦

Graduate Program A: Program A is fairly selective, accepting 30% of applicants. Program A relies on letters of recommendation from academic advisors that are given ratings by Program A's selection committee. The ratings have a validity coefficient of .10 for predicting success in Program A.

Graduate Program B: Program B uses the Miller Analogies Test (MAT) in its selection of applicants. A recent study has determined that the correlation between MAT scores and success in Program B is .15. Program B is not highly selective, as it admits 90% of applicants.

Graduate Program C: Program C relies on an Aptitude for Graduate Study (AGS) measure that was developed by two of its own graduate faculty members. A study of the AGS has revealed a validity coefficient of .30 for predicting success in Program C, which accepts 40% of its applicants.

Graduate Program D: Program D is the most selective of the four programs, with an applicant acceptance rate of only 10%. Program D uses a weighted average of GRE subtest (Verbal, Quantitative and Analytical/Writing) scores. A study has found that the correlation between the weighted average GRE score and success in Program D is .45.

SUMMARY TABLE						
Graduate Program	**Base Rate of Success**	**Validity of Measure**	**Percentage of Applicants to Be Accepted**	**Percentage Successful Using Measure to Select Applicants**	**Success Rate With Measure - Base Rate**	**Incremental Increase Using Measure**
A	.60	.10	30%	.64	.64 - .60	.04, or 4%
B	.60					
C	.60					
D	.60					

11. For each graduate program, indicate how many applicants selected with the measure would succeed and how many would fail.

Graduate Program A: *[.64 x 30% = 19.20] Out of every 30 applicants accepted, about 19 will succeed and about 11 will fail;* _____

Graduate Program B: _____
_____

Graduate Program C: _____
_____

Graduate Program D: _____
_____

12. Based on the incremental validity information, to which graduate program(s) would you recommend continued use of the primary selection measure? Explain your answer. _____
_____
_____

B. Utility Theory and Decision Analysis (text pp. 511-512)

13.   Use of the Taylor-Russell tables requires that the criterion be a _____ variable, but it would be much more effective to use a _____ of job performance as the criterion.

14.   Equations used in utility theory and decision analysis are complex; for example, one must estimate the _____ associated with different levels of job performance.

15.   Another approach (Raju et al., 1993) estimates the value of the individual in the workplace from the total value of his or her _____.

C. Value-Added Employee Assessments (text pp. 513-516)

This section focuses on issues, methods, and challenges involved in the appraisal of teachers on the basis of student performance.

16.   The **value-added approach to teacher assessment** suggests that teachers should be promoted when their students perform well and denied reappointment when their students perform poorly. What is a major challenge to this approach? _____

_____

17.   To address this challenge, statistical modeling is used to estimate the _____ _____ of students over the course of a school year, and then analysts use multiple regression techniques to identify whether, on average, a class of students outperformed or underperformed .

18.   In the table below, summarize the major problems that are associated with the value-added approach to teacher assessment (from pp. 513-515).

Difficulties in measuring growth	
Teachers with disadvantaged students	
Assortative selection	
Teaching to the test	
Decline in numbers of teachers	
Consequences of transparency	

D. Incremental Validity (text pp. 517-518)

19.   What is *incremental validity*? _____

_____

_____

20.   Research findings on the prediction of behavior in particular situations have yielded what results?

_____

_____

_____

21.   Why are these results (described in 20., above) relevant to the question of incremental validity of

psychological tests? _____

_____

22.   Studies examining the validity of employment interviews have found that situational interviews are

more valid than _____ interviews, structured interviews are more valid than unstructured

ones, and _____ -based interviews had the lowest validity of all categories studied.

III. PERSONNEL PSYCHOLOGY FROM THE EMPLOYEE'S PERSPECTIVE: FITTING PEOPLE TO JOBS (text pp. 518-520)

A. The Myers-Briggs Type Indicator (text p. 519)

1.   Describe the four ways of experiencing the world, according Carl Jung.

Sensing: _____

Intuition: _____

Feeling: _____

Thinking: _____

2.   What is the purpose of the Myers-Briggs Type Indicator (MBTI)? _____

_____

_____

3.   Researchers have used the MBTI to study what types of variables? _____

_____

_____

_____

B. Tests for Use in Industry: Wonderlic Personnel Test (text pp. 519-520)

4.   The Wonderlic Personnel Test is a quick test of _____ in adults that is used to help make employment, placement, and promotion decisions; it was revised in _____ .

IV. MEASURING CHARACTERISTICS OF THE WORK SETTING (text pp. 520-524)

A. The Social Ecology Approach (text pp. 521-522)

1.   *Social ecology* is the study of _____ .

2.   What aspects of the ecology of the workplace are important to job satisfaction? _____

_____

_____

3.   Lit some applications of the social ecology approach in clinical and health psychology. _____

_____

_____

B. Classifying Environments (text pp. 522-524)

4.   Use the classification system created by Moos (1973) to identify an original example of each of the six characteristics of your current college environment.

a. *ecological dimensions* _____

b. *behavioral settings*: _____

c. *organizational structure*: _____

d. *inhabitants*: _____

e. *psychosocial and organizational climate*: _____

f. *functional or reinforcing properties*: _____

5.   Recognizing that environment affects behavior, in your view, what specific characteristics of your college environment have a:

Positive effect on your productivity? _____

_____

_____

Negative effect on your productivity? _____

_____

_____

V. JOB ANALYSIS (text pp. 525-527)

1.   In the table below, briefly describe five methods of measuring characteristics of jobs and workplaces.

Be sure to note both strengths/benefits and weaknesses/limitations of each method.

Method	Description	Strengths/benefits of method	Weaknesses/limits of method
Checklists			
Critical Incidents			
Observations			
Interviews			
Questionnaires			

VI.   MEASURING THE PERSON-SITUATION INTERACTION (text pp. 527-529)

1.   Studies using analysis of variance (ANOVA) have determined the importance of
_____ between the person and the situation in explaining behavior.

2.   What is the *template-matching technique*? _____
_____
_____

3.   Describe one problem with the template matching approach. _____
_____
_____

Key Concepts, Terms, and Tests to Know from Chapter Eighteen

Industrial/organizational psychology

Personnel psychology

Organizational psychology

Cutting score

Hit rate

Base rate

False negative

False positive

Detection rate

Taylor-Russell tables

Value-added assessment

- Assortative selection

Incremental validity

Myers-Briggs Type Indicator (MBTI)

Carl Jung's theory
- Sensing
- Intuition
- Feeling
- Thinking

Wonderlic Personnel Test (WPT)

Environmental psychology

Ecological psychology

Social ecology

Multiphasic environmental assessment procedure

Job Analysis
- Checklists
- Critical incidents
- Observations
- Interviews
- Questionnaires

Occupational Information Network

Person-situation interaction

analysis of variance

Error variance

Template-matching technique

Aptitude-treatment interaction

CHAPTER 18 PRACTICE QUIZ

1.   **Reviewers of research on employment interviews have concluded that**

   a. interviewers generally look for positive and favorable evidence about an interviewee.
   b. communication skills, eye contact, and enthusiasm do not influence the outcomes of interviews.
   c. few if any studies have examined the influence of personal characteristics such as age, gender, and race on interview outcomes.
   d. structured interview formats are far superior to unstructured interview formats.

2.   **If a test is being used to make a dichotomous decision (e.g., suitable or unsuitable for the job), the _____ marks the point of decision.**

   a. base rate
   b. cutting score
   c. hit rate
   d. criterion score

3.   **Christopher was selected for a job on the basis of a test score. However, he performed so poorly he was fired just two months later. This case illustrates**

   a. a false negative.
   b. a base rate.
   c. a hit rate.
   d. a false positive.

4.   **A tool for evaluating the validity of a test in relation to the amount of information it contributes beyond the base rates is the**

   a. Taylor-Russell tables.
   b. critical incident analysis.
   c. selection ratio.
   d. meta analysis.

5.   **Equations based on utility theory to calculate the value of test data used in selection decisions**

   a. require that the criterion be a dichotomous variable.
   b. are widely used among managers who make personnel decisions.
   c. require the estimation of dollar values associated with different performance levels.
   d. shifts the subjective judgment to estimating the coefficient of variation of the criterion.

6.   Imagine that the National Football League was considering using a test to help make decisions about which players would be drafted into the professional league. The percentage of people who are drafted into the National Football League without the use of the test is the

        a. selection ratio.
        b. base rate.
        c. cutting score.
        d. hit rate.

7.   Which of the following is <u>not</u> a mode through which we experience the world, according to Carl Jung?

        a. feeling
        b. sensing
        c. creating
        d. thinking

8.   A quick intelligence test used to help make employment decisions in business and industry is the

        a. Myers-Briggs Type Indicator.
        b. Revised Minnesota Paper Form Board Tests.
        c. Differential Aptitude Test.
        d. Wonderlic Personnel Test.

9.   Incremental validity refers to

        a. the degree to which a test accurately predicts success on a criterion measure.
        b. the amount of information a test provides beyond what is known without using the test.
        c. the extent to which a test is valid for inferences involving success in employment settings.
        d. evidence that a test is a cost-effective tool to aid in decision-making.

10.   Which of the following would be of least interest to a social ecologist?

        a. the relationship between room temperature and productivity in the workplace
        b. the influence of workers' self-esteem on responses to performance feedback
        c. the impact of an enforced dress code on student learning
        d. the relationship between number of hours on-call and medical residents' stress levels

✍Student Workbook Assignment 18.1

⊸ Developing a College Instructor Selection Program ⊷

◆ DESCRIPTION OF THE ASSIGNMENT

As you have read in Chapter 18, Industrial/Organizational psychologists assist in the development of employee selection programs.

According to the Society for Industrial/Organization Psychology (SIOP; www.siop.org/), development of a selection program involves several steps: (1) identification of relevant job performance dimensions; (2) identification of knowledge, skills, and abilities (KSAs) necessary for the job, and (3) development and validation of assessment tools and strategies to measure KSAs.   (See figure below.)

For this assignment, imagine that you have been asked to be a member of a committee at your college or university that is charged with developing a program to help select new instructors. Directions for completing this assignment are on the next page.

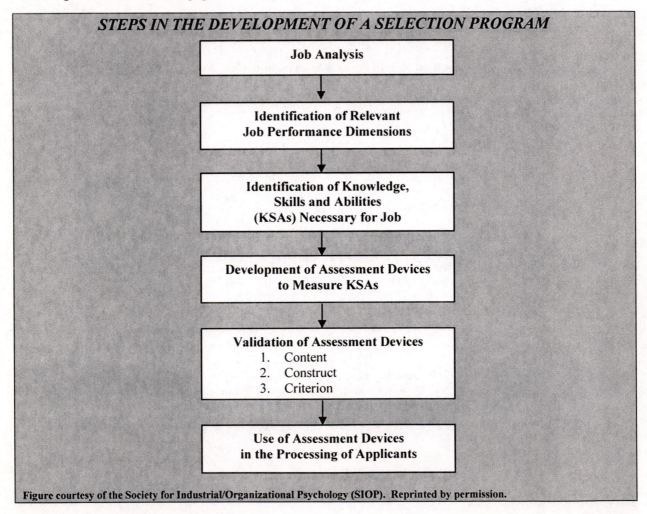

STEPS IN THE DEVELOPMENT OF A SELECTION PROGRAM

Job Analysis

↓

Identification of Relevant Job Performance Dimensions

↓

Identification of Knowledge, Skills and Abilities (KSAs) Necessary for Job

↓

Development of Assessment Devices to Measure KSAs

↓

Validation of Assessment Devices
1. Content
2. Construct
3. Criterion

↓

Use of Assessment Devices in the Processing of Applicants

Figure courtesy of the Society for Industrial/Organizational Psychology (SIOP). Reprinted by permission.

◆ DIRECTIONS

➔ **Before beginning this assignment, make sure you have read Chapter 18.**

(1) Identify four dimensions of an instructor's job at your college or university. If you are having trouble coming up with four dimensions, ask a few of your professors about their work.

(2) Identify the knowledge, skills, and abilities (KSAs) required for each dimension.

(3) Write descriptive criteria reflecting excellent, adequate, and poor performance on each dimension.

(4) Identify at least one tool or strategy by which each dimension-specific set of KSAs could be evaluated.

An example is presented in the shaded box below.

JOB DIMENSION: Developing written materials and handouts for students

KSAs required:

Content knowledge beyond what is presented in the textbook; writing skills; understanding of students' level of knowledge, skills; and learning styles; ability to present information in a clear and engaging way; creativity and originality

Performance Standards:

Excellent: Handouts are very well written and organized; information presented in the handouts is accurate; information is presented in a very clear and engaging fashion; handouts substantially contribute to students' understanding of course material beyond what the text provides.

Adequate: Handouts are fairly well written and organized; information presented in the handouts is accurate; information is presented in a somewhat clear and engaging fashion; handouts contribute to students' understanding of course material beyond what the text provides.

Poor: Handouts are poorly written and/or organized; information presented in the handouts is inaccurate; information is presented in a fashion that confuses, rather than clarifies, concepts; handouts do not contribute to students' understanding of course material (and may even detract from it) beyond what the text provides.

Evaluation tools or strategies:

Strategy #1: External judges (e.g., psychology professors, students) could rate the quality of a representative sample of handouts created by the instructor for one or more courses.

Strategy #2: The instructor could be provided information about a particular subject and given a limited amount of time (e.g., one hour) to develop a handout that presents the information. External judges could rate the quality of the work sample.

Validation of evaluation tool or strategy:

Pre-employment ratings of the samples could be correlated with students' ratings of course materials developed by the instructor in one or more courses during the academic term.

⊸ CHAPTER 19: *Test Bias* ⊢

Chapter 19 Outline

CHAPTER 19 EXERCISES

I.   WHY IS TEST BIAS CONTROVERSIAL? (text pp. 532-534)

🖝 *Chapter 19 focuses on the question of whether cross-group differences in standardized aptitude and intelligence test scores can be explained by test bias. Although the possibility that biological and environmental factors may explain these differences is not addressed at length in this chapter, Focused Examples 19-1 and 19-2 introduce you to these interesting areas of research.*

1.   A significant controversy exists over *why* African Americans, on average, score _____ points (or about _____ standard deviation) lower than white Americans on standardized IQ and some other aptitude tests.

2.   A 2011 College Board report summarizing SAT scores indicated that one in four students did not disclose their _____, so it is difficult to determine why the performance gap between ethnic groups has not narrowed over a number of years.

3. For what reasons might students decline to report their race/ethnicity on the SAT? _____

_____

_____

_____

> **Focused Example 19-1, *Genes and Improving IQ***
> Focused Example 19-1 discusses the fact that over the last 60 years, IQ scores have steadily increased. Increases in IQ scores are more dramatic among African Americans than white Americans in recent years. •Why do these trends call into question the extent to which genetic factors determine intelligence?

> **Focused Example 19-2, *Can Stereotyping Affect Test Performance?***
> Focused Example 19-2 examines research suggesting that being a member of a group that is negatively stereotyped may adversely affect college grades, standardized test performance, and employment testing.
> • What were the methods and findings of Steele and Aronson's experiments on this issue?

II. TEST FAIRNESS AND THE LAW (text pp. 534-536)

1.   Title VII of the 1964 Civil Rights Act created the _____ _____ _____ _____ (EEOC), which in 1970 and 1978 published formal guidelines for the use of _____ in education and in industry.

2.   How is **adverse impact** defined by the 1978 EEOC guidelines? _____
_____
_____

3.   If a selection procedure—including one utilizing psychological tests—results in adverse impact, the employer must show that the procedure has _____ for the inferences the employer wants to make.

III. THE TRADITIONAL DEFENSE OF TESTING (text pp. 537-545)

 Section III examines the question of whether standardized achievement, aptitude, and intelligence tests are as valid for African American and other minority examinees as they are for white examinees. It is very important to understand the point that when a particular group of examinees—defined by gender, race, socioeconomic status, etc. –obtains a lower mean score on a test than another group of examinees, it does not necessarily mean the test is biased against the first group. In this section, pay close attention to the types of evidence that would potentially support the charge that standardized tests are biased against particular groups.

1.   The term _____ validity refers to the possibility that scores on a test have different meanings for different groups of examinees (for example, scores on an aptitude test might predict job performance for one, but not for all, groups of examinees).

A. Content-Related Evidence for Validity (text pp. 537-542)

2.   Accusations that the content of standardized aptitude and intelligence tests are biased against individuals from disadvantaged backgrounds are founded on several claims. What are these claims?
_____
_____
_____

3.   Flaugher (1978) contended that accusations of test bias sometimes arise from a misunderstanding about how test scores are usually interpreted. Specifically, Flaugher suggested that people incorrectly assume *what* about the distinction between a fair test and a biased test? _____

_____

_____

4.   Flaugher points out that test developers evaluate the validity of their tests by examining correlations between test scores and _____; in other words, they are more concerned about the meaning of overall test scores than about individual items on the test.

5.   Researchers have failed to find evidence that biased items in well-known standardized tests explains differences in scores among racial/ethnic groups. In the table below, summarize the specific findings of two different approaches that have attempted to find such evidence.

Approach	Findings
Experts judge the unfairness of items; potentially biased items are then removed from the test	
Types or categories of items more likely to be missed by minority examinees are identified and removed	

6.   The Educational Testing Service (ETS) is particularly concerned with investigating the possibility of standardized test bias, since significantly different scores are obtained by various groups of examinees on the Graduate Record Examination (GRE), the Scholastic Assessment Test (SAT-I) and the Law School Admissions Test (LSAT) – all of which are published by ETS. Describe some of these between-group score differences.

_____

_____

_____

7.   ETS has developed an approach called _____ _____

_____ **(DIF) analysis** which identifies items that are biased against any ethnic, racial, or gender group.

8.   Describe the method of DIF. _____

_____

_____

_____

9.   In one study, DIF was used to eliminate items from the SAT, but this procedure had only slight effects on minimizing differences between ethnic groups. Why? _____

_____

10.   Although some research indicates the depiction of _____ as characters in intelligence test items occurs with disproportionate frequency, there is no evidence that the frequency with which different groups appear in items affects test scores.

11.   In one sentence, summarize conclusions drawn regarding evidence of bias in standardized aptitude and intelligence test items. _____

_____

B. Criterion-Related Sources of Bias (text pp. 542-545)

12.   Bias might also be demonstrated if a test has differential _____ power (or validity) for two or more groups of examinees.

The next three Workbook pages explore how regression plots are used to investigate whether criterion-related sources of bias might explain differences in test scores between groups of examinees. Rread through text pp. 542-545 before going on.

The first figure shown at left (and on text p. 542) depicts a simple regression plot from which one might predict a criterion score, such as grade point average, from a test score. The shaded ellipse, called an **isodensity curve,** simply shows the performance of a certain group of examinees. Imagine the shaded ellipse is full of data points, with each point representing the intersection between one examinee's test score and his/her criterion score. The question of differential validity can be addressed by looking at two or more groups (represented by ellipses) on a single plot. Of most interest would be a comparison of the slopes and intercepts of the two (or more) groups to see if they are similar or different.

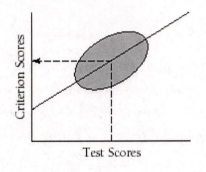

Regression Plot 1

Regression Plot 1 (also shown on p. 543) shows two groups of examinees, A and B, who took the same test. Again, imagine that each ellipse is full of data points. If you look at the horizontal axis, you can see that almost all the examinees in Group B got higher scores on the test than examinees in Group A, although there is some overlap. Also, if you look at the vertical axis, you can see that Group B got higher scores on the criterion, although once again there is some overlap. You can see that examinees who score lower on the test are expected to perform less well on the criterion. The important thing to focus on in this plot is the regression line. There is just one line which describes both Group A and Group B data sets equally well. This means that the relationship between test scores and performance on the criterion is the same for both Group A and Group B. Thus, there is no evidence that the test adequately predicts the criterion for one group, but not for the other group (i.e., there is no evidence of test bias).

13.   Imagine that an examinee from Group A charged that the test he took was biased because almost all the examinees in his group got lower scores than examinees in Group B. Using Regression Plot 1, how might you respond to this examinee's accusation? _____

_____

_____

_____

_____

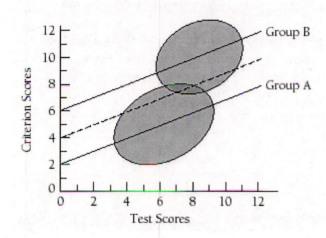

Regression Plot 2

The first thing you will notice about **Regression Plot 2** (also shown on text p. 543) is that there are two regression lines (these are the solid lines). It should be obvious that one regression line could not have represented Group A and Group B equally well. The regression lines have different y-intercepts, but they are parallel – they have exactly the same slope.

If you knew that an examinee got a test score of 6, would that score predict poor or good performance on the criterion? It depends on which group the examinee is in! If the examinee is in Group A, a score of 6 predicts a criterion performance score of about 4. However, if the examinee is in Group B, a score of 6 predicts a criterion performance score of about 8. So, the fact that there are two regression lines with the same slope but different intercepts suggests that test scores predict different criterion scores depending on one's group.

14.   Look at the dashed line running between the two regression lines. This dashed line depicts what would happen if the two separate regression lines were combined. If you use the combined regression line to predict the performance on the criterion of an examinee who got a score of 6 on the test, what criterion score would you predict? _____

15.   If the examinee was in Group A, would his/her actual performance on the criterion probably be higher or lower than the predicted performance on the criterion? _____

What if the examinee was in Group B? _____

16.   Describe how use of the SAT to predict college performance resembles Regression Plot 2. _____

_____

_____

_____

_____

17.   When the relationships between test scores and criterion scores among different groups are best described by two (or more) regression lines with _____ slopes, there is little evidence that the test has differential validity.

Regression Plot 3

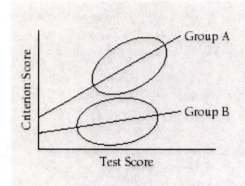

Regression Plot 3 (also on text p. 523) shows a situation that is very rarely encountered. As you can see, there are two regression lines. However, unlike Regression Plot 2, the two regression lines in this figure do not have the same intercept *or* the same slope.

The slope of the regression line that describes Group B data is much less (is flatter) than the slope of the regression line that describes Group A data. In fact, we could ask whether the test predicts anything of value for Group B examinees, since a very low test score and a very high test score predict only marginally different criterion scores.

18.   Regression Plot 3 depicts evidence of a biased test. Explain why. _____

_____

_____

_____

_____

_____

ᛟ Focused Example 19-5, *Scoring the WISC-R for Inner-City Children: The Evolution of Strict Scoring Rules*

Focused Example 19-5 describes research on the effects of alterations in WISC-R administration procedures on responses to test items of inner-city children in the Baltimore area. •What were the method and findings of this Johns Hopkins study? • On what grounds was the research challenged? • How might alterations in the administration and scoring procedures of standardized tests affect their reliability? • How might alterations affect criterion-related validity?

IV. OTHER APPROACHES TO TESTING MINORITY GROUP MEMBERS (text pp. 545-552)

1.   Two alternatives for dealing with unfair tests have been suggested by those who believe that much more needs to be done to end discrimination against minority group members. What are these two alternatives?

a. _____

b. _____

A. Ignorance Versus Stupidity (text pp. 545-547)

2.   "Ignorance versus stupidity" was the rather insensitive phrase used by a California judge to describe two potential explanations for why some children do more poorly on standardized aptitude tests than other children. In the table below, describe the two potential explanations in more academic terms and then identify at least one implication of each explanation.

Explanation for why minority children do not perform as well on standardized tests	Implications of the explanation

B. The Chitling Test (text pp. 547-548)

3.   What was the purpose of the Chitling Test when it was developed in the late 1960s? _____

_____

_____

_____

_____

C. The Black Intelligence Test of Cultural Homogeneity (text pp. 548-549)

4.   The term _____ is used by some to describe the view that because achievement and intelligence tests are supported by empirical validity studies, their use as instruments of racial discrimination is a more subtle and insidious form of racism.

5.   R. L. Williams and his colleagues contend that whereas traditional assessments of IQ indicate the likelihood of succeeding in the white community, a _____ _____ (SQ) is a more important predictor of success in the African American community.

6. In the table below, summarize characteristics of the Black Intelligence Test of Cultural Homogeneity (BITCH).

Characteristic	Description
Measures	
Items	
Differences in mean scores across groups	
Psychometric properties (reliability and validity)	

D. The System of Multicultural Pluralistic Assessment (text pp. 549-552)

7. Mercer developed the System of Multicultural Pluralistic Assessment (SOMPA) based on an important set of assumptions regarding cultural groups and their performances on IQ tests. What were these assumptions?

_____

_____

_____

_____

_____

8. Because of Mercer's concerns about the misclassification of minority children as mentally retarded, the SOMPA was designed to integrate three different assessment approaches. In the table below, describe the rationale for each component of SOMPA. Then identify how each component is assessed.

Component	Rationale	Assessment
Medical		
Social System		
Pluralistic		

9.   Mercer counters criticisms about the modest validity of the SOMPA by stating that only the

_____ component should be validated through school performance criteria, whereas

the appropriate criterion in validity studies of ELPs should be the percentage of WISC-R scores that can be

explained by _____ variables.

V. SUGGESTIONS FOR SOLUTIONS (text pp. 553-561)

A. Ethical Concerns and the Definition of Test Bias (text pp. 532-535)

1.   In the table below, summarize three ethical positions on how individuals representing different groups

should be treated with regard to selection decisions.

Ethical position	Description of position
Unqualified individualism	
Use of quotas	
Qualified individualism	

❧ *Questions 2. through 4. relate to Table 19-2 on text p. 555, which describes four different statistics-based models of selection procedures.*

2.   The regression model reflects _____ _____, because

separate regression lines are used for different groups, and individuals with the highest predicted criterion scores

are selected. The result of this approach is that few _____ group members may be

selected.

3.   The _____ system also use separate regression lines, but a predetermined proportion of

people predicted to score highest on the criterion are selected from *each* group. This procedure may lead to

greater _____ rates among some groups.

4.   Two other models result in some increases in the number of minority group members selected, along

with _____ on average criterion performance.

B. Thinking Differently: Finding New Interpretations of Data (text pp. 535-537)

5.   Rather than indicating genetic variation or social deficits, group differences in test scores may reflect what? _____

_____

6.   Goldman's _____ _____ theory suggests that different kinds of strategies lead to effective solutions for many types of tasks.

7.   Summarize research findings on relative strengths (on tests) of various cultural minority groups.

_____

_____

_____

⚹ Focused Example 19-6, *The Bell Curve*
This Focused Examples discusses Hernstein and Murray's (1994) controversial book about the meaning and implications of racial differences in intelligence test scores. In *The Bell Curve*, Hernstein and Murray contend that intelligence is of paramount importance in the prediction of everything from leadership, job performance, and economic attainment to school drop-out rates, unemployment, and crime. • On what grounds was *The Bell Curve* criticized?

C. Developing Different Criteria (text pp. 537-539)

8.   Regarding criterion-related evidence for the validity of standardized tests, what does the author's statement that "the criterion may be the test dressed in different clothes" mean? _____

_____

_____

_____

9.   What are the arguments for and against the use of classroom grades as the criterion in validity studies of standardized tests?

For classroom grades as criterion: _____

_____

_____

_____

Against classroom grades as criterion: _____

_____

_____

_____

10.   As discussed on pp. 560-561 (and in Focused Example 19-6), what is a primary problem with criterion measures used to validate the Medical College Admissions Test (MCAT) and the Law School Admissions Test (LSAT)? _____

_____

_____

_____

VI. CHANGING THE SOCIAL ENVIRONMENT(text pp. 540-542)

1.   Examine Figure 19-9 on text p. 562. In the spaces provided below, indicate the approximate mean SAT-I verbal score and SAT-I math score for examinees from families in the income groups listed.

Annual Family income	Mean SAT-I verbal score	Mean SAT-I math score
Less than $10,000	_____	_____
$50,000-$60,000	_____	_____
more than $100,000	_____	_____

2.   Why do you think there is such a strong relationship between family income and SAT-I scores?

_____

_____

_____

_____

_____

> ♀ **Focused Example 19-7, *Consequences of the University of California Decison to Drop SAT-I***
> This Focused Example examines the basis and consequences of University of California's decision to stop using the SAT-I for admissions decisions (but to continue to use the SAT-II). As reported in Chapter 5, a study of over 70,000 University of California freshmen found that the SAT-II was a better predictor of college grades than was the SAT-I. . • What were the consequences of the University of California's decision?

3.   Examine Table 19-3 on text p. 564, which summarizes arguments for and against the use of aptitude and intelligence tests to make important selection/admissions decisions. Which side do you agree with more? Why? _____

_____

_____

_____.

_____

Terms, Concepts, and Tests to Know From Chapter Nineteen

EEOC Guidelines

Uniform Guidelines on Employee Selection Procedures

Adverse impact

Differential validity

Differential Item Functioning (DIF) analysis

The Chitling Test

The Black Intelligence Test of Cultural Homogeneity (BITCH)

Scientific racism

The System of Multicultural Assessment (SOMPA)

Estimated learning potentials (ELPs)

Test bias

Unqualified individualism

Quotas

Qualified individualism

CHAPTER 19 PRACTICE QUIZ

1.   Research indicates that on standardized aptitude and intelligence tests, African Americans tend to score, on average, about _____ standard deviation(s) lower than white Americans.

      a. .5
      b. 1.0
      c. 1.5
      d. 2.0

2.   Which of the following methods is used to identify biased test items by equating groups on the basis of overall test scores and then evaluating differences between groups of examinees on particular items?

      a. regression analyses
      b. adverse impact analysis
      c. differential item analysis
      d. differential validity

3.   The _____ published standards that specifically address the use of psychological tests in selection procedures.

      a. Equal Employment Opportunities Commission
      b. Educational Testing Service
      c. United States Supreme Court
      d. Federal Trade Commission

4.   Which of the following tests specifically addresses the problem of minority children being misclassified as mentally retarded by examining medical, social-system, and pluralistic factors?

      a. The Chitling Test
      b. The SOMPA
      c. The BITCH
      d. The WISC

5. Which of the following findings most clearly reflects test bias?

      a. significantly different slopes in the regression lines predicting criterion scores for male versus female examinees
      b. consistent and significant differences in mean test scores between Asian American and Caucasian American examinees
      c. significant differences in standard deviations, but not means, of test scores between native speakers of the language and non-native speakers of the language
      d. the same slopes but different intercepts in the regression lines predicting criterion scores for African American and white American examinees

6.   An item on an intelligence test designed by a British test developer reads, "What does one do in a *loo*?" Because the term *loo* is unfamiliar to most American children, they would probably answer this item incorrectly. This is an example of

        a. adverse impact.
        b. criterion-related bias.
        c. differential validity.
        d. content-related bias.

7.   **Quota systems**

        a. result in the selection of few minority group members.
        b. select individuals with the highest predicted criterion score.
        c. have been termed "color blind" selection procedures.
        d. select predetermined percentages of individuals from different groups.

8.   **Studies demonstrate that minority children obtain relatively lower scores on contemporary standardized intelligence tests (such as the WISC). Most researchers agree that racial differences in test scores**

        a. are obtained because the majority of the items in these tests are culturally loaded.
        b. are a result of only a few, but heavily-weighted, culturally loaded items.
        c. cannot be attributed to culturally loaded items.
        d. are found in a small minority of studies that examine racial differences in test scores.

9.   **Unqualified individualists would most likely**

        a. accept the use of quotas in the selection of employees.
        b. consider race or gender in the selection process if these variables were valid predictors of job success.
        c. reject the notion that if a test is shown to be a valid predictor, it is a fair test.
        d. be more concerned about discrimination than about job performance.

10.   **Studies have shown that professional school entrance exams such as the MCAT and LSAT**

        a. are poor predictors of grades in the relevant professional programs.
        b. are poor predictors of real-life professional performance and success.
        c. currently are used much less frequently by professional programs to select students than in the past.
        d. are highly correlated with non-cognitive predictors of success in professional practice.

✍**Student Workbook Assignment 19.1**

⊷ **Creating a Culturally Biased Aptitude Test** ⊶

♦ **DESCRIPTION OF THE ASSIGNMENT**

As you know, one way that test items can be biased is if they contain information or images more familiar to one group than to other groups of examinees. Your text uses the hypothetical example of an intelligence test containing items asking examinees to define the terms *shilling* and *petrol*; although British examinees would probably answer these items correctly, most American examines would fail these items. This example illustrates **content-biased** items.

This assignment asks you to create content-biased items for an ability test. The objective of the assignment is to encourage you to consider ways in which subtle content bias might affect the test scores of different groups.

♦ **DIRECTIONS**

➔ **Before beginning this assignment, make sure you have read Chapter 19.**

(1) Identify a broadly defined "cultural group" for which item content will be very familiar. Examples of these groups include: individuals from a particular area or region of the country (e.g., the South, the Northeast); people who were raised in rural (e.g., farming, ranching) vs. urban areas; psychology vs. non-psychology majors; sports-minded vs. non-sports minded people; artists vs. non-artists, etc.

(2) Create two verbal-type items and two performance (nonverbal)-type items for your culturally-biased ability test. Examples of content-biased items that would favor football fans are presented below.

Example of a biased verbal-type test item:

Crossing the line of scrimmage before the snap, the defensive end was flagged for being _____.

       a. out-of-bounds
       b. off-sides
       c. premature
       d. under center

Example of a biased nonverbal-type test item.

What important part is missing from the object shown below?

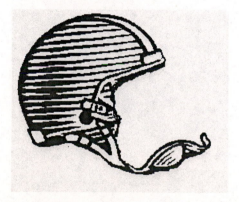

⊸ CHAPTER 20: *Testing and the Law* ⊱

CHAPTER 20 EXERCISES

I. LAWS GOVERNING THE USE OF TESTS (text pp. 569-580)

A. Federal Authorities (text pp.569-577)

1.   The federal government regulates _____ _____, or business activity that involves two or more states. In practice, this term can apply to virtually all business activity, including the sale and distribution of psychological tests.

2.　　　The federal government can also regulate the use of tests indirectly by controlling spending. Give an example of how the federal government might indirectly influence whether, and which, standardized tests are used by a public school district. _____

_____

_____

3.　　　The federal government exerts most of its control over use of psychological tests through its interpretation of the **14ᵗʰ Amendment** of the Constitution, which guarantees all citizens _____

_____

4.　　　When Congress enacted the **Civil Rights Act of 1964**, the Equal Employment Opportunity Commission (EEOC) was created. EEOC guidelines defining fair employee-selection procedures were published in 1970, then revised and re-published in 1978. The *Uniform Guidelines on Employee Selection Procedures* affect whom? _____

_____

5.　　　Complete the following statements regarding EEOC guidelines for employee selection procedures. The EEOC guidelines state that

a. an employer cannot discriminate on the basis of: _____

_____

b. the federal government will look for evidence of selection procedures that might have *adverse impact,* which is defined by the **four-fifths rule**: the government will view an employee-selection procedure as having adverse impact if the selection rate: _____

_____

c. when psychological tests are used in selection decisions that result in adverse impact (or overselection in a group), the employer must: _____

_____

♀ Psychological Testing in Everyday Life 20-1, *EEOC Guidelines for Criterion Validity*
PTEL Box 20-1 is rather lengthy, but it contains very important information about how the EEOC defines and evaluates criterion-related validity evidence of employee selection procedures. Standards for criterion-related validity studies are described with regard to: (1) technical feasibility of conducting a study; (2) analysis of the job to determine measures of work behavior that are relevant to the job; (3) criterion measures; (4) representativeness of the sample in the study; (5) degree of statistical relationships between selection procedure scores and criterion measures; (6) operational use of selection procedures; (7) degree to which validity findings have been overstated; (8) studies of unfairness, including definitions of unfairness, when unfairness studies must be conducted, and requirements of unfairness studies.

6.   The EEOC requires an organization with more than _____ employees to submit a form every year specifying the number of _____ and members of four different _____ groups employed in nine job categories within the organization.

7.   In 1980, the EEOC published guidelines on **sexual harassment** in the workplace. How did the EEOC define sexual harassment? _____

_____

C.   Specific Laws (text pp. 577-579)

🖙 *The story of how the New York Truth in Testing Law came about is a fascinating one. It begins with a watchdog/public advocacy group, the New York Public Interest Research Group (NYPIRG), taking issue with the enormous wealth, success, and power of the Educational Testing Service (ETS), which publishes such widely-used graduate school entrance tests as the Graduate Management Admission Test (GMAT), the Law School Admission Test (LSAT), and the Graduate Record Exam (GRE). The story ends with the enactment of the controversial New York Truth in Testing Law, which gives students taking these tests some rights which might surprise you! Questions 8.-10. address this law.*

8.   Spurred by an investigation by NYPIRG, the Truth in Testing Law requires testing companies such as ETS to do what three things?
   (1) _____
   (2) _____
   (3) _____

9.   What concerns have been expressed about the third component of the Truth in Testing Law? _____

_____

_____

_____

_____

_____

10.   Do you agree or disagree with the statement, "Truth-in-testing legislation has done more harm than good to test takers."? Explain your answer. _____

_____

_____

_____

_____

_____

_____

C.   No Child Left Behind (NCLB) (text pp. 579-580)

11.   No Child Left Behind (NCLB), also known as Public Law 107-110, reauthorized federal programs designed to improve performance of students in _____ and _____ schools.

12.   In addition to giving parents more flexibility in choosing where their children would go to school, NCLB mandated that schools must be accountable for their performance by demonstrating student progress on tests; poorly performing schools would lose funding. One of the most controversial aspects of NCLB led critics to suggest that it encouraged teachers to "teach to the test." Discuss this criticism below.

_____

_____

_____

_____

_____

_____

_____

13. In 2008, George W. Bush announced that No Child Left Behind had been effective. However, critics maintained that there was little evidence that school performance had improved. Describe the bases of this criticism below. _____

_____

_____

_____

_____

_____

_____

_____

II. MAJOR LAWSUITS THAT HAVE AFFECTED PSYCHOLOGICAL TESTING (text pp. 580-599)

This section of the textbook contains descriptions of over a dozen different lawsuits related to the use of psychological tests in education and employment settings. The most important aspects of these cases for you to know are (1) the case name, (2) the issue raised, and (3) the outcome and relevance of the case. Complete the table on the next two pages, which will help you organize this information for further study. A few of the cells have been filled in for you as examples.

312

CASE NAME Text page numbers	ISSUE	OUTCOME & RELEVANCE OF THE CASE
Plessy v. Ferguson *(1896)* pp. 580-581	Whether school segregation violates the 14th Amendment (equal protection)	U.S. Supreme Court ruled that as long as schools were "separate but equal," the 14th Amendment was not violated.
Brown v. Board of Education (1954) pp. 580-581		
Stell v. Savannah-Chatham County Board of Education p. 582		GA court ruled that in the best interest of all children, the Savannah school district should not desegregate. Judge agreed integration would lead to feelings of inferiority/frustration & antisocial behavior among African American children. The validity of IQ test scores, the primary "evidence" in this case, was never debated. [This GA decision was later overturned].
Hobson v. Hansen *(1967)* pp. 582-583		
Diana v. State Board of Education pp. 583-584		
Larry P. v. Wilson Riles (1979) pp. 584-586		Many experts testified on both sides of test bias issue. California judge ruled IQ tests are racially and culturally biased, and their use discriminatory and not validated. CA must discontinue using them to place African-American children in EMR classes. *Larry P* is a frequently cited case.[Ruling expanded in 1986 to ban use of IQ tests w/all African American students in CA.]
Parents in Action on Special Education v. Hannon p. 586		
Crawford et al. v. Honig et al. (1991) pp. 586-590		

Marchall v. Georgia (1981) pp. 590-591		
Debra P. v. Turlington (1979) pp. 591-593	Argued that Florida's (high school) minimum competence test should not be used for minority students with inferior educational opportunities.	Florida judge ruled in favor of defendants – minimum standards should be absolute. Although validity of test was not challenged, use of it was suspended for four years until segregated students graduated.
Regents of the University of California v. Bakke pp. 593-594		
Golden Rule Insurance Company et al. v. Washburn et al. (1984 p. 594	Illinois insurance company sued ETS over "culturally biased" insurance licensing exam it created. Study showed 77% of white, but only 52% of black, examinees passed exam.	Case was settled out of court. ETS admitted no guilt, but agreed to change item selection criteria to minimize race differences: proportion of correct answers for white and African American examinees can differ by no more than .15. *Golden Rule* sets precedent in testing industry.
Adarand Constructors, Inc. v. Pena, Sec. of Trans. et al.(1995) pp. 594-595		
Grutter v. Bollinger (2003) & *Gratz v. Bollinger (2003)* pp. 595-597		
Parents v. Seattle (2007) pp. 597-598		
Meredith v. Jefferson Co. Board Of Educ (2007) pp. 598-599		
Fisher v. University of Texas (ongoing) p. 599		

III. PERSONNEL CASES (text pp. 599-606)

1.   Describe the unfair or discriminatory conditions experienced by African American employees of the Duke Steam Plant in North Carolina, which later became the defendant in *Griggs v. Duke Power Company.*

_____

_____

_____

2.   In response to a formal complaint, the Duke Power Company constructed a test that all employees had to pass in order to gain advancement. The _____ of this test became the central issue in *Griggs v. Duke Power Company.*

3.   What was the U.S. Supreme Court's decision in this case? _____

_____

4.   What was the argument put to the U.S. Supreme Court in *Watson v. Fort Worth Bank and Trust* (1988)?

_____

_____

5.   What had lower courts previously ruled in this case? _____

_____

6.   What was the U.S. Supreme Court's ruling in *Watson v. Fort Worth Bank and Trust*? _____

_____

_____

7.   In *Wards Cove Packing Company v. Antonia*, the U.S. Supreme Court reversed an important component of the *Griggs* decision. What did the Court decide in the *Wards Cove* case? How did the court's decision affect plaintiffs in equal employment opportunity cases? _____

_____

_____

8.   In reaction to the Supreme Court's ruling, the Congress enacted the **1991 Civil Rights Act**. The 1991 Civil Rights Act:

a. put the burden of proving that employee selection procedures were valid and reliable back on the

_____.

b. forbids the use of different cutoff scores associated with _____.

9.	In *Ricci v. DeStafano* [2009], 20 firefighters brought suit against the city of New Haven, Connecticut.

a.	What did the plaintiffs claim? _____

_____

_____

b.	What did the city claim? _____

_____

_____

c.	What did the Supreme Court rule? _____

_____

_____

10.	What did the U.S. Supreme Court decide in *Detroit Edison Co. v. N. L. R. B.*? _____

_____

_____

10.	In *Connecticut v. Teal*, The Supreme Court was asked to consider whether discrimination had occurred against an individual employee in the absence of adverse impact. (In this case, even though the initial written employment screening test had no relation to the job and reduced the number of African Americans in the applicant pool, the total number of African Americans hired after the entire screening process had been completed did not show adverse impact). What did the Court decide? _____

_____

_____

_____

11.	In contrast to *Connecticut v. Teal*, the Supreme Court allowed testing that excluded some groups when the test was shown to be _____, in *Association of Mexican-American Educators v. California, 1996.*

12.	Obtaining evidence to prove bias in job discrimination cases is a major challenge. In lawsuits involving blue-collar jobs, evidence of bias usually focuses on a test's _____ validity and ratio of _____ applicants the test selects.

13.	The use of tests in employee selection and advancement has been advocated by _____ employees, even though evaluation of these employees typically does not involve tests; this is viewed by some as a troubling double-standard.

A. Cases Relevant to the Americans with Disabilities Act (text pp. 604-605)

14.   Summarize the rights *related to achievement or aptitude testing* afforded people with disabilities by the **Americans with Disabilities Act (ADA).** _____

_____

_____

_____

15.   In what ways does the ADA conflict with the American Psychological Association's *Standards for Educational and Psychological Tests*? _____

_____

_____

16.   In *Brookhart v. Illinois State Board of Education*, the plaintiffs were a group of disabled students (some with learning disabilities) who were denied their high-school diplomas because they failed a minimum competency test. What did the federal court decide in this case? _____

_____

_____

_____

17.   The Hawaii Department of Education was a defendant in a case revolving around the question of the type and amount of assistance on a statewide graduation test the ADA afforded a learning-disabled student. What did the court rule in this case? _____

_____

_____

_____

B. A Critical Look at Lawsuits (text p. 582)

18.   Summarize some of the problems that can arise when the use of psychological tests is determined in the courtroom. _____

_____

_____

_____

_____

_____

_____

_____

Concepts, Terms, and Cases to Know from Chapter Twenty

Law
- Statutes
- Constitutions
- Judicial opinion

Interstate commerce

14th Amendment

Civil Rights Act of 1964

Equal Employment Opportunity Commission (EEOC)

Uniform Guidelines on Employee Selection Procedures

Adverse impact

Four-fifths rule

Validity

EEOC guidelines for criterion validity

Sexual harassment

1991 Civil Rights Bill

New York Truth in Testing Law

New York Public Interest Research Group

Education testing Service (ETS)

No Child Left Behind (NCLB)

"teaching to the test"

Plessy v. Ferguson

Brown v. Board of Education

Stell v. Savannah-Chatham County Brd of Educ

Hobson v. Hansen

Diana v. State Board of Education

Larry P. v. Wilson Riles

Parents in Action on Special Education v. Hannon

Crawford et al. v. Honig et al.

Marchall v. Georgia

Debra P. v. Turlington

Regents of the University of California v. Bakke

Golden Rule Insurance Company et al. v.

Washburn et al.

Adarand Constructors, Inc. v. Pena, Secretary of Transportation et al.

Grutter v. Bollinger

Gratz v. Bollinger

Parents v. Seattle

Meredith v. Jefferson County Board of Education

Fisher v. University of Texas

Griggs v. Duke Power Company

Watson v. Fort Worth Bank and Trust

Wards Cove Packing Company v. Antonio

Ricci v. DeStafno

Detroit Edison Co. v. N.L.R.B.

Connecticut v. Teal

United States v. City of Buffalo

Assoc of Mexican-American Educators v. Ca.

Americans with Disabilities Act (ADA)

Brookhart v. Illinois State Board of Education

CHAPTER 20 PRACTICE QUIZ

1.   **Which Constitutional Amendment is most relevant to the issue of school segregation?**

    a. 11th
    b. 14th
    c. 18th
    d. 21st

2.   **Which case forced the Educational Testing Service (ETS) to change the way items on some of its tests were selected?**

    a. *Regents of the University of California v. Bakke*
    b. *Wards Cove Packing Company vs. Antonia*
    c. *Diana v. State Board of Education*
    d. *Golden Rule Insurance Company et al. v. Washburn et al.*

3.   **_____ was the first case in which the Supreme Court ruled that schools must provide nonsegregated facilities for African American and white students.**

    a. *Brown v. Board of Education*
    b. *Diana v. State Board of Education*
    c. *Plessy v. Ferguson*
    d. *Stell v. Savannah-Chatham County Board of Education*

4.   **As a result of the court ruling in *Larry P. vs. Wilson Riles*,**

    a. schools were forced to provide special EMR classes for non-white children.
    b. IQ testing was no longer used to place African-American children in EMR classes.
    c. standardized achievement tests could no longer be used with bi-lingual children.
    d. all handicapped children were guaranteed a free, appropriate public education.

5.   **The first major case to examine the validity of psychological tests was:**

    a. *Debra P. v. Turlington.*
    b. *Regents of the University of California v. Bakke.*
    c. *Stell v. Savannah-Chatham County Board of Education.*
    d. *Hobson v. Hansen.*

6.   In *Regents of the University of California v. Bakke*, the plaintiff argued that he was

  a. not provided the special accommodations he needed to take a law school admissions test.
  b. sexually harassed by a professor and not given adequate support and counsel because of his gender.
  c. kept out of better-paying supervisory positions on a grounds maintenance crew because of his race.
  d. denied admission to medical school because he was not a minority group member.

7.   The *Truth in Testing Law* requires

  a. publishers of academic entrance tests to disclose actual test items and their correct answers to examinees who request this information.
  b. psychologists who use intelligence tests to provide actual test items, but not answers to items, before the test is administered to examinees who make the request.
  c. organizations utilizing psychological tests in their employment decisions (e.g., hiring, advancement, firing) to provide copies of the test to employees who request them.
  d. state-funded colleges and universities to disclose the degree to which subjective judgments and biases influence decisions about which students they accept or reject.

8.   Equal Employment Opportunity Commission (EEOC) guidelines define adverse impact in term of

  a. test standardization.
  b. the four-fifths rule.
  c. criterion validity.
  d. use of quotas.

9.   _____ requires public elementary and secondary schools to demonstrate accountability through the use of tests of student progress.

  a. No Child Left Behind
  b. 1991 Civil Rights Act
  c. Equal Employment Opportunities Commission (EEOC) guidelines
  d. Americans with Disabilities Act (ADA)

10.   Currently, _____ in employment discrimination cases have the burden of proof with regard to showing that employee selection procedures are valid and reliable.

  a. judges
  b. employers (defendants)
  c. employees (plaintiffs)
  d. psychologists or expert witnesses

✍**Student Workbook Assignment 20.1**

⊶ **Creating a Case Law Matching Game** ⊷

♦ **DESCRIPTION OF THE ASSIGNMENT**

Chapter 20 describes numerous court decisions relevant to psychological testing; this assignment will help you to organize and learn this information. The assignment is based on a children's game that uses playing cards to test spatial (or location) memory. In the children's version of the game, a deck of cards is spread out and turned face-down on a flat surface. The goal is to turn one card over, try to remember where the matching card is, and then turn that card over. The person who has the most matched pairs at the end of the game is the winner. Assignment 20.1 requires you to create a set of cards on which are written the names, central issues, and outcomes of court cases related to psychological tests.

♦ **DIRECTIONS**

➔ **Before beginning this assignment, make sure you have read Chapter 20.**

(1) You will need about 45 unlined 3"x5" index cards to make one set.

(2) On 15 of the cards, write the names of 15 cases (e.g., *Plessy v. Ferguson*). On another 15 cards write the central issue or question raised in the case. On the remaining 15 cards, write the outcomes of the cases. Thus, each case will have 3 cards. See the example for *Diana v. State Board of Education*, below

(3) Once you have created your set of cards, play the matching game (and ace the exam on Chapter 20)!

Card 1	Card 2	Card 3
Diana v. State Board of Education	The plaintiffs argued that individual standardized tests for placing bilingual children in EMR classes violated the 14th Amendment – these tests had been standardized only on white children.	This case did not go to court because the California Board of Education changed its policies for testing Mexican-American and Chinese-American children – changes included testing children in their primary language and using new tests normed for bilingual children.

◄ CHAPTER 21: *Ethics and the Future of Psychological Testing* ►

<u>**Chapter 21 Outline**</u>

I. Issues Shaping the Field of Testing (text pp. 610-621)

      A. Professional Issues (text pp. 610-614)

      B. Moral Issues (text pp. 614-619)

      C. Social Issues (text pp. 619-621)

II. Current Trends (text pp. 621-624)

      A. The Proliferation of New Tests (text pp. 621-622)

      B. Higher Standards, Improved Technology, and Increasing Objectivity (text pp. 622-623)

      C. Greater Public Awareness and Influence (text pp. 623-624)

      D. The Computerization of Tests (text p. 624)

      E. Testing on the Internet (text p. 624)

III. Future Trends (text pp. 624-627)

      A. Future Prospects for Testing Are Promising (text p. 625)

      B. The Proliferation of New and Improved Tests Will Continue (text pp. 625-626)

      C. Controversy, Disagreement, and Change Will Continue (text pp. 626-627)

      D. The Integration of Cognitive Science and Computer Science Will Lead to Several Innovations in Testing (text p. 627)

CHAPTER 21 EXERCISES

I. ISSUES SHAPING THE FIELD OF TESTING (text pp. 610-621)

A. Professional Issues (text pp. 610-614)

1.   All psychological tests are based on assumptions about human functioning. The professional issue for testers concerns whether these assumptions are valid. The two primary assumptions testers make are that people possess characteristics and response tendencies that (1) are relatively stable over time, and (2) are relatively stable across situations (i.e., exist independently of context or environment).   To what extent are these two assumptions accurate?

Assumption (1) _____

_____

_____

Assumption (2) _____

_____

_____

2.   The text authors suggest that a theory consistent with research data would hold that all people possess the ability to adapt to changing circumstances. This ability involves a combination of factors termed the

_____ .

3.   Describe the concept you identified in 2., above. _____

_____

_____

_____

4.   Another professional issue involves the question of whether even the best tests have strong enough psychometric properties to warrant their use. Address this issue, below. _____

_____

_____

_____

_____

_____

5.   A third professional issue concerns the accuracy of clinical approaches to prediction versus actuarial approaches to prediction. Describe both approaches below.

Clinical approach: _____

Actuarial approach: _____

6.   Describe research findings indicating that actuarial approaches are superior to clinical approaches.

_____

_____

_____

_____

7.   Under what circumstances might the predictions of trained practitioners be better than predictions made on the basis of actuarial formulas? _____

_____

8.   What are some potential abuses that might accompany the use of computer software to interpret psychological tests? _____

_____

_____

B. Moral Issues (text pp. 614-619)

9.   Individuals have a right not to be tested and usually must provide their informed consent to be tested. There are three circumstances, however, in which informed consent to testing is *not* required according to APA ethical guidelines. What are these circumstances?

a. _____

b. _____

c. _____

10.   Test takers also have a right to know their test _____ and _____, as well as the bases of any decisions that affect their lives.

11.   Other rights of test takers include the right to know who will have _____ to their test scores and the right to _____ of test results.

12.   What are the dangers of assigning labels such as "learning disabled" or "schizophrenic" to people?

_____

_____

_____

_____

_____

_____

13.   What are the two sides of the "invasion of privacy" issue with regard to psychological testing?

a. _____

_____

_____

b. _____

_____

_____

14.   Both APA ethical codes and state laws regulating the practice of psychology state that *except under specified circumstances*, personal information obtained through testing is communicated to others only with the examinee's consent. What are these specified limits of confidentiality? _____

_____

_____

15.   Give an example of a situation in which a psychologist might be faced with a dilemma involving conflicting loyalties. _____

_____

_____

_____

16.   How are potential ethical dilemmas related to potentially divided loyalties addressed? _____

_____

_____

17.   What are three practices recommended by the APA Code of Ethics with regard to testing diverse populations?

a. _____

_____

b. _____

_____

c. _____

_____

18.   What information must be provided by test constructors in test manuals? _____

_____

_____

C. Social Issues (text pp. 619-621)

19.   In what ways might psychological testing have the potential to be dehumanizing? _____

_____

_____

_____

20.   An important social issue in testing is whether tests are useful to society. Identify one risk and one benefit of psychological tests to society.

Risk: _____

Benefit: _____

21.   Increasingly, expensive psychological, neurological, and psychiatric assessments are available only to whom? _____

II. CURRENT TRENDS (text pp. 621-627)

A. The Proliferation of New Tests (text pp. 621-622)

1.   One reason for the proliferation of new tests is that test developers disagree about the best ways to measure human characteristics. What are two other reasons why new tests continue to be created and published?

a. _____

b. _____

2.   One reason for the proliferation of nontraditional tests, in particular, is the need for new tests based on more recent psychological theories and research. What are two other reasons for the proliferation of nontraditional psychological tests?

a. _____

b. _____

B. Higher Standards, Improved Technology, and Increasing Objectivity (text pp. 622-623)

3.   In the table below, give a specific example or piece of evidence illustrating each trend in testing.

Trend in Testing	Specific example or evidence
Higher standards	
Improved technology	
Increased objectivity	

C. Greater Public Awareness and Influence (text pp. 623-624)

4.   Discuss the most significant benefit of the public's increased awareness of psychological tests.

_____

_____

_____

_____

D. The Computerization of Tests (text p. 624)

5.   List three ways in which computers are used in psychological testing.

a. _____

b. _____

c. _____

E. Testing on the Internet (text p. 624)

There are no questions over this very brief section.

III. FUTURE TRENDS (text pp. 624-627)

A. Future Prospects for Testing Are Promising (text p. 625)

1.   Identify two pieces of evidence in support of the text authors' statement that *the future prospects for testing are promising.* _____

_____

_____

_____

_____

B. The Proliferation of New and Improved Tests Will Continue (text pp. 625-626)

2.   Identify two pieces of evidence in support of the text authors' statement that *the proliferation of new and improved tests will continue.* _____

_____

_____

_____

_____

C. Controversy, Disagreement, and Change Will Continue (text pp. 626-627)

Although there are no Workbook questions on this very brief section of the text, be sure to read it carefully.

D. The Integration of Cognitive Science and Computer Science Will Lead to Several Innovations in Testing (text p. 627)

3.   Identify two innovations in testing resulting from the integration of cognitive science and computer science.

a. _____

_____

b. _____

_____

Concepts and Terms to Know from Chapter Twenty-One

Theoretical concerns about tests

Index of competency

Concerns about the adequacy of tests

Actuarial vs. clinical prediction

human rights

labeling

invasion of privacy

divided loyalties

responsibilities of test users

responsibilities of test constructors

dehumanization

usefulness of tests

access to psychological testing services

CHAPTER 21 PRACTICE QUIZ

1.   **One assumption of questionable accuracy made by testers is that human characteristics and traits**

     a. are strongly influenced by the context or environment.
     b. cannot be reliably measured.
     c. are variable across situations.
     d. are stable over time.

2.   **The interpretation of test results using a set of rules or formulas reflects a(n) _____ approach to prediction.**

     a. clinical
     b. unbiased
     c. inflexible
     d. actuarial

3.   **Which of the following is <u>not</u> correct with regard to the rights of test takers?**

     a. In order to evaluate an individual's decisional capacity, examiners are required to obtain the individual's consent.
     b. Individuals have a right to know what their own test scores and interpretations are.
     c. If other people will have access to an individual's test results, the individual has a right to know who these people are.
     d. When an examiner uses tests to make important decisions about an individual's life, the examiner is required to give the individual information about how the decisions were reached.

4.   **With regard to psychological testing, ethical guidelines concerning _____ focus specifically on the question of who has access to examinees' test results.**

     a. the responsibilities of test developers
     b. informed consent
     c. confidentiality
     d. test security

5.   **Stigma, the self-fulfilling prophecy, and passivity are all potential consequences of**

     a. divided loyalties.
     b. labeling.
     c. actuarial prediction.
     d. invasion of privacy.

6. **Which trend has generated concerns about inadequate involvement of clinicians in the assessment process?**

    a.   increased use of computers to interpret tests
    b.   stricter ethical guidelines regarding test use
    c.   the proliferation of tests based on empirical research findings
    d.   increased cost of psychological testing services

7. **In one study reported in the text, researchers were able to access 850,000 cases in an evaluation of the psychometric properties of a brief IQ test. The unusually large sample size in this study is explained by the fact that**

    a. the brief IQ test was on the Internet.
    b. examinees received monetary incentives for completing the IQ test.
    c. the data set was collected over a period of 20 years.
    d. most examinees completed the IQ test several times.

8. **In recent years, the National Education Association and others have called for the development and use of _____ testing as an alternative assessment approach in the public school system.**

    a.   standardized
    b.   performance
    c.   norm-referenced
    d.   high-stakes

✍Student Workbook Assignment 21.1

⤙ **Identifying Ethical Violations** ⤚

♦ **DESCRIPTION OF THE ASSIGNMENT**

The ethical use of tests is of paramount importance to psychologists. In this assignment, you will identify ethical violations committed by a test-user in a hypothetical case. Then you will describe more ethical behavior with regard to use of tests in the case.

♦ **DIRECTIONS**

➔ **Before beginning this assignment, make sure you have read Chapter 21.**

(1) Read the case presented below.

(2) Refer to Chapter 21 and Appendix 5, *Code of Fair Testing Practices in Education*, to help you identify three specific ethical violations committed by Dr. Colby.

(3) Then, for each violation, describe a more ethical practice.

Dr. Colby administered a battery of psychological tests to Martin, a 9-year-old boy. Martin was referred for psychological testing by his elementary school because the boy was showing significant academic and behavioral problems. After examining Martin, Dr. Colby stated in his written report, "Martin's test results indicated high levels of psychasthenia, suggesting that he is fixated at the phallic stage. It is very possible that he will experience a psychotic breakdown in the near future." Dr. Colby also wrote, "Martin's Full-Scale IQ score on the WAIS-III was below the 2nd percentile, indicating mental deficiency." After Dr. Colby gave Martin's parents a verbal summary of his findings, they were very upset. They asked Dr. Colby for copies of Martin's test scores and the written report. Dr. Colby refused, stating that giving unauthorized individuals these materials would compromise the validity of the tests. Upon leaving the psychologist's office, Martin said to his distraught parents, "That was a test to see if I can go to soccer camp this summer, right? The doctor never said so, but I know that's why! I can't wait for camp!"

⊷ CHAPTER 1 ⊶

I. Basic Concepts
1. page numbers given

III. Historical Perspective
1. pp. 11-12
2. p. 12
3. p. 12
4. sensory and motor functioning, including reaction time, visual acuity, and physical strength
5. mental test
6. pp. 13-14
7. pp. 14-15
8. p. 15
9. The Army Alpha required reading ability, whereas the Army Beta measured the intelligence of illiterate adults.
10. p. 16
11. answers will vary
12. p. 17
13. p. 17-18
14. p. 18
15. p. 19
16. a method of finding the minimum number of dimensions, called factors, to account for a large number of variables
17. 1949
18. p. 20
19. p. 21
20. Psychologists were not allowed to conduct psychotherapy independent of physicians, and this created frustration and resentment regarding the "technician" role in service of physicians
21. pp. 21-22

CHAPTER 1 PRACTICE QUIZ
1. c; 2. a; 3. d; 4. c; 5. b;
6. a; 7. c; 8. d; 9. a; 10. e

⊷ CHAPTER 2 ⊶

II. Scales of Measurement
1. rules; numbers
2. pp. 27-29
3. pp. 29-31
4. ratio; ordinal; nominal; interval; ratio
5. nominal; ordinal; interval; ratio

III. Frequency Distributions
1. see figure 2-3 on p. 33

IV. Percentile Ranks
1. what percent of the scores fall below a particular score

2. Keisha: 80th; Thomas: 47th; Joe: 13th; Corey: 93rd; Marcia: 7th

V. Percentiles
1. a) 10; b) 6; c) 17
2. Answers will vary, but something along the lines of: "Blair, your UAT score of 12 puts you at the 53rd percentile rank, which means that about 53% of students who took the UAT got scores lower than yours."

VI. Describing Distributions
1. 10.6
2. variation
3. all $\Sigma x_1/N = 0$
4. a) 0; b) .67; c) 12
5. a) 0; b) .82; c) 3.46
6. a) 0; b) .89; c) 3.79
7. N=15; ΣX=159; ΣX^2=1935; S=4.22
8. 2.16; 6.38; 10.6; 14.82; 19.04
9. a) Joe's score of 6 places him about 1 SD below the mean; b) Keisha's score of 15 places her about 1 SD above the mean; c) Thomas' score of 11 places him just above the mean; d) Corey's score of 17 places him about 1 ½ SDs above the mean.
10. standardized
11. Joe: -1.09; Keisha: 1.04; Thomas: .10
12. (-3.00) <1st; (-2.00) 2nd; (-1.00) 16th; (+1.00) 84th; (+2.00) 98th; (+3.00) 99.9th
13. (-2.00) 2.28; (-1.30) 9.68; (-.50) 30.58; (+.50) 69.15; (+1.80) 96.41; (+2.00) 97.72
14. (-2.28) 1.13; (-1.77) 3.84; (-.63) 26.43; (+.19) 57.53; (+1.55) 93.54; (+2.06) 98.03
15. (12th) -1.17 or -1.18; (62nd) +.31; (44th) -.15; (95th) +1.64 or +1.65; (29th) -.55; (75th) +.67
16. (-2.28) 27.2; (-1.77) 32.3; (-.63) 43.7; (+.19) 51.9; (+2.55) 75.5; (+3.06) 85.6
17. fourths; 50th; 75th; 100th
18. 20th; 50th; 70th
19. 1; 9; standard nine; 5; 2

VII. Norms
1. percentiles, Z scores, T scores
2. pp. 53-54
3. age
4. tracking
5. (see Figure 2-10) Madeline: 25th; 36.5; Yes; Fiona: 36.0; 39.5; No; Hannah: 24 mos; Yes
6. Fiona: At 36 mos., she is not as long/tall as expected. Her length has not changed substantially from what it was at 24 mos.
7. p. 59
8. pp. 59-62

CHAPTER 2 PRACTICE QUIZ
1. b; 2. a; 3. b; 4. b; 5. a
6. d; 7. a; 8. b; 9. e; 10. c

335

⊰ CHAPTER 3 ⊱

I. The Scatter Diagram
1. see p. 67-68

II. Correlation
1. a) negative; b) no correlation; c) positive
2. c
3. UAT scores and GPA appear to be positively correlated; higher UAT scores are associated with higher GPAs

III. Regression
1. predictions
2. best-fitting
3. see pp. 69-70
4. answers will vary (Find the UAT score of 14 on the x axis. Go straight up until you hit the regression line you drew, then straight over to the left until you identify a GPA).
5. responses will vary

Worksheet 1: $\Sigma X=159$; $\Sigma Y= 47.70$; $\Sigma X^2=1935$; $\Sigma Y^2=155$; $\Sigma XY=525.05$; $N=15$; $\overline{X}=10.60$; $\overline{Y}=3.18$; $(\Sigma X)^2=25281$; $(\Sigma Y)^2=2275.29$; $(\Sigma X)(\Sigma Y)=7584.30$

6. 2.355; .0778
7. (4) Y'=2.67; (10) Y'=3.13; (17) Y'=3.68
8. (4) Y=2.95; (10) Y=2.50 and 3.60; (17) Y=3.40
9. standardized; z
10. (N=10): .t=69, no, --; (N=40): t=1.46, no, --; (N=80): t=2.09, yes, $p<.05$; (N=200): t=3.33, yes, $p<.01$
11. unrelated
12. the mean of Y

IV. Other Correlation Coefficients
1. p. 82
2. see Table 3-4 on p. 82

V. Terms and Issues in the Use of Correlations
1. page numbers given in the table

VI. Multivariate Analysis
1. predictors; outcome
2. linear
3. answers will vary
4. the coefficients in the linear composite are greatly affected by the range of values taken on by the variables; to compare the coefficients to one another, it is necessary to transform the variables into similar units
5. p. 90
6. answers will vary
7. when the task is to find a linear combination of variables that provides maximum discrimination between *categories*

8. I) 2, 6, 8; II) 4, 7, 9; III) 1, 3, 5
9. answers will vary, but the labels should reflect ways in which the 3 items loading on each scale are similar to one another

CHAPTER 3 PRACTICE QUIZ

1. a;   2. c;   3. b;   4. b;   5. b;
6. a;   7. c;   8. d;   9. a;   10. b

⊰ CHAPTER 4 ⊱

I. History and Theory of Reliability
1. true; measurement
2. reliable; unreliable
3. p. 102
4. product moment correlation; Spearman
5. observed score; true score; error
6. random
7. no; explain using pp. 104-105
8. *normal (bell-shaped) distribution curve should be drawn*
9. pp. 104-105
10. standard; error; measurement
11. (a) c; (b) a; (c) answers will vary, but should emphasize the degree of score dispersion represented in each curve
12. standard deviation

II. The Domain Sampling Model
1. sample
2. error
3. true score
4. p. 106

III. Item Response Theory
1a. & 1.b pp. 107-108

IV. Models of Reliability
1. correlation; variance of the true scores; variance of the observed scores
2. p. 108
3. answers will vary
4. p. 109
5. change over time
6. p. 109
7. carryover; overestimates
8. p. 110
9. p. 110
10. p. 111
11. p. 111
12. p. 111-112
13. p. 112
14. .82
15. different

16. $\Sigma pq=1.78$; $\Sigma X=87$; $\Sigma X^2=599$; $S^2=6.74$; $KR_{20}=.79$ (differences of $\pm$ .01 could be due to rounding)

17. when items are not dichotomously scored (e.g., items do not have a correct or incorrect answer)

18. measure the same ability or trait

19. factor analysis

20. p. 116

21. z (standardized)

22. p. 116

23. .475

V. Reliability in Behavioral Observation Studies

1. p. 118

2. judges; same

3. p. 118

4. kappa; chance

VI. Connecting Sources of Error with Reliability Assessment Method

1. see Table 4-2 on p. 120

VII. Using Reliability Information

1. the attribute is measured accurately; the attribute is measured accurately

2. .74

3. true score

4. Clint: 14.26-15.74 (68%), 13.55-16.45 (95%); Marianne: 10.26-11.74 (68%), 9.55-12.45 (95%); Jennifer: 18.26-19.74 (68%), 17.55-20.45 (95%) Anthony: 7.26-8.74 (68%), 6.55-9.45 (95%)

5. a) research; b) focused, complex; c) .95

6. p. 126

7. N=2.39; 2.39x10= 23.90; 23.90-10=13.90; so, about 14 items would have to be added to the 10-item UAT to bring its reliability up to .90.

8. the added items come from the same pool as the original items and they have the same psychometric properties

9. factor analysis; discriminability analysis

10. to estimate what the correlation between two measures would have been if they had not been measured with error

CHAPTER 4 PRACTICE QUIZ

1. b;	2. a;	3. a;	4. a;	5. c;
6. a;	7. a;	8. d;	9. a;	10. c

⇥ CHAPTER 5 ⇤

I. Defining Validity

1. p. 134

2. answers will vary (p. 134)

3. construct-related, criterion-related, content-related

II. Aspects of Validity

1. answers will vary (pp. 135-136)

2. p. 136

3. One possible answer is that examinees can more easily manipulate item scores (e.g., "fake good")

4. p. 136

5. adequately represent the conceptual domain the test is designed to cover

6. pp. 136-137

7. the failure to capture important components of a construct

8. answers will vary

9. p. 137

10. answers will vary

11. a) predictive; b) concurrent; c) concurrent; d) predictive

12. the relationship between a test and a criterion; tells the extent to which the test is valid for making statements about the criterion; when the validity coefficient is squared, it tells the proportion of variation in the criterion that can be explained by the test (coefficient of determination)

13. p. 140

14. the STASS; number of service hours; .36; .13; 13%; service hours; STASS scores; answers will vary, but possibly amount of time students spend working in paid employment, college major, whether students have their own transportation, etc.

15. pp. 143-148

16. pp. 146-147 (section on restricted range)

17. answers will vary

18. a) showing that a test measures the same things as other tests used for the same purpose; b) demonstrating specific relationships that we can expect if the test is measuring what it purports to measure (i.e., hypothesis testing)

19. pp. 149-151

20. Why should anyone create (and therefore purchase and use) a new test if there is already one available that does the same thing?

21. low, unrelated

22. .78 (between OPS and POT)

23. yes; explanations will vary

24. .21 (between BSEI and POT)

25. yes; explanation will vary

26. pp. 153-154

27. .87; .82; .77; .71; .65

28. pp. 154-155

CHAPTER 5 PRACTICE QUIZ

1. a;	2. b;	3. c;	4. b;	5. c;
6. c;	7. b;	8. a;	9. b;	10. c

⇥ CHAPTER 6 ⇤

I. Item Writing

1. acceptable; unacceptable (terminology may be too advanced for age group); unacceptable (double-barreled question: dizzy *and* head hurts); unacceptable (too long and convoluted, also this is a double-barreled question)
2. answers will vary
3. a) simplicity, ease of administration, quick scoring, require absolute judgment; b) less reliable, less precise, do not allow test taker to show understanding
4. p. 160
5. p. 160
6. no one ever selects it (or it is selected by all or nearly all examinees)
7. pp. 160-161
8. 25%; correction, guessing; guessing threshold
9. (1) correct answer is c, *ineffective* because contradictions among options allow one to eliminate the incorrect options; (2) correct answer is c, *ineffective* because information provided in the next item provides the answer; (3) correct answer is a, *ineffective* because information in the previous item provides the answer; (4) correct answer is d, *ineffective* because there is grammatical inconsistency between the stem and the incorrect options but not the correct option.
10. answers will vary; see pp. 162-163
11. a) groupings, rated; b) endpoints, reminded; c) 10; d) visual analogue
12. answers will vary

II. Item Analysis

1. the number (actually, the proportion) of people who get a particular item correct
2. (1) .53; (2) .73; (3) .87; (4) 1.00; (5) .13
3. halfway between 100% of the respondents getting the item corrects and the level of success expected by chance alone
4. (chance performance level is .20); .40+.20=.600
5. .30; .70
6. determines whether the people who have done well on particular items have also done well on the whole test
7. Discrimination indexes: (1) .60; (2) .60; (3) .00; (4) .00; (5) .40
8. (1) discriminates well; (2) discriminates well; (3) does not discriminate; (4) does not discriminate; (5) discriminates well
9. Point-biserial correlations: (1) .51; (2) .69; (3) .01; (4) 0.00; (5) .54
10. see pp. 174-177
11. Total score 1-6: (1) 0; (2) 0; (3) .66; (4) 1.0; (5) 0; Total score 7-10: (1) .75; (2) .75; (3) 1.0; (4) 1.0; (5) 0; Total score 11-14: (1) .40; (2) 1.0;

(3) 1.0; (4) 1.0; (5) 0; Total score 15-18: (1) 1.0; (2) 1.0 (3) .66; (4) 1.0 (5) .60
12. see pp. 174-177
13. see pp. 175-177 and Figure 6.8
14. *retained*: item 1. and maybe item 2.; *eliminated*: items 3., 4., and 5.
15. the level of difficulty of items that can be answered correctly
16. those who do well or poorly on the exam will have different levels of performance
17. answers will vary
18. pp. 178-179 and Figure 6-9
19. p. 179-180
20. pp. 180-181
21. clearly specifying the objectives by writing clear and precise statements about what the learning program is attempting to achieve
22. give the test to two groups, one of which has not been exposed to the learning unit
23. antimode or least frequent score; those above the antimode are considered to have met the objective of the test
24. answers will vary
25. pp. 182-183

CHAPTER 6 PRACTICE QUIZ

1. d; 2. c; 3. a; 4. b; 5. b;
6. a; 7. d; 8. c; 9. c; 10. a

⇥ CHAPTER 7 ⇤

I. The Examiner and the Subject

1. pp. 186-187
2. p. 187
3. procedures for properly administering an IQ test are very specific and race does not have an effect
4. when examiners are given more discretion about the use of the tests
5. how items are presented – explanations, listening to the test rather than reading it
6. p. 189
7. psychiatrists; psychologists
8. pp. 189-190
9. test results can be affected by what an experimenter expects to find
10. very consistent; small magnitude
11. answers will vary
12. pp. 192-193
13. clearly spell out the directions for administration so that they can be duplicated in all situations; include exact words to be read to the test takers; include questions that testers will likely ask and instructions on how to answer them
14. p. 195

15. individuals were more likely to disclose socially undesirable information on computer than during personal interview; individuals had the most positive experience with the computer
16. cannot replace clinical judgment, computerized scoring routines that have errors or are poorly validated
17. pp. 196-197
18. educational
19. pp. 197-198

II. Behavioral Assessment Methodology
1. p. 198
2. answers will vary; see pp. 199-200
3. pp. 200-201
4. p. 201
5. tendency to ascribe positive attributes independently of the observed behavior; page 201

CHAPTER 7 PRACTICE QUIZ
1. c; 2. d; 3. d; 4. a; 5. b;
6. d; 7. a; 8. b; 9. d; 10. b

⊷ CHAPTER 8 ⊶

I. The Interview as a Test
1. pp. 206-207
II. Reciprocal Nature of Interviewing
1. p. 208
III. Principles of Effective Interviewing
1. interpersonal attraction—the degree to which people share a feeling of understanding, mutual respect, similarity, etc.
2. pp. 208-209
3. p. 209
4. answers will vary
5. a) to discover how someone deals with stress or responds to evaluation, hostility, etc.; b) answers will vary, but possibilities include interviews with police officers who will encounter hostility and resistance, government agents who may be taken hostage and interrogated, etc.
6. p. 210
7. p. 211
8. answers will vary
9. they imply the interviewer is listening, and the interviewee should continue talking
10. answers will vary
11. answers will vary
12. p. 213
13. pp. 215-217
14. see text pp. 215-217
IV. Types of Interviews
1. discrepancies between a) what the person is and what he or she wants to become; b) what the person

says about himself or herself and what he or she does; c) the person's perception of himself or herself and the interviewer's experience of the person
2. p. 218
3. p. 218
4. pp. 218-219
5. pp. 222-223
6. to understand individuals' backgrounds so that one can accurately interpret individual test scores
7. answers will vary
8. p. 224
9. answers will vary; see pp. 224-225
10. p. 225
V. Sources of Error in Interviews
1. answers will vary
2. pp. 226-227
3. pp. 227-229
4. pp. 229-230

CHAPTER 8 PRACTICE QUIZ
1. b; 2. d; 3. a; 4. d; 5. a;
6. a; 7. b; 8. c; 9. b; 10. c

⊷ CHAPTER 9 ⊶

I. The Problem of Defining Intelligence
1. answers will vary
2. p. 234
3. a) examines the properties of a test through an evaluation of its correlates and underlying dimensions; b) examine the processes that underlie how we learn and solve problems; c) focuses on how humans adapt to real world demands
4. to recommend a procedure for identifying so-called subnormal (intellectually limited) children
II. Binet's Principles of Test Construction
1. pp. 235-236
2. tasks that could be completed by between 66.67% and 75% of the children of a particular age group and also by a smaller proportion of younger children but a larger proportion of older ones
3. p. 237
4. 12 years
5. p. 237
III. Spearman's Model of General Mental Ability
1. consists of one general factor plus a large number of specific factors
2. pp. 237-238
3. the shared variance underlying performance on a diverse set of tests

4. fluid intelligence allows us to reason, think, and acquire new knowledge; crystallized intelligence is the knowledge and understanding we have acquired

IV. The Early Binet Scales
1. pp. 239-240
2. p. 240
3. verbal, language, reading ability

V. Terman's Stanford-Binet Intelligence Scales
1. 1911
2. p. 242
3. IQ = Mental Age / Chronological Age x 100
4. 100; 140; 88.6; 58.3; 65
5. 19.5
6. p. 243
7. 16; belief that mental age ceased to improve after 16
8. p. 244
9. p. 245
10. tasks that showed an increase in the percentage passing with an increase in age; tasks that correlated highly with scores as a whole
11. a) 100, 16; b) mental age; c) percentile
12. 2100

VI. The Modern Binet Scales
1. hierarchical; multidimensional
2. p. 247
3. Thurstone; primary mental abilities
4. point scales (description on p. 247 & 249)
5. Figure 9-9, p. 249
6. similar; difficulty
7. start point
8. a) level at which a minimum criterion number of correct responses is obtained; b) level at which a certain number of incorrect responses indicates the items are too difficult
9. 10; 3
10. 100; 15
11. pp. 250-252

CHAPTER 9 PRACTICE QUIZ
1. c; 2. b; 3. a; 4. d; 5. d;
6. c; 7. a; 8. b; 9. d; 10. c

⇥ CHAPTER 10 ⇤

I. The Wechsler Intelligence Scales
1. single score; nonintellective
2. p. 257
3. pp. 257-258
4. pp. 258-259

II. From the Wechsler-Bellevue Intelligence Scale To the WAIS-IV
1. 1081 whites from the eastern United States

2. 1955, 1981, 1997; 2008
III. Scales, Subtests, and Indexes
1. the capacity to act purposefully and to adapt to the environment
2. pp. 260-265
3. 10, 3
4. inferential norming; norms
5. core; 100; 15
6. p. 266 and Figure 10.6
8. 100; 15; general intelligence

IV. Interpretive Features of the Wechsler Tests
1. a) the verbal score has been confirmed and examinee appears to have intellectual deficits; b) other factors, such as education, language, and culture have influenced the verbal score
2. discrepancies
3. p. 268
4. hypotheses

V. Psychometric Properties of the Wechsler Adult Scale
1. pp. 270-271

VI. Evaluation of the Wechsler Adult Scales
1. the reliability of the individual subtests is lower and makes pattern analysis dubious, if not hazardous

VII. Downward Extensions of the WAIS-IV: The WISC-IV and the WPPSI-III
1. 6; 16; 11
2. VIQ-PIQ; indexes
3. a) VCI core subtests are comprehension, similarities, & vocabulary subtests, and supplemental subtests are information & word reasoning; b) PRI core subtests are block design, picture concepts,& matrix reasoning, and supplemental subtest is picture completion; c) PSI core subtests are coding & symbol search, and supplemental subtest is cancellation; d) WMI core subtests are digit span & letter-number sequencing, and supplemental subtest is arithmetic
4. p. 272
5. p. 273
6. pp. 273-275
7. Preschool; Primary
8. pp. 275-276
9. 2; 6; 3; 11
10. pp. 276-277

CHAPTER 10 PRACTICE QUIZ
1. d; 2. b; 3. a; 4. b; 5. c;
6. a; 7. b; 8. c; 9. d; 10. c

⊸ CHAPTER 11 ⊷

1. p. 280
I. Alternative Individual Ability Tests Compared With the Binet and Wechsler Scales
1a. and 1b. pp. 280-281 and Table 11-1 (p. 282)
II. Alternatives Compared With One Another
1. pp. 282-283
2. p. 283 and Table 11-2
III. Specific Individual Ability Tests
1. a) to evaluate mentally retarded adults; b) nonverbal test for adolescent delinquents; c) performance tests for non-English-speaking adult immigrants to the US
2. a) Brazelton Neonatal Scales on pp. 284-286; b) Gesell Developmental Schedules on pp. 286-288; c) Bayley Scales on pp. 288-290; d) Catell Infant Intelligence Scale on pp. 290-291
3. 2 ½ ; 8 ½
4. a) composite score; b) 100, 16; c) reflects how well the child has integrated prior learning experiences and adapted them to the demands of the scales; d) see Figure 11-7
5. .81; .71
6. pp. 292-294
7. 3; 18
8. p. 294
9. achievement; nonverbal
10. 10; 3; 100; 15
11. a) sequential-simultaneous and mental processing achievement; b) African American; c) gifted; d) Mexican Americans
12. p. 295-296
13. a) Columbia Mental Maturity Scale on pp. 296-297; b) Peabody Picture Vocabulary Test on pp. 297-298; c) Leiter International Performance Scale on pp. 299-300; d) Porteus Maze Test on p. 300
IV. Testing Learning Disabilities
1. severe discrepancy between a child's potential to achieve and his/her actual school achievement
2. a) Individuals, Disabilities, Education; b) every eligible child with a disability to a free appropriate public education; c) have a disability and also have his or her educational performance adversely affected by the disability
3. disorganization, careless effort, forgetfulness, refusal to do schoolwork or homework, slow performance, poor attention, moodiness
4. p. 301-302 and Table 11-4 on p. 303
5. 2; 10; general language, spoken language, and written language
6. general intellectual ability, specific cognitive abilities, scholastic aptitude, oral language, and achievement
7. p. 304
8. p. 305

9. p. 305
10. p. 305
11. require a subject to copy various designs
12. p. 306
13. a) Benton Visual Retention Test on p. 306; b) Bender Visual Motor Gestalt Test on pp. 306-307; c) Memory- For-Designs Test on pp. 307-308
14. the ability to be original, to combine known facts in new ways, to find new relationships between known facts
15. pp. 308-309
16. answers will vary
17. reading; spelling; arithmetic
18. grade-level reading

CHAPTER 11 PRACTICE QUIZ
1. c;   2. b;   3. d;   4. c;   5. a;
6. a;   7. c;   8. b;   9. d;   10. d

⊸ CHAPTER 12 ⊷

I. Comparison of Group and Individual Ability Tests
1. In group tests, there are no safeguards to prevent a person for receiving a low score for reasons other than low ability, such as lack of motivation, high anxiety, or lack of cooperation.
2. p. 314 and Table 12-2 on p. 315
3. pp. 314-315 and Table 12-2 on p. 315
II. Overview of Group Tests
1. paper-and-pencil; multiple-choice
2. p. 316
III. Group Tests in the Schools: K-12th Grade
1. a) learned; content; b) potential; criterion; c) future; generally
2. pp. 318-320
3. pp. 320-322
IV. College Entrance Tests
1. 1926
2. 500; 20; 80; 420; 480
3. The test developers re-normed the test, thus restoring the national average to 500; the new norms pushed up national SAT averages about 75 points on Verbal (new average score was 504) and 20 points on Math (new average score was 516).
4. 200; 800; 2400
5. 45; p. 323
6. pp. 323-324
7. middle; answers will vary
8. .40; 16%
9. African American, Latino/Latina, and female students
10. 1955; undertake additional schooling
11. representativeness

12. 2005; non-native speakers of English

13. English, mathematics usage, social studies reading, natural science reading

14. 19; 5

15. SAT; high (in the high .80s)

V. Graduate and Professional School Entrance Tests

1. verbal; quantitative; analytic reasoning

2. p. 326

3. majors

4. p. 326

5. 500; 100

6. a) reasoning, identification of opposites, use of analogies, paragraph comprehension; b) arithmetic reasoning, algebra, geometry

7. pp. 327-329

8. p. 329

9. verbal; quantitative; analytical; a corresponding increase in non-U.S. test-takers who tend to core higher on GRE-Q and lower on GRE-V

10. verbal; relationships

11. predictive; 25-34; 35-44

12. facing bias

13. a) reading comprehension; b) logical reasoning; c) analytical reasoning

14. undergraduate GPA and LSAT scores

15. reliability; first-year grades; resemble the ones needed for success in the first year of law school.

16. p. 333

17. answers will vary

VI. Nonverbal Group Ability Tests

Answers to sample matrices-type items: (1) 6; (2) 3

1. pp. 333-337

2. employment in government agencies

3. p. 338

4. 1952; 18; 54; 11

5. p. 338

6. Defense; occupational training

7. p. 338

8. p. 339

CHAPTER 12 PRACTICE QUIZ

1. b; 2. d; 3. c; 4. c; 5. b;
6. a; 7. d; 8. b; 9. c; 10. a

⇥ CHAPTER 13 ⇤

1. p. 342

2. p. 343

I. Strategies of Personality Test Construction

1. p. 344

2. p. 344

3. pp. 344-345

4. p. 345

5. the item content does not matter

6. p. 345

7. a) to find the minimum number of factors that accounts for as much variability in the data as possible; b) by ascertaining what the items related to a particular factor have in common.

8. p. 346

II. The Logical-Content Strategy

1. p. 346

2. p. 347

3. Bernreuter Personality Inventory could be used with examinees as young as 13; both produced more than one score

4. p. 347

5. that the subject takes a normal approach to the test, complies with instructions, reads each item, answers honestly, and interprets the test items in the same way as the test constructor or test user

6. answers will vary

III. The Criterion-Group Strategy

1. a) true or false; b) fake bad, fake good;
c) psychological disorders; d) anger; e) T, 50, 10;
f) major psychiatric disorders; g) 6th, 8th

2. pp. 350-351, also Table 13-1

3. to make sure that the items were valid for new criterion and control groups

4. p. 352

5. p. 352-353, also Table 13-2

6. 70; 2; 65; 1.5

7. the two highest scales (two-point code)

8. *in order from top to bottom of the table*:
(6) Paranoia; (2) Depression; (1) Hypochondriasis;
(0) Social introversion; (7) Psychasthenia;
(3) Hysteria; (9) Hypomania; (8) Schizophrenia;
(5) Masculinity-femininity; (4) Psychopathic deviate); two-point code: 8-6

9. 86* 97" 2' 40- 3/ 15: (note: last 2 symbols, "/" and ":" are not presented in the text)

10. pp. 355-357

11. p. 357

12. age, gender, race, place of residence, intelligence, education, socioeconomic status

13. pp. 358-359

14. normally adjusted

15. pp. 359-360

16. p. 360

IV. The Factor Analytic Strategy

1. dimensions

2. p. 361

3. pp. 361-363

4. p. 363

5. .83

6. .75; second-order

7. Table 13-4 on p. 362

8. common; unique

V. The Theoretical Strategy

1. predictions are made about the nature of the scale, which is based on a theory; if the predictions hold up, the validity of the scale is supported
2. pp. 364-365
3. p. 365
4. consistency
5. p. 366
6. p. 367
7. p. 367-368
8. F; social desirability
9. research; normal
10. pp. 368-369
11. p. 368-369

VI. Combination Strategies

1. answers will vary
2. answers will vary
3. p. 370
4. .80s; .90s; .80s
5. a) Conscientiousness; b) Openness to Experience; c) Extroversion; d) Agreeableness; e) Neuroticism
6. p. 372
7. crystallized intelligence
8. p. 373

VII. Frequently Used Measures of Positive Personality Traits

1. Page numbers given in table

VII. Future of Positive Personality Research

1. Answers to all 3 questions on pp. 378-379

CHAPTER 13 PRACTICE QUIZ

1. a;   2. d;   3. c;   4. d;   5. a;
6. a;   7. d;   8. b;   9. a;   10. a

➤ CHAPTER 14 ➤

I. .The Projective Hypothesis

1. p. 383

II. The Rorschach Inkblot Test

1. psychological disorders
2. p. 385
3. black and gray; black, gray, and red;
4. p. 386
5. free association
6. p. 386
7. inquiry
8. *Location*: circled area indicates a D or Dd response; *Determinant*: What it was that led the examinee to see the percept; Form, Movement (M, FM. or m), Color, Shading; "it looks like a horse because of its shape (F)…this leg just looks like it is moving (FM)"; *Form Quality*: The extent to which the percept matches the properties of the inkblot; F+, F, F-; answers will vary; *Content*: The content of the percept; many scores possible; "looks like a …horse (A)"; *Popular*: how frequently is the percept seen; popular or original; answers will vary, although this would probably <u>not</u> be a popular response
9. p. 387
10. motor; internal
11. interact
12. p. 391
13. pp. 391-392
14. they capitalized on the Barnum effect; they gave different and even contradictory analyses for an individual client, but they were able to use other test data to support their analyses; they had vast experience with the Rorschach
15. Comprehensive System
16. pp. 393-399
17. administration

III. An Alternative Inkblot Test: The Holtzman

1. one response; standardized; alternate; objective
2. p. 399
3. p. 399

IV. The Thematic Apperception Test

1. p. 400 and Table 14-3
2. needs
3. p. 400
4. structured; ambiguous
5. p. 401
6. administration; scoring
7. pp. 401-402
8. Because an unusually long reaction time might indicate a specific problem in the area
9. judgment; intuition
10. *Hero*: young man; *Needs*: answers will vary, but possibly needs for abasement, autonomy, infavoidance, or succorance; *Press*: answers will vary, but possibly financial situation and family stress; *Themes*: answers will vary, but possibly resentment toward women and disempowerment; *Outcomes*: answers will vary, but the general outcome appears to be negative
11. projective hypothesis
12. unstandardized
13. achievement need
14. content; criterion
15. .19; .22

V. Alternative Apperception Procedures

1. *Family of Man*; Southern Mississippi
2. 3; 10; animal
3. Latino/Latina
4. p. 405

VI. Nonpictorial Projective Procedures

1. page numbers given in the table

CHAPTER 14 PRACTICE QUIZ

1. c.   2. a;   3. b;   4. c;   5. d;
6. b;   7. a;   8. b;   9. a.   10. a

343

⇥ CHAPTER 15 ⇤

I. Cognitive-Behavioral Assessment Procedures
1. pp. 413-414 and Table 15-2
2. p. 415, also Table 15-3
3. p. 417
4. that the person's responses reflect individual differences and measure some other observable behavior; the face validity of the subject's responses
5. pp. 418-419
6. situations involving fear and avoidance behaviors, e.g., of open places, snakes, etc.
7. pp. 419-420, also see Table 15-5
8. p. 420
9. p. 421
10. It assumes that both normal and disordered behaviors develop according to the same laws and differ only in extremes.
11. pp. 421-422
12. Schemas organize prior experience, guide the interpretations of new experiences, and shape expectancies and predictions.
13. answers will vary
14. p. 422
15. beliefs and expectations
16. 100
17. anxiety; depression
18. 50; cognitions
19. p. 423
20. p. 424
21. *environmental antecedents* include socializing with friends at a bar, work stress, and that his friends buy him drinks because he has not told them he is abstaining; *cognitive antecedents* include his belief that he is "in control" of his drinking, that he deserves a drink as a reward, that his friends might be offended if he refuses a drink, that he should be able to drink like others, and that drinking helps him interact socially
22. *environmental consequences* include more social interaction with friends and attractive women; *cognitive consequences* (short-term) include feeling relaxed, having fun, and the belief that alcohol use enhances his attractiveness to women.
23. answers will vary
24. p. 425

II. Psychophysical Procedures
1. p. 426
2. increases in blood pressure, skin conductance
3. p. 426
4. p. 426-427
5. several problems mentioned on p. 427

III. Computers and Psychological Testing
1. p. 427

2. p. 427
3. p. 428
4. pp. 428-429
5. Tests that measure negative affect (e.g., depression, anxiety) show elevated scores among computer-anxious individuals; computer anxiety also affects educational tests, especially tests of math skills.
6. p. 429
7. projective
8. essay; Project Essay Grade
9. p. 431
10. p. 432
11. p. 432
12. p. 433
13. p. 433
14. p. 434
15. ability
16. Because only items necessary for the evaluation of the test taker are administered, so there are fewer items on the test.
17. p. 435
18. GRE, GMAT, TOEFL
19. schizophrenia
20. transfer; iconic
21. interval; slowly
22. backward; mentally retarded
23. pp. 438-439

CHAPTER 15 PRACTICE QUIZ
1. b; 2. c; 3. d; 4. a; 5. c;
6. b; 7. c; 8. b; 9. d; 10. a

⇥ CHAPTER 16 ⇤

I. Measuring Interests
1. Carnegie
2. 80; Strong; Kuder
3. p. 443
4. p. 443
5. a) 54, 32; b) occupational, population;
c) 50, 10; d) 300; e) job satisfaction;
f) relatively stable; g) 17; h) gender, theory
6. Strong-Campbell
7. p. 444
8. Table 16-1 on p. 445
9. pp. 444-445
10. 1985
11. p. 446
12. Strong Interest Inventory (SII); Campbell Interest and Skill Survey
13. 200; skill
14. Holland's; 50; 10
15. Likert; 41; technology; normative

16. p. 449
17. interests; people employed in various occupations
18. college majors
19. pp. 451-452
21. a) reliabilities; b) college major; c) their knowledge of themselves; d) Men; women; e) career preferences
22. pp. 452-454
23. p. 454
24. answers will vary
25. p. 456
26. p. 456

II. Measuring Personal Characteristics for Job Placement
1. Holland's; tests
2. p. 457
3. pp. 457-458
4. cause; entities; times
5. situations; dispositions or trait

CHAPTER 16 PRACTICE QUIZ
1. c;   2. b;   3. a;   4. d;   5. b;
6. a;   7. c;   8. a;   9. d;   10. b

⊣ CHAPTER 17 ⊢

I. Neuropsychological Assessment
1. p. 462
2. a) both focus on sensations, perceptions, and motor movements; b) both study mood and adaptations to psychosocial situations; c) both use psychological tests
3. p. 463
4. neuro-imaging
5. p. 463
6. speech; left; cerebral cortex; function
7. p. 465
8. p. 465
9. alcoholic; Huntington's; recent
10. p. 455 and Figure 17-2
11. two-thirds; left
12. p. 466
13. To provide an initial baseline, and then to identify neurological changes over time.
14. brain plasticity (p. 468)
15. adaptive; attention
16. p. 469
17. focus execute; sustain; encode; shift
18. dyslexia; single words; 80
19. faking
20. p. 470
21. verbal ability, coordination, visual-spatial ability

22. p. 471
23. MMPI; WAIS
24. Table 17-2 on p. 474
25. hemispheres; left
26. p. 473
27. p. 475
28. standardized
29. 269; 24
30. Table 17-3 on p. 476
31. learning; errors
32. p. 478
33. a) they may do well on early trials but reach a plateau where more trials don't show improvement; b) they may show inconsistent recall across trials
34. pp. 478-479
35. mild to severe learning disabilities; attention deficit disorder; mental retardation; neurological disorders; psychiatric disorders
36. national
37. 480-481

II. Anxiety and Stress Assessment
1. definitions: pp. 481-482; examples: answers will vary
2. worry, apprehension and tension, also activation of autonomic nervous system
3. p. 482
4. a) 20; b) .73; .86; inconsistent; c) concurrent
5. p. 483
6. emotional problems (panic disorder); Japanese
7. problem-solving, growth, wishful thinking, advice-seeking, minimizing threat, seeking support, self-blame
8. p. 484
9. activities and attitudes people use to avoid stress; strategies for working through stressful events; socialization responses—how each strategy helps the examinee cope with a specific stressful event
10. p. 484
11. pp. 484-485

III. Quality of Life Assessment
1. answers will vary
2. "Health is a complete state of physical, mental, and social well-being and not merely absence of disease."
3. p. 486
4. Medical Outcome Study Short Form-36
5. p. 487
6. p. 487
7. pp. 488-489
8. p. 489
9. a) sensors, b) monitors, c) mobile phones
10. real, everyday life experiences
11. pp. 489-490
12. p. 490
13. cognitive, emotional, motor, sensory function

14. physical and biological sciences, verbal reasoning, and writing skills
15. psychological, social, and biological; 95; 55
16. p. 494
17. 44; 72; tobacco use, lipids, blood pressure

CHAPTER 17 PRACTICE QUIZ

1. b;   2. d;   3. c;   4. d;   5. b;
6. c;   7. c;   8. a;   9. b;   10. d

⊸ CHAPTER 18 ⊢

I. Personnel Psychology: The Selection of Employees

1. *Personnel psychology* is the study and practice of job analysis, job recruitment, employee selection, and the evaluation of employee performance; *Organizational psychology* focuses on leadership, job satisfaction, employee motivation, and the functioning of organizations
2. structured
3. p. 501
4. p. 501
5. cutting score
6. Table 18-1 on p. 502
7. pp. 502-503
8. answers will vary
9. answers will vary
10. *Answers for Summary Table, by row*: Program B: .15, 90%, .61, .61-.60, .01 or 1%; Program C: .30, 40%, .71, .71-.60, .11 or 11%; Program D: .45, 10%, .87, .87-.60, .27 or 27%.
11. Program B: Out of every 90 applicants accepted, about 55 will succeed and about 35 will fail; Program C: Out of every 40 applicants accepted, about 28 will succeed and about 12 will fail; Program D: Out of every 10 applicants accepted, about 9 will succeed and 1 will fail.
12. Programs C and D; explanations will vary
13. dichotomous; continuum
14. dollar value
15. compensation package
16. students come into the classroom with different levels of ability
17. growth trajectories
18. pp. 513-515
19. determination of how much information a test contributes beyond a simpler method of prediction
20. p. 517
21. Because simple self-reports are often as good as complex, expensive, and time-consuming personality tests
22. job-related; psychologically

II. Personnel Psychology From the Employee's Perspective: Fitting People to Jobs

1. p. 519
2. p. 519
3. p. 519
4. mental ability or intelligence; 2007

III. Measuring Characteristics of the Work Setting

1. human behavior and events that occur in relation to environmental and behavioral settings
2. answers will vary
3. pp. 521-522
4. answers will vary (see Table 18-6 on p. 523)
5. answers will vary

IV. Job Analysis

1. pp. 525-527

V. Measuring the Person-Situation Interaction

1. interactions
2. p. 528
3. p. 529

CHAPTER 18 PRACTICE QUIZ

1. d;   2. b;   3. d;   4. a;   5. c;
6. b;   7. c;   8. d;   9. b;   10. b

⊸ CHAPTER 19 ⊢

I. Why is Test Bias Controversial?

1. 15; 1
2. ethnicity
3. p. 533

II. Test Fairness and the Law

1. p. 514
2. a screening procedure has adverse impact if it systematically rejects higher proportions of minority than nonminority applicants.
3. validity

III. The Traditional Defense of Testing

1. differential
2. pp. 537-538
3. That a fair test asks questions examinees can answer, and a biased test does not ask about things an examinee knows.
4. external criteria
5. p. 540
6. p. 540
7. differential item functioning
8. pp. 540-541
9. Because the items that differentiated the groups tended to be the easiest items, so the test was more difficult for everyone.
10. white males

11. p. 542

12. predictive

13. answers will vary, but should emphasize the idea that the test predicts performance for both groups equally well

14. 6

15. lower; higher

16. pp. 543-544

17. different

18. answers will vary, but should emphasize the fact that if the test was used to predict criterion performance of all examinees, it would be biased against Group B examinees since it does not seem to be related to the criterion for this group.

IV. Other Approaches to Testing Minority Group Members

1. p. 545

2. pp. 545-546

3. p. 547

4. scientific racism

5. survival quotient

6. pp. 548-549

7. p. 550

8. pp. 550-551

9. social-system; sociocultural

V. Suggestions for Solutions

1. p. 553

2. unqualified individualism; minority

3. quota; failure

4. reduced scores

5. patterns of problem solving that characterize different subcultures

6. differential process

7. p. 557

8. Most of the tests used to assess the potential of children are simply valid predictors of how well children will do on *other* standardized tests.

9. pp. 558-560

10. pp. 560-561 (Focused Example 19-6)

VI. Changing the Social Environment

1. *Less than $10,000*: about 425 (V), about 445 (M); *$50,000-$60,000*: about 515 (V), about 520 (M); *more than $100,000*: about 565 (V), about 575(M)

2. answers will vary

3. answers will vary

CHAPTER 19 PRACTICE QUIZ

1. b; 2. c; 3. a; 4. b; 5. a;

6. d; 7. d; 8. c; 9. b; 10. b

⌐ CHAPTER 20 ⌐

I. Laws Governing the Use of Tests

1. interstate commerce

2. answers will vary

3. due process and equal protection under the law

4. public employment and institutions that receive public funds

5. a) race, color, gender, national origin, religion; b) is less than four-fifths of the group with the highest rate; c) must present evidence for the validity of the selection procedure

6. 100; women; minority

7. p. 576

8. a) disclose all studies on the validity of a test; b) provide a complete disclosure to students about what scores mean and how they were calculated; c) on request by a student, provide a copy of the test questions, the correct answers, and the student's answers

9. p. 578

10. answers will vary

11. primary; secondary

12. p. 579

13. p. 580

II. Major Lawsuits That Have Affected Psychological Testing

1. page numbers on which cases can be found are listed in the table

III. Personnel Cases

1. p. 599

2. validity

3. employment tests must be valid and reliable

4. any procedure that appears to discriminate because of the ratio of minorities selected violates the law

5. p. 600

6. statistical selection ratios are sufficient evidence of adverse impact

7. pp. 600-601

8. a) employer; b) race, gender, or ethnic background

9. pp. 601-602

10. to release a copy of the test to the employee to check scoring

10. Title VII protects individuals, not just the groups to which they belong; African American applicants had been discriminated against by the use of a test that did not have validity for the particular job

11. well-constructed

12. criterion; minority

13. white-collar

14. p. 605

15. p. 605

16. the test need not be modified to ensure a passing grade for a person unable to learn because of a disability

17. readers could be provided for portions of the test that did not measure reading competency

18. p. 606

CHAPTER 20 PRACTICE QUIZ
1. b; 2. d; 3. a; 4. b; 5. d;
6. d; 7. a; 8. b; 9. a; 10. b

⊣ CHAPTER 21 ⊢

I. Issues Shaping the Field of Testing
1. pp. 610-614
2. index of competency
3. p. 612
4. p. 613
5. trained professionals interpret test results; test results are interpreted using a set of rules and statistical formulas
6. p. 614
7. when clinicians use data from several sources such as a test battery, an interview, and a case history
8. p. 615
9. p. 615
10. scores; interpretations
11. access; confidentiality
12. pp. 615-616
13. p. 616
14. when withholding information causes danger to the person or society, and when the case records are subpoenaed by the court
15. p. 617
16. p. 617
17. p. 618
18. p. 618
19. p. 619
20. answers will vary
21. those who can afford them (out-of-pocket) and those who have good insurance coverage

II. Current Trends
1. p. 621
2. pp. 621-622
3. answers will vary; see pp. 622-623
4. pp. 623-644
5. p. 624

III. Future Trends
1. p. 625
2. pp. 625-626
3. p. 627

CHAPTER 21 PRACTICE QUIZ
1. d; 2. d; 3. a; 4. c; 5. b
6. a; 7. a; 8. b

⊷ SECTION 4: *MEASURES* ⊶

IMPORTANT NOTE TO STUDENTS: Do not complete the measures in this section until your instructor directs you to do so.

Contents

⊸ PES (1st Administration) ⊱

DIRECTIONS: Circle the number corresponding to the extent to which you agree with each of the 10 statements below. Be as accurate and honest as you can when responding to each statement, and try not to let your answers to one question influence your answers to other questions. There are no correct or incorrect answers.

	Strongly agree	Moderately agree	Slightly agree	Slightly disagree	Moderately disagree	Strongly disagree
1. When I get what I want it's usually because I worked hard for it.	6	5	4	3	2	1
2. When I make plans I am almost certain to make them work.	6	5	4	3	2	1
3. I prefer games involving some luck over games requiring pure skill.	1	2	3	4	5	6
4. I can learn almost anything if I set my mind to it.	6	5	4	3	2	1
5. My major accomplishments are entirely due to my hard work and ability.	6	5	4	3	2	1
6. I usually don't set goals because I have a hard time following through on them.	1	2	3	4	5	6
7. Competition discourages excellence.	1	2	3	4	5	6
8. Often people get ahead just by being lucky.	1	2	3	4	5	6
9. On any sort of exam or competition I like to know how well I do relative to everyone else.	6	5	4	3	2	1
10. It's pointless to keep working on something that's too difficult for me.	1	2	3	4	5	6

From Paulhus, D. (1983). Sphere-specific measures of perceived control. *Journal of Personality and Social Psychology, 44,* 1253-1265. Used with permission.

⊷ LOT-R (1ˢᵗ Administration) ⊶

DIRECTIONS: Circle the number corresponding to the extent to which you agree with each of the 10 statements below. Be as accurate and honest as you can when responding to each statement, and try not to let your answers to one question influence your answers to other questions. There are no correct or incorrect answers. Answer according to your own feelings, rather than how you think "most people" would answer.

	I agree a lot	I agree a little	I neither agree nor disagree	I disagree a little	I disagree a lot
1. In uncertain times, I usually expect the best.	4	3	2	1	0
2. It's easy for me to relax.	4	3	2	1	0
3. If something can go wrong for me, it will.	0	1	2	3	4
4. I'm always optimistic about my future.	4	3	2	1	0
5. I enjoy my friends a lot.	4	3	2	1	0
6. It's important for me to keep busy.	4	3	2	1	0
7. I hardly ever expect things to go my way.	0	1	2	3	4
8. I don't get upset too easily.	4	3	2	1	0
9. I rarely count on good things happening to me.	0	1	2	3	4
10. Overall, I expect more good things to happen to me than bad.	4	3	2	1	0

From Carver, C. S., at www.psy.miami.edu/faculty/ccarver/sclLOT-R.html. (Permission for use not required).

⊶ WOFO-C (1ˢᵗ Administration) ⊷

DIRECTIONS: Circle the number corresponding to the extent to which you agree with each of the 5 statements below. Be as accurate and honest as you can when responding to each statement, and try not to let your answers to one question influence your answers to other questions. There are no correct or incorrect answers.

	Strongly agree	Somewhat agree	Neither agree nor disagree	Somewhat disagree	Strongly disagree
1. I enjoy working in situations involving competition with others.	5	4	3	2	1
2. It is important to me to perform better than others on a task.	5	4	3	2	1
3. I feel that winning is important in both work and games.	5	4	3	2	1
4. It annoys me when other people perform better than I do.	5	4	3	2	1
5. I try harder when I'm in competition with other people.	5	4	3	2	1

From *Achievement and Achievement Motives: Psychological and Sociological Approaches* by Janet Spence © 1983 by W.H. Freeman and Company. Used with permission.

⇥ ICQ (1ˢᵗ Administration) ⇤

DIRECTIONS: Circle the number corresponding to the extent to which you agree with each of the 8 statements below. Be as accurate and honest as you can when responding to each statement, and try not to let your answers to one question influence your answers to other questions. There are no correct or incorrect answers.

	Strongly agree	Agree	Neutral	Disagree	Strongly disagree
1. I perform better when I am competing against someone rather than when I am the only one striving for a goal.	5	4	3	2	1
2. I do *not* feel that winning is important in both work and games.	1	2	3	4	5
3. When I win an award or game it means that I am the best compared to everyone else that was playing. It was only fair that the best person win the game.	5	4	3	2	1
4. In school, I always liked to be the first one finished with a test.	5	4	3	2	1
5. I have always wanted to be better than others.	5	4	3	2	1
6. When nominated for an award, I focus on how much better or worse the other candidates' qualifications are as compared to mine.	5	4	3	2	1
7. I would want an A because that would mean I did better than other people.	5	4	3	2	1
8. Because it is important that a winner is decided, I do not like to leave a game unfinished.	5	4	3	2	1

From Griffin-Pierson, S. (1990). The Competitiveness Questionnaire: A measure of two components of competitiveness. *Measurement and Evaluation in Counseling and Development, 23,* 108-115. Used with permission.

⊸ AEAS (1ˢᵗ Administration) ⊶

DIRECTIONS: Circle the number corresponding to the extent to which you agree with each of the 12 statements below. Be as accurate and honest as you can when responding to each statement, and try not to let your answers to one question influence your answers to other questions. There are no correct or incorrect answers.

	Strongly agree	Agree	Neutral	Disagree	Strongly disagree
1. I might cut class if I think that the lecture material will not be on the test.	1	2	3	4	5
2. I sometimes wonder if I am really "college material".	1	2	3	4	5
3. In a "pass-fail" course, I try to exert just enough effort to avoid failing.	1	2	3	4	5
4. Anytime that I really need to get a good grade on a test, I can get it.	5	4	3	2	1
5. I plan my study sessions in advance and pretty much stick to the plan.	5	4	3	2	1
6. Sometimes I feel unaware of how to get good grades.	1	2	3	4	5
7. My goal is to get the best grade I can without expending a lot of effort on my school work.	1	2	3	4	5
8. Test anxiety lowers my grades a lot.	1	2	3	4	5
9. I tend to study in spurts rather than at a regular consistent pace.	1	2	3	4	5
10. I worry a great deal that I may not get the grade I need in a class.	1	2	3	4	5
11. I try to work just hard enough to get the grade I need in a course.	1	2	3	4	5
12. I am pretty good at guessing the questions on tests beforehand.	5	4	3	2	1

From Davidson, W., Beck, H., & Silver, N. (1999). Development and validation of scores on a measure of six academic orientations in college students. *Educational and Psychological Measurement, 59*, 678-693. Used with permission.

⊸ VOCABULARY TEST (1st Administration) ⊢

DIRECTIONS: Circle the correct answer. If you are not sure what the correct answer is, take your best guess. Unanswered items will be counted incorrect.

1. A **vista** is a:

   (a) reason   (b) view   (c) body of water   (d) memory

2. A **guileless** person is:

   (a) watchful   (b) serene   (c) exuberant   (d) straightforward

3. To **parody** is to:

   (a) imitate   (b) despise   (c) inquire   (d) placate

4. An **impetus** is:

   (a) an advancement   (b) an incentive   (c) a barrier   (d) a declaration

5. To **acquiesce** is to:

   (a) comply   (b) forgive   (c) discard   (d) challenge

6. An **erudite** person is:

   (a) wealthy   (b) honorable   (c) knowledgeable   (d) adventurous

7. **Onerous** means:

   (a) terrifying   (b) burdensome   (c) prestigious   (d) clandestine

8. A **panacea** is a:

   (a) remedy   (b) delicacy   (c) microbe   (d) surprise

9. **Rancor** refers to:

   (a) fear   (b) pleasure   (c) malice   (d) shame

10. To **promulgate** is to:

    (a) explore   (b) require   (c) exacerbate   (d) proclaim

Vocabulary Test created by the author.

⇥ PES (2nd Administration) ⇤

DIRECTIONS: Circle the number corresponding to the extent to which you agree with each of the 10 statements below. Be as accurate and honest as you can when responding to each statement, and try not to let your answers to one question influence your answers to other questions. There are no correct or incorrect answers.

	Strongly agree	Moderately agree	Slightly agree	Slightly disagree	Moderately disagree	Strongly disagree
1. When I get what I want it's usually because I worked hard for it.	6	5	4	3	2	1
2. When I make plans I am almost certain to make them work.	6	5	4	3	2	1
3. I prefer games involving some luck over games requiring pure skill.	1	2	3	4	5	6
4. I can learn almost anything if I set my mind to it.	6	5	4	3	2	1
5. My major accomplishments are entirely due to my hard work and ability.	6	5	4	3	2	1
6. I usually don't set goals because I have a hard time following through on them.	1	2	3	4	5	6
7. Competition discourages excellence.	1	2	3	4	5	6
8. Often people get ahead just by being lucky.	1	2	3	4	5	6
9. On any sort of exam or competition I like to know how well I do relative to everyone else.	6	5	4	3	2	1
10. It's pointless to keep working on something that's too difficult for me.	1	2	3	4	5	6

From Paulhus, D. (1983). Sphere-specific measures of perceived control. *Journal of Personality and Social Psychology, 44,* 1253-1265. Used with permission.

⊸ LOT-R (2ⁿᵈ Administration) ⊱

DIRECTIONS: Circle the number corresponding to the extent to which you agree with each of the 10 statements below. Be as accurate and honest as you can when responding to each statement, and try not to let your answers to one question influence your answers to other questions. There are no correct or incorrect answers. Answer according to your own feelings, rather than how you think "most people" would answer.

	I agree a lot	I agree a little	I neither agree nor disagree	I disagree a little	I disagree a lot
1. In uncertain times, I usually expect the best.	4	3	2	1	0
2. It's easy for me to relax.	4	3	2	1	0
3. If something can go wrong for me, it will.	0	1	2	3	4
4. I'm always optimistic about my future.	4	3	2	1	0
5. I enjoy my friends a lot.	4	3	2	1	0
6. It's important for me to keep busy.	4	3	2	1	0
7. I hardly ever expect things to go my way.	0	1	2	3	4
8. I don't get upset too easily.	4	3	2	1	0
9. I rarely count on good things happening to me.	0	1	2	3	4
10. Overall, I expect more good things to happen to me than bad.	4	3	2	1	0

From Carver, C.S., at www.psy.miami.edu/faculty/ccarver/sclLOT-R.html. (Permission for use not required).

⊶ WOFO-C (2ⁿᵈ Administration) ⊷

DIRECTIONS: Circle the number corresponding to the extent to which you agree with each of the 5 statements below. Be as accurate and honest as you can when responding to each statement, and try not to let your answers to one question influence your answers to other questions. There are no correct or incorrect answers.

	Strongly agree	Somewhat agree	Neither agree nor disagree	Somewhat disagree	Strongly disagree
1. I enjoy working in situations involving competition with others.	5	4	3	2	1
2. It is important to me to perform better than others on a task.	5	4	3	2	1
3. I feel that winning is important in both work and games.	5	4	3	2	1
4. It annoys me when other people perform better than I do.	5	4	3	2	1
5. I try harder when I'm in competition with other people.	5	4	3	2	1

From *Achievement and Achievement Motives: Psychological and Sociological Approaches* by Janet Spence © 1983 by W.H. Freeman and Company. Used with permission.

⫷ ICQ (2ⁿᵈ Administration) ⫸

DIRECTIONS: Circle the number corresponding to the extent to which you agree with each of the 8 statements below. Be as accurate and honest as you can when responding to each statement, and try not to let your answers to one question influence your answers to other questions. There are no correct or incorrect answers.

	Strongly agree	Agree	Neutral	Disagree	Strongly disagree
1. I perform better when I am competing against someone rather than when I am the only one striving for a goal.	5	4	3	2	1
2. I do *not* feel that winning is important in both work and games.	1	2	3	4	5
3. When I win an award or game it means that I am the best compared to everyone else that was playing. It was only fair that the best person win the game.	5	4	3	2	1
4. In school, I always liked to be the first one finished with a test.	5	4	3	2	1
5. I have always wanted to be better than others.	5	4	3	2	1
6. When nominated for an award, I focus on how much better or worse the other candidates' qualifications are as compared to mine.	5	4	3	2	1
7. I would want an A because that would mean I did better than other people.	5	4	3	2	1
8. Because it is important that a winner is decided, I do not like to leave a game unfinished.	5	4	3	2	1

From Griffin-Pierson, S. (1990). The Competitiveness Questionnaire: A measure of two components of competitiveness. *Measurement and Evaluation in Counseling and Development, 23*, 108-115. Used with permission.

◄ AEAS (2ⁿᵈ Administration) ►

DIRECTIONS: Circle the number corresponding to the extent to which you agree with each of the 12 statements below. Be as accurate and honest as you can when responding to each statement, and try not to let your answers to one question influence your answers to other questions. There are no correct or incorrect answers.

	Strongly agree	Agree	Neutral	Disagree	Strongly disagree
1. I might cut class if I think that the lecture material will not be on the test.	1	2	3	4	5
2. I sometimes wonder if I am really "college material".	1	2	3	4	5
3. In a "pass-fail" course, I try to exert just enough effort to avoid failing.	1	2	3	4	5
4. Anytime that I really need to get a good grade on a test, I can get it.	5	4	3	2	1
5. I plan my study sessions in advance and pretty much stick to the plan.	5	4	3	2	1
6. Sometimes I feel unaware of how to get good grades.	1	2	3	4	5
7. My goal is to get the best grade I can without expending a lot of effort on my school work.	1	2	3	4	5
8. Test anxiety lowers my grades a lot.	1	2	3	4	5
9. I tend to study in spurts rather than at a regular consistent pace.	1	2	3	4	5
10. I worry a great deal that I may not get the grade I need in a class.	1	2	3	4	5
11. I try to work just hard enough to get the grade I need in a course.	1	2	3	4	5
12. I am pretty good at guessing the questions on tests beforehand.	5	4	3	2	1

From Davidson, W., Beck, H., & Silver, N. (1999). Development and validation of scores on a measure of six academic orientations in college students. *Educational and Psychological Measurement, 59*, 678-693. Used with permission.

⤙ VOCABULARY TEST (2nd Administration) ⤚

DIRECTIONS: Circle the correct answer. If you are not sure what the correct answer is, take your best guess. Unanswered items will be counted incorrect.

1. A **vista** is a:

    (a) reason   (b) view   (c) body of water   (d) memory

2. A **guileless** person is:

    (a) watchful   (b) serene   (c) exuberant   (d) straightforward

3. To **parody** is to:

    (a) imitate   (b) despise   (c) inquire   (d) placate

4. An **impetus** is:

    (a) an advancement   (b) an incentive   (c) a barrier   (d) a declaration

5. To **acquiesce** is to:

    (a) comply   (b) forgive   (c) discard   (d) challenge

6. An **erudite** person is:

    (a) wealthy   (b) honorable   (c) knowledgeable   (d) adventurous

7. **Onerous** means:

    (a) terrifying   (b) burdensome   (c) prestigious   (d) clandestine

8. A **panacea** is a:

    (a) remedy   (b) delicacy   (c) microbe   (d) surprise

9. **Rancor** refers to:

    (a) fear   (b) pleasure   (c) malice   (d) shame

10. To **promulgate** is to:

    (a) explore   (b) require   (c) exacerbate   (d) proclaim

Vocabulary Test created by the author.

DIRECTIONS FOR CALCULATING SCORES

►CALCULATING SCORES ON THE MEASURES

PES (Personal Efficacy Scale)
Scores for the PES are determined by summing the 10 item scores. PES total scores can range from 10 to 60. Higher scores indicate higher degrees of perceived personal efficacy.

LOT-R (Life Orientation Test-Revised)
Scores for the LOT-R can be determined by summing the scores on the following 6 items: 1, 3, 4, 7, 9, and 10. (Items 2, 5, 6, and 8 are filler items and should <u>not</u> be included in the total LOT-R score). LOT-R total scores can range from 0 to 24, with higher scores indicating greater dispositional optimism.

WOFO-C (Work and Family Orientation Questionnaire-Competitiveness scale)
Scores for the WOFO-C are determined by summing the 5 item scores. WOFO-C total scores can range from 5 to 25. Higher scores indicate greater competitiveness.

ICQ (Interpersonal Competitiveness Questionnaire)
Scores for the ICQ are determined by summing the 8 item scores. ICQ total scores can range from 8 to 40. Higher scores indicate greater interpersonal competitiveness.

AEAS (Academic Efficacy and Apathy Scale)
Scores for the AEAS are determined by summing the 12 item scores. AEAS total scores can range from 12 to 72. Higher scores indicate greater academic efficacy and a learning vs. a grade orientation.

Vocabulary Test
Scores on the Vocabulary Test are determined by summing the number of correct responses. Total scores can range from 0 to 10, with higher scores indicating more extensive vocabulary. Correct responses are: (1) b, (2) d, (3) a, (4) b, (5) a, (6) c, (7) b, (8) a, (9) c, (10) d.

►CALCULATING STUDY HOURS INDEX (SHI)

Estimate the number of hours you spend studying (including reading class material, writing papers, completing homework assignments, studying for exams, etc.) for your academic courses in an average 7-day week. Then divide this number by the number of academic credit hours you are enrolled in this semester. Do not include study or credit hours for "activity" courses such as studio art, music or theater performance, athletics, internship, etc.

Example:

Course	Academic Credit Hours
U.S. History	3
Organic Chemistry	4
Psych Assessment	3
Photography II	not counted
Psych of Learning	3
Soccer	not counted
TOTAL	13

Number of Study Hours per Week = 22 (*Note*: this does not include hours spent on Photography or Soccer)

→ **Number of Study Hours/Number of Academic Credit Hours = 22/13 = 1.69**

♦ ♦ ♦ *SCORE REPORT FORM* ♦ ♦ ♦

DIRECTIONS:

(1) Write your code number on the Score Report Form in the space provided.
(2) Look at "Directions for Calculating Scores".
(3) Calculate your scores for each of the measures labeled "1st Administration". Write your scores in the appropriate column on the Score Report Form.
(4) Calculate your scores for each of the measures labeled "2nd Administration". Write your scores in the appropriate column on the Score Report Form.
(5) Write your current cumulative grade point average (GPA) in the space provided.
(6) Calculate the Study Hour Index (SHI) according to "Directions for Calculating Scores".
(7) Submit the Score Report Form to your instructor

Write your CODE NUMBER here: _____		
MEASURE	*1st* Administration	*2nd* Administration
Personal Efficacy Scale (PES)		
Life Orientation Test (LOT-2)		
Work and Family Orientation Questionnaire-Competitiveness scale (WOFO-C)		
Interpersonal Competitiveness Questionnaire (ICQ)		
Academic Efficacy/Apathy Scale (AEAS)		
Vocabulary Test (VOC)		
Your Current Grade Point Average		
Study Hours Index (SHI)		